South Asia Economic and Policy Studies

Series Editors

Sachin Chaturvedi, Director General, RIS for Developing Countries, New Delhi, India
Mustafizur Rahman, Distinguished Fellow, Centre for Policy Dialogue (CPD), Dhaka, Bangladesh
Abid Suleri, Executive Director, Sustainable Development Policy Institute, Islamabad, Pakistan
Dushni Weerakoon, Executive Director, Institute of Policy Studies of Sri Lanka, Colombo, Sri Lanka

D1823924

The Series aims to address evolving and new challenges and policy actions that may be needed in the South Asian Region in the 21st century. It ventures into niche and makes critical assessment to evolve a coherent understanding of the nature of challenges and allow/facilitate dialogue among scholars and policymakers from the region working with the common purpose of exploring and strengthening new ways to implement regional cooperation. The series is multidisciplinary in its orientation and invites contributions from academicians, policy makers, practitioners, consultants working in the broad fields of regional cooperation; trade and investment; finance; economic growth and development; industry and technology; agriculture; services; environment, resources and climate change; demography and migration; disaster management; globalization and institutions among others.

More information about this series at http://www.springer.com/series/15400

Sachin Chaturvedi · Sabyasachi Saha
Editors

Manufacturing and Jobs in South Asia

Strategy for Sustainable Economic Growth

South Asia Centre for
Policy Studies (SACEPS)

Editors
Sachin Chaturvedi
Research and Information System
for Developing Countries (RIS)
New Delhi, India

Sabyasachi Saha
Research and Information System
for Developing Countries (RIS)
New Delhi, India

ISSN 2522-5502 ISSN 2522-5510 (electronic)
South Asia Economic and Policy Studies
ISBN 978-981-13-8263-5 ISBN 978-981-10-8381-5 (eBook)
https://doi.org/10.1007/978-981-10-8381-5

This Springer imprint is published by the registered company Springer Nature Singapore Pte Ltd.
The registered company address is: 152 Beach Road, #21-01/04 Gateway East, Singapore 189721, Singapore

Foreword

The past three decades have witnessed rapid economic growth in South Asian countries, which is impressive in comparison with their own performance in the past and with other developing countries' performance in the present. GDP growth rates in South Asia since the mid-1980s, which provide a sharp contrast with near stagnation in the colonial era and modest growth in the preceding four decades, are much higher than those in other parts of the developing world, particularly Africa and Latin America, even if they do not match the performance of East Asia, especially China.

This has led to a significant reduction in absolute poverty and some improvement in the living conditions of people. Yet, impressive economic growth has not always been transformed into meaningful development which improves the well-being of ordinary people. The underlying reason is the triangular relationship between growth, poverty, and inequality. Rapid growth did help reduce absolute poverty in South Asia but not as much it could have, in part because the initial income distribution was unequal and in part because of rising income inequality. At the same time, economic growth did not lead to commensurate employment creation. Indeed, employment growth was distinctly slower than output growth and the gap widened over time.

In 2016, as many as 24% of the people on earth lived in South Asia, but the contribution of the region to world GDP, in current prices at market exchange rates, was less than 4%. It is no surprise that South Asia is home to 35–45% of the world's poor, depending on where we draw the poverty line. For the region as a whole, in terms of 2011 purchasing power parity (PPP) dollars, in 2013, 16% of its population lived below the poverty line of PPP $1.90 per day, while 54% of its population lived below the poverty line of PPP $3.20 per day. The former are the perennial poor probably unable to reach the critical minimum even in terms of nutrition, while the latter might have been able to reach the critical minimum in terms of food and clothing plus some basic needs but not an appropriate shelter or adequate health care and education. The people between the two poverty lines, as many as 640 million people in South Asia, were vulnerable to any shock such as a bad harvest, high inflation, jobs lost, or an illness in the family. But that is not all.

Social indicators of development, on health and education status, are still among the worst in the world, with the possible exception of sub-Saharan Africa. Clearly, we have miles to go in our journey if the destination is the well-being of our people.

It is obvious that South Asia has much to learn from the rest of Asia about industrialization as an imperative, the critical importance of employment, a focus on human development, and the fundamental role of governments in transforming economies. The social and economic transformation of Asia over the past five decades has been remarkable. In Asia's stunning performance, East Asian countries have been the leaders, while South Asian countries have been the laggards, with Southeast Asian countries somewhere in the middle. South Asia has experienced not only jobless growth but also a premature de-industrialization. Even where jobs have been created, the quality of employment remains poor. What is more, the existing manufacturing sectors have not really managed vertical diversification (the spread remains horizontal) or technological upgrading (there is little capacity for innovation).

In the quest for development in South Asia over the next 25 years, there are many things that remain to be done. Among these, the importance of manufacturing cannot be stressed enough. Economic development is not only about economic growth but also about the capabilities of economies to transform their productive activities. This is simply not possible without industrialization. The economic history of the now developed high-income countries provides confirmation. So does the more recent experience of the East Asian success stories in development. Indeed, the experience of latecomers to development since 1950 shows that no country has achieved even middle-income status without industrialization. Manufacturing also shows faster growth in lower-income countries, so that it narrows the productivity gap more rapidly, suggesting an unconditional convergence to the frontier. It must, of course, be recognized that the world economy has changed. There could be a return to protectionism in industrialized countries. The next industrial revolution on the horizon driven by technological progress—robotics, artificial intelligence, 3D printing, or the Internet of things—that replaces labour in production processes could constrain manufactured exports from developing countries.

Even so, the rationale for a renewed focus and emphasis on manufacturing in South Asia is strong. First, it is the path to employment creation. Most new entrants to the labour force are unskilled or low-skill workers, whose employment is the only means of mobilizing South Asia's most abundant resource—people—for development. Second, it is a potential source of economic growth, not only for labour absorption at the extensive margin, but also for labour use at the intensive margin, with a potential for moving workers from lower to higher productivity in manufacturing. Moreover, given the low shares of manufacturing in GDP and in employment, juxtaposed with the large size of the domestic market in most South Asian countries, the potential for growth in the manufacturing sector is considerable.

This perspective provides the *raison d'etre* for the present study, which seeks to focus on manufacturing and jobs in South Asia. It analyses past development experience to examine what has constrained the manufacturing sector and why it has not created as much employment as it could have. The explanation might lie in structural constraints that are almost folklore: pathetic infrastructure, poor connectivity, rigid labour laws, and difficulties of doing business, quite apart from a workforce without primary or secondary education, combined with limited possibilities for skill formation. In addition, the study suggests that policy regimes in the spheres of international trade and international investment have not been conducive to industrialization, while there has been little in terms of trade policy, industrial policy, technology policy, or exchange rate policy that has been supportive of industrialization. It would seem that South Asia has made minimal attempts to learn from the experience of East Asia or even Southeast Asia. Notwithstanding this past, the book explores future possibilities to emphasize manufacturing as the only way forward that could create jobs, provide decent work, and make growth inclusive. Indeed, the essential hypothesis is that manufacturing which creates employment is the strategy for sustainable economic growth and social progress in South Asia.

The editors set the stage with an overview in an introduction which also outlines the objective, structure, and scope of the study. The book is divided into two parts. The first part is constituted by country studies on Bangladesh, India, Nepal, Pakistan, and Sri Lanka with a focus on the manufacturing sector and employment creation in each of the countries. There are, in fact, two studies on India, which consider manufacturing trade and employment linkages, and employment in manufacturing for exports. The second part of the study comprises two cross-country thematic essays. Of these, one analyses the relationship between economic growth and employment creation, to examine the nature of employment challenges in South Asia and stress the need for manufacturing-led growth, while the another examines skill formation, competitiveness, and industrial development, to suggest that the transition from a traditional to a modern industrial sector, capable of upgrading and diversification, requires a revamping of national innovation systems. In the concluding chapter, the editors draw together the findings of this study on manufacturing and employment in South Asia, for each of the country chapters and thematic chapters, to highlight the frustrations and the aspirations, many of which are common across these countries, while reflecting on what these countries might learn from past experience to chart a path to a better future.

This study has been commissioned and conducted by the South Asia Centre for Policy Studies—SACEPS—as an integral part of its work programme. SACEPS is a network organization engaged in addressing issues of common concern in South Asia. Leading research institutions and think tanks in South Asian countries are actively associated with SACEPS as partners and stakeholders. In fact, the country studies have been carried out in collaboration with its partner institutions. For those who might not know, SACEPS is an independent non-governmental organization working at the intersection of research and policy. The objective of SACEPS is to create a meeting space that facilitates interaction not only between public intellectuals, policy practitioners, the business community, civil society, and media persons, but also with an even wider constituency of people, concerned citizens, who are committed to the idea of South Asia. These countries have much in common that is embedded in their histories: languages, cultures, arts, music, and cuisines. Yet, politics creates divides that have become barriers to economic cooperation.

It is hoped that this study on manufacturing and jobs, both critical for the future of South Asia, will be of interest to governments, parliamentarians, policymakers, media, and civil society, as much as it would be to academics, researchers, and citizens. There is so much that we—the people of this populous subcontinent—can learn from each other to create a better world for ourselves.

New Delhi, India   Prof. Deepak Nayyar

Deepak Nayyar is Emeritus Professor of Economics at Jawaharlal Nehru University, New Delhi, and Honorary Fellow of Balliol College, Oxford. He was Distinguished University Professor of Economics at The New School for Social Research, New York. Earlier, he taught at the University of Oxford, the University of Sussex, and the Indian Institute of Management Calcutta. He served as Vice Chancellor of the University of Delhi and as Chief Economic Adviser to the Government of India. He has published widely in academic journals. His books include *Catch Up: Developing Countries in the World Economy*, *Stability with Growth: Macroeconomics, Liberalization and Development*, *Governing Globalization: Issues and Institutions* and *The Intelligent Person's Guide to Liberalization*.

Endorsements

"South Asia is the quintessential example of the phenomenon of jobless growth. This is largely due to the neglect of the manufacturing sector. This book containing case studies of the structure and trend of the manufacturing sector, problems besetting it and, outlining the policy measures to revive it, will, I hope, redirect policy focus to the revival of manufacturing which is job creating, inclusive and sustainable."

—Prof. Muchkund Dubey, *President, Council for Social Development, New Delhi*

"I am happy to commend this book in which leading scholars from 5 countries try to analyze reasons for a relative failure of South Asia in harnessing the job-creating potential of manufacturing sectors. Given its rich evidence base covering both internal and external factors, I hope that this book will be read widely for the analytical insights and policy lessons that are offered."

—Dr. Nagesh Kumar, *Director and Head of the South and South-West Asia (SSWA) Office of the United Nations Economic and Social Commission for Asia and the Pacific (UNESCAP) based in New Delhi*

Contents

About the Editors

Sachin Chaturvedi is Director General of the Research and Information System for Developing Countries (RIS), a New Delhi-based autonomous think-tank. He was also a Global Justice Fellow at the MacMillan Center for International Affairs at Yale University. His work addresses issues related to development cooperation policies and South–South cooperation. He has also worked on trade and innovation linkages with a special focus on the World Trade Organization (WTO). Dr. Chaturvedi has served as a Visiting Professor at Jawaharlal Nehru University (JNU) and has also worked as a consultant to the UN Food and Agriculture Organisation, World Bank, UN-ESCAP, UNESCO, OECD, the Commonwealth Secretariat, IUCN, and to the Government of India's Department of Biotechnology and the Ministry of Environment and Forests.

Sabyasachi Saha is an Assistant Professor at the Research and Information System for Developing Countries (RIS), New Delhi. He specialises in innovation economics, technology transfer, industrial development and trade. He has published research articles in academic journals and edited volumes, and has presented his research at prominent international conferences. He previously worked as a senior member of research staff at the New Delhi based Indian Council for Research on International Economic Relations (ICRIER) and Jawaharlal Nehru University (JNU), and has received the WIPO prize, a DAAD-funded fellowship, and a Government of India grant. He has also participated in numerous high-level policy/think-tank forums in India and abroad.

The support for this publication comes from The Asia Foundation. The views and opinions expressed in this publication are that of the authors and not of The Asia Foundation.

Introduction: Challenges Confronting a Rising South Asia—Industry and Employment

Sachin Chaturvedi and Sabyasachi Saha

1 Background

South Asia is large by relative share of the world population and also in terms of share of world's poor people. Riding on steady economic progress (growth in per capita GDP), poverty headcount ratio (at $1.90 a day for 2011 PPP) for South Asia fell from 44.4% in 1990 to 15.1% in 2013. However, this may be seen in light of the fact that extreme poverty is getting concentrated in Sub-Saharan Africa and South Asia among all regions.

South Asia, a historically dynamic region, witnessed decline in wealth creation due to de-industrialization during first and second industrial revolution largely due to colonial nature of its relation with the West that emerged as industrial powers in the nineteenth and the twentieth century. Habib (2006) explains that de-industrialisation, first used as a phrase in 1940, means 'reduction or destruction of a nation's industrial capacity'. In the case of India, the decline of traditional artisanal industries was not replaced or adequately compensated by newer or more advanced forms of industrial production. Thus, India's traditional industries declined in the face of the influx of British manufactured goods that were sold under colonial conditions that benefited foreign manufactures. Consequently, industrial workers in India were pushed into agriculture and other low-paying occupations. This process is referred to as the 'de-industrialization of India'. Apparently, by the middle of the nineteenth century, India had lost all of its export market and much of its domestic market. Quantitative evidence on the overall level of economic activity in eighteenth- and nineteenth-century India is scant, let alone evidence on its breakdown between agriculture, industry and services.

Technological advancement has been driver of wealth creation during phases of industrialization witnessed in the West. East Asian countries promoted assimila-

S. Chaturvedi (✉) · S. Saha
Research and Information System for Developing Countries (RIS), New Delhi, India
e-mail: dg@ris.org.in

© Springer Nature Singapore Pte Ltd. 2019
S. Chaturvedi and S. Saha (eds.), *Manufacturing and Jobs in South Asia*, South Asia Economic and Policy Studies,
https://doi.org/10.1007/978-981-10-8381-5_1

tion of new knowledge, learning and competence building for technological catch-up. Enhanced physical and human capital accumulation, high-savings rate, careful industrial policy and calibrated integration with the world economy all contributed in achieving high economic growth for East Asian countries during the second half of the last century.

Given prolonged closed economies, South Asia on the other hand registered very slow pace of physical capital accumulation and due to weaker policies and institutions failed to push human capital formation as well.[1] Savings rate remain high, but their conversion into investment has been weak. South Asian countries have encouraged skill development at the top of the pyramid. This had effects in terms of widening the inequality despite enhancing the competitiveness of their knowledge-intensive sectors. While catching-up was not easy, India which occupies a disproportionately larger space in South Asia in terms of geography and population has been able to leverage its knowledge capabilities and skills in greater measure over crude labour resources in production of goods and services in select sectors of the economy.

Persistence of poverty and inequality in South Asia is a major concern. Even as, South Asia has been able to lift millions out of absolute poverty partly by achieving high-income growth over the last three decades, absolute numbers remain among the highest in the world with poor record of well-being of amongst its citizens reflected in low scores across development indicators. Persistence of absolute poverty offers the most resounding alarm about dangers of income inequality even as widening income disparity and slowing economic mobility is on record. Majority of non-agricultural employment in South Asia is informal in nature. The challenge appears insurmountable at this point due to the population bulge in the middle, except in the case of Sri Lanka which is experiencing an ageing population. The challenges are also complex given variety of exclusions in access to opportunities that hinder formation and utilization of human capital leading to greater incidence of inequality. Social sector policies, affirmative action, efforts on gender equality in education, and support for entrepreneurship are among measures frequently applied in the region to address concerns on unequal access to opportunities.

However, Governments in the region are increasingly convinced that in order to sustain economic growth and check rising inequality there has to be commensurate expansion of the productive sectors of the economy (and productivity) and expansion in the share of decent jobs (with guarantees of minimum wage and social security) for greater equality in distribution of the benefits of economic growth. The Sustainable Development Goals (SDG) have emphasized on high economic growth coupled with creation of decent jobs as a priority under SDG 8. There is a strong belief that manufacturing sector would install productive capacities, deepen value addition and guarantee decent job creation. The relative stagnation of the manufacturing sector has been due to poor policy environment that failed to transform rural economies into

---

[1] This varied across countries and sectors in South Asia. India's strong push for specialized institutions of higher learning primarily focused on science and engineering is reflected in the establishment of various Indian Institute of Technology (IIT) in the decades following Independence. Sri Lanka made commendable efforts at education and skill development.

industrial ones, even as urban centres were being driven by the services sector. The primary sectors of the economies in South Asia have long been under distress due to poor institutional support, low investments and lack of competence building. Greater value addition in terms of agriculture-based manufacturing and rural industrialization is also an important tool for poverty reduction at the bottom of the pyramid.

Manufacturing sector was the major driver of economic growth in East and South-East Asia and China with huge positive impact on employment creation. While mass manufacturing activities in Asia have been driven by low labour costs, wages have increased as countries moved into more skill intensive segments. It is not unreasonable to consider a similar trajectory for South Asia, particularly so, since manufacturing sector has shown dynamism in pockets and are increasingly contributing to national incomes. Skill distribution has been highly uneven in South Asia. The effect is visible in terms of how countries have specialized in industrial production. While India is increasingly exporting high and medium technology-intensive products, Bangladesh's success in industrial production remains confined to low-tech product segments (majorly textile and apparel). Even as Nepal lags in industrialization, Sri Lanka has wider spread of education and skills aligned with higher end services sector. Industry has played historically important roles in wealth creation and employment generation in India and Pakistan. Pakistan still specializes in low technology-intensive industrial production, while India has experienced strong dualism in industrial performance with rising share of high-tech and medium-tech production and divergence between performance of small and large firms. World Bank (2017) notes that almost 80% of the region's export growth from 2001 to 2013 came from selling the same goods to the same destinations, and remaining 20% came from selling the same products to new markets. It further notes, while the sophistication of exports has increased in India, it has remained low in the rest of South Asia and quality (as measured by the prices its products fetch in international markets) has generally remained low and has declined for some countries.

With sustained economic growth, of the four LDC countries in the region, Bangladesh and Bhutan are poised to graduate out of the LDC status. As per UN norms, it is necessary that at least two of the three graduation criteria—Gross National Income (GNI) per capita, the Human Assets Index (HAI) and the Economic Vulnerability Index (EVI)—are met for eligibility. Bangladesh has been able to satisfy all the three criteria. To some extent, this justifies the importance of sustained economic growth towards accelerating economic progress in resource-poor countries like Bangladesh. Economic growth prospect for the region is strongly influenced by India which accounts for four-fifths of the region's GDP. India maintains strong economic growth outlook and is currently the fastest growing large economy globally. Other economies including Nepal, Bangladesh, Pakistan and Sri Lanka remain on track with average growth rate of over 4% despite periodic fluctuations.

Greater integration with the world economy has meant greater inflow of FDI in the region. India has consistently received the major share and is among the top five recipient economies in Asia. South Asia has also shown consistent performance in registering increased flow of FDI in recent times unlike other developing regions in the world. Pakistan has also seen a sharp rise in its FDI inflows following new impetus in economic relations with larger regional neighbours like China. Both Bangladesh and Nepal are also poised to attract increased quantum of FDI in the near future. Historically, as World Bank (2017) notes, merchandise trade-to-GDP and FDI-to-GDP ratios in the region remained sub-optimum in comparison to other comparator regions. However, UNCTAD (2017) highlights India and other South Asian countries are linking up with regional value chains and infrastructure networks. Indian manufacturing industries have started to integrate significantly into the strong and sophisticated regional production networks in East and South-East Asia. Trade liberalization has contributed significantly to the rate of economic growth in South Asia. Trade-to-GDP ratio in India has touched 40.6% in 2017 suggesting robust openness of the economy similar to that of countries like Australia (42%), Indonesia (40%), Russia (47%) and China (44%).

One of the foremost debates on economic policies in South Asia in the post-economic liberalization period has been around ascertaining the contested evidence on jobless economic growth. The dominant character of economic growth in the region has been that of economic growth being overwhelmingly determined through the performance of the service sector. However, commensurate employment generation in the formal segments within manufacturing and services has not taken place. Increasing informalization of the labour force has been the main challenge even as rising informal workforce did not contribute to the rise in poverty. Share of industry in employment has been highest for India in the region (and Nepal and Bhutan having very low levels of industrial employment). Agriculture continues to support bulk of the workforce in South Asia. In the Indian context, manufacturing is still the largest employer outside agriculture. Contribution of the services sector in employment creation may go up keeping in view its share in the GDP but employment in this sector mostly dominated by non-tradables would most certainly not be of desirable quality.

Expansion of formal sector manufacturing employment is therefore a credible strategy for reducing inequality and for job creation. The challenge one encounters here is that of nature of the industrial sector itself. Evidence suggests, as in the case of India, preponderance of very small units in manufacturing and services with limited scope of employment generation, even as absolute numbers may be large.[2] Informal employment is therefore rampant and sharply on the rise. The challenge therefore is not only for expanding the manufacturing sector but also creating larger share of decent jobs. It is in this context that the macro-policy regime for determining main drivers and constraints for manufacturing sector growth in South Asia has to be revisited. Assessment of the experience of economic liberalization and deeper integration in the case of South Asia suggests greater resilience. This prompts us to believe that South Asia might further exploit the external sector in aiding its economic growth as well as strengthening economic transformations. Economic reforms that have always been closely linked with integration with the world economy have to be inspired by ideas around transformation, sustainability of economic growth and

---

[2]As per the Sixth Economic Census of India (2013–14), 58.5 million establishments were found to be in operation employing 131.29 million persons. Out of 58.5 million establishments, 1.4% establishments were in organized sector (establishments employing 10 or more persons).

equity rather than solely by notions of inefficiencies derived in regulatory controls and extended presence of the public sector.

The idea of full employment had captured the imagination of economists as early as in the nineteenth century and constitutes one of the most enduring policy dilemmas till date. Full employment was also followed as one of the most critical economic dogmas in several developed as well as developing countries. Countries of late, including India, are once again experimenting with policies on full employment with governments playing a proactive role in directing resources to sectors that may create employment. However, with deeper integration with the world economy, full employment policies cannot be effective in isolation and benchmark competitiveness has to be ensured across the board. One of the key challenges in making policies on employment more effective is the unavailability of useful, timely, regular and appropriate labour market data. India with its robust statistical system again has to make labour surveys/census more comprehensive and timely particularly to capture large informal sector employment opportunities and character.

The demise of Washington consensus and the subsequent evolution of the policy regimes have forced national governments to look for alternatives. Across the countries, the issue is how factor price equalization would move with jobless growth. The prescriptions may vary. One has to have the ability to differentiate short-term gains and long-term advantages. The development paradigm has to have a clear strategy for inter-balancing factors of production, viz., land, labour and capital, and of course, technology. It should be relevant for smaller countries and far more relevant for bigger countries with huge population. It is in this context, what Douglas North said about the role of institutions. Institutions play an important role, not only in achieving this inter-balance among these factors of production but also in guiding markets and bringing in elements that are essential in policymaking. If one per cent of population is getting overwhelming expansion in their wealth, the inequality that would emerge out of such a system would derail several measures that inter-balancing of factors of production may intend to achieve.

2 Grand Industrial Transitions and Developing Countries

The paradigm of the Fourth Industrial Revolution (Industry 4.0) currently unfolding suggests total knowledge-based economic progress. It would be important to understand the changes that have shaped economies, societies and politics, through the course of industrial revolutions, keeping governance and development at the core. The fourth revolution showcases a new era that builds and extends the impact of digitization in new and unanticipated ways. Scientific advancements and technological breakthroughs are getting interwoven with development and governance, making socio-economic challenges more complex and apparent.

The twenty-first-century global challenges are emanating out of anti-globalization, fragility, insecurity, environmental crisis, lack of employment opportunities, demographic imbalances and the exclusionary technological advancements.

When we are moving towards hyper-digital future with universal connectivity, decentralized energy production and digital business models and greater automation, obvious questions are: Who controls this process? What market structure is required to facilitate? What would happen to international trade regime, whether all of us are committed for multilateralism? How technological unemployment would be addressed? And what would be the nature of work we are looking at? There are debates emerging all across on these and many other issues, suggesting a serious rethinking of our development strategy and our focus on localization of our development priorities.

The long-standing debate between monetarists and structuralists has also influenced the role of technology that is envisaged in the larger development paradigm. Role of market and the incentivization has also relevance in terms of how specific policy choices are made. Let us have a look at how development narratives have influenced patterns of industrial revolutions. The very term 'industrial revolution', as you may imagine, is not free from contestations. Intense debates are there on its contours, its focus and its very evolutionary process, if at all associated with it. The first industrial revolution can be exemplified as an evolutionary phenomenon, which transformed the industrial organizations from being rooted in rules, excessive manpower, hierarchic and centralized structures of power and authority towards management and mass production. The first industrial revolution, characterized by developments in textiles, iron and steam led by Britain, differentiates from a 'second' revolution of the 1850s onwards, characterized by steel, electrics and automobiles led by the US and Germany, moving further to the 'third' revolution around the 1990s, characterized by technological advancements like IT, biotechnologies and materials in industrialized countries. It is essential to understand that imperialism was a major factor impeding the spread of the industrial revolution. While Britain was experiencing 'industrialization', colonialised countries digressed on the path of 'de-industrialisation', characterized with slavery, expropriation of indigenous peoples, imperial expansion and assertion of sovereignty over people and land by foreign governments. Gunnar Myrdal in his seminal work on South Asia captures the postcolonial aspirations of industrialization in South Asia from this perspective.

India witnessed the European 'cotton imperialism', which was also evident in sectors like sugar, tobacco and mining, exploited through large-scale commercial plantation production, fueling the Industrial Revolution. In terms of Science and Technology, through introduction of railways and machinery, the developed West was not intending for technological advancements in the colonies nor to provide a competitive edge. Although science and technology advanced significantly, the era encountered serious consequences of industrialization, in the form of increased child labour, urbanization, dehumanization of factory systems and social degradation.

The second industrial revolution shifted the power play from Great Britain to United States and Germany. A country like India stood at the crossroads of modern science and traditional knowledge, amidst national movements and economic transformations, in the later part of the second industrial revolution. From 1947 to 1970, science became the focal point of economic progress and development—growth of scientific institutions, thrust for industrialization, scientific advancements, etc.

In India and China, ideas were to abridge the inequalities of colonialism and hegemonic west, through the realm of S&T and incorporation of transformative economic reforms, trade policies and regulations serving the national interests.

The advent of third industrial revolution, as Cooper and Kaplinsky in their (1989) paper showed, brought technological advancements to another pedestal with ICT, biotechnology and other scientific advancements. But the gap between LDCs, developing countries and developed counterparts widened further. Contrastingly, it has been argued that the industrial revolution in the west, acted as a compelling force for countries like India and China to adopt a techno-nationalistic and globally competitive perspective, as Sanjay Lall in his paper in (1992) demonstrated, through catching-up, technological leap-frogging and capability upgradation. Countries like India, China, Brazil and Argentina have been characterized by high indigenous science and technological capacities, but low economic strength. Thus, it was essential to build strong scientific base to aid developing countries in challenging technological dominion of the developed countries, which tend to dictate through international regulations and policies.

Furthermore, two themes that had characterized both the first and second industrial revolutions were observably perpetuated by the third revolution—intense exploitation of natural resources deepened within the third industrial revolution, to the point of significant *natural-resource depletion,* for example, as Freeman and Louçã (2001) documents.

- intensification globally in the burning of petroleum derivatives as staple sources of fuel;
- inefficient waste management mechanisms;
- climate change;
- decrease in biodiversity as a result of habitat destruction, in order to expand agriculture, housing, etc.;
- despite computing and production systems that emerged during the third revolution, 'reprogramming' of systems ultimately required substantial human intervention.

Some of the leading scholars in the arena of economic history, innovation studies and systems of innovations, have postulated three key features attributing to the fourth industrial revolution. First, ease in flow of information and exchange between inventors and the market, through technologies like 3D printing and prototypes, which would reduce cost of innovation and commercialization. Second, the wave of artificial intelligence and robotics will improve problem-solving to achieve goals in a diverse set of real-world scenarios, which would offer new avenues to economic growth and novel employment opportunities. Third, the systems of innovation will set foundation for integrating different scientific and technical disciplines, facilitating innovation and knowledge production through diverse funding avenues, capability enhancements and infrastructural support.

In the case of fourth industrial revolution, what is extremely fascinating is the likelihood of integration across various scientific and technical disciplines, whereby outcomes of one stream may become input for the other. It assumes a greater importance with several sectors and geographical locations that are still waiting for third industrial revolution to descend for them. The blurring away of barriers with 3D printing between inventors and markets, lowering cost of bridging ideas of people with specific products. OECD in its reports to the G20 in 2016 and 2017 presented a rather brighter picture, defining as Next Production Revolution (NPR). According to them, the set of technologies is likely to be important for production across several Global Value Chains (GVCs), presenting a combinatorial nature of technologies. This largely represents growth convergence of technological applications in the realm of biotechnology, nanotechnology and information and communication technology. This combinatorial nature of technology will bring in five different kinds of applications. As OECD presents, this may include (1) digital technologies that are transformational for production, based on data-driven innovation; (2) bio-based revolution in production bringing in artificial photosynthesis and microorganisms that produce biofuels; (3) nanotechnology; (4) 3D printing and last, and (5) advances in materials science. These technologies are likely to boost productivity and speed up sectoral transformation with greater track for economic growth. Preparedness of developing countries at the entrepreneurial level to compete and survive against the obliterating approaches of the digitally advanced economies would be a major issue.

As consumption patterns are evolving inclination and push for fourth industrial revolution is very natural. In the first three industrial revolutions, employment could not change in single generation. It evolved from farmers to factories and from factories to knowledge work. But it all happened very gradually. Total employment is not destroyed but multiplied. Under the G20 process West is worried about informalization, about jobs and economy. India has always witnessed informality in economy and uncertainty in employment.

In India, since the pre-independence era, the importance has been on social and economic development and use of S&T, which is evident in various 5-year plans, policies and regulations. The subsequent S&T policies, viz. Technology Policy Statement of 1983, Science and Technology Policy of 2003 and the most recent Science, Technology and Innovation Policy (STIP) of 2013, have reiterated the broad vision of the foremost policy while expanding and enriching it further. At the Indian Science Congress 2017, the Indian PM mentioned Socially Responsible Science which sets the prelude for responsible innovation in the policy framework.

Incorporation of responsible research and innovation (RRI) in the context of Indian Science and Technology policies has been shaped by the concerns that the application of science and technology should enable faster socio-economic development for all sections of the society and they should benefit from scientific and technological advances. The main priorities of the Indian S&T Policy thus would be to ensure access, equity and inclusion (AEI). AEI would mean providing all the sections of the society with affordable and accessible innovative solutions based on S&T. Given the nature of challenges before the Indian society which involves even the lack of basic needs to majority of the population, it can be further argued that a framework based on Access, Equity and Inclusion (AEI) is more pragmatic and appropriate in the Indian context. This institutionalization of an operational framework based on

AEI keys is not supposed to be seen as an alternative framework to RRI, but as a more practical, pragmatic and operational approach inspired by the overall notion of responsibility of research and innovation, amidst the complexities arising in the present and future with the dawn of industrial revolution.

3 The Layout of the Volume

The volume takes a comprehensive view in order to promote manufacturing sector and job creation in South Asia taking into account stage of development, macro-policy regime, comparative advantages and competitiveness, industrial policies, trade and investment, labour market issues, and structural constraints. The volume has two parts. Part A explores country cases in detail for select countries in South Asia, primarily focusing on opportunities and challenges of job creation in the manufacturing sector. The countries covered for this purpose are Bangladesh, India, Nepal, Pakistan and Sri Lanka. The core issues include the contours of the manufacturing sector in the wider context of the national economy with focus on employment creation over the past three decades or so; analysis of what constrained growth of the manufacturing sector in the past, and how they are associated with employment creation. The relative importance of the external sector has been looked into in detail from the point of view of manufactured exports as well as integration with global value chains. Part B presents key chapters on carefully identified topics that may lead to deeper understanding of strategies on industrialization and employment creation in the context of South Asia.

Chapter 2, by Moazzem and Halim, explores the context of Bangladesh by assessing extent of job creation in the manufacturing sector in recent decades focusing on sectoral composition of the manufacturing sector and employment trend in different subsectors. The paper examines national policies related to industrial development and their implications for growth in specific sectors of the manufacturing industry. The paper also identifies the major challenges confronting long-term growth of the manufacturing sector and employment generation in Bangladesh. Bangladesh, contrary to other South Asian countries, has maintained a rising share of the manufacturing sector in GDP, promoted mainly through local private investment. The composition of manufacturing in Bangladesh appears similar to other South Asian countries. Major manufacturing industries include textiles, RMG, food and non-metallic mineral products which comprised 73.5% of total establishments in 2012 (79.9% in 2000). Industries with export intensity include RMG (95% of total production), transport equipment (82%), leather and leather goods (74%) and textiles products (57%). RMG sector has gradually become the major source of manufacturing employment by replacing textiles which was the major source of employment in early 1990s. The other sectors contributing to employment generation include food processing non-metallic minerals, recorded media, pharmaceuticals and leather. Nevertheless, Bangladesh suffers from the lack of diversified industrial base, and hence further growth of employment in industry could be challenging. The chapter also vividly discusses labour market issues of employability, skills, wages, employment conditions, etc. in keeping with the context of this volume.

Chapter 3 by Khanal and Pandey focuses on the economy of Nepal and presents a detailed assessment of the role played by the manufacturing sector in employment generation. This chapter deeply engages in the policy questions with regard to structural bottlenecks, the absence of competitiveness, low FDI and integration with GVCs, transit and trade facilitation issues and coordination and implementation failures. In comparison with other South Asian countries, Nepal, which is a landlocked country, faces more challenges in the domain of economic growth and employment. In the last four decades, the average economic growth rate in Nepal has been around 4.0%. However, in the last decade and half-economic growth further slowed to 3.7% during 2001–2002 to 2015–2016 with meager growth in manufacturing value added at 1.4% on average with almost stagnating growth in the agricultural sector, which holds the largest share in GDP. Although unemployment rate is estimated to be only 2.2%, it conceals structural unemployment and underemployment problems. The chapter presents statistics to underline the difficult employment situation in Nepal. The inter-census economically active population data shows a sharp deceleration in overall employment growth in recent years, from 2.7% during the period of 1991–2001 to 0.6% during the period of 2001–2011. During the period of 2001–2011, sectors like electricity, manufacturing and trade registered a negative employment growth at 16, 3.7 and 1.3%, respectively. Out of total economically active population, the share of manufacturing employment had reached 8.8% in 1991 from 2% in 1981. This ratio has fallen to 5.5% in 2011.

In its estimation of coefficients of structural change, the chapter concludes that perhaps no significant structural change has taken place over the years for the overall economy although structural change in value added might have been faster compared to the manufacturing industries themselves. Similarly, high degree of rank correlation coefficient for different periods suggests that the sector shares are highly correlated without major structural changes between the two periods (i.e. 1995–1996 to 2011–2012 and 2006–2007 to 2011–2012). This reflects the absence of any leading sector in the manufacturing industry in Nepal. Even in the presence of an industrial policy framework with benefits for the manufacturing sector, the textile industry has shrunk in share and number allegedly due to liberal economic policies in recent times. However, alongside food and beverages and non-metallic mineral products, wood products, rubber and plastic products, chemicals and chemicals products, furniture, and fabricated metal products sectors have expanded between 1996–1997 and 2011–2012. For Nepal, employment elasticity of manufacturing industries ranges from minimum 0.25 to maximum 0.70 with no firm trend across industries. The overall elasticity remains low with exception of a few industries like textile, apparel and light manufacturing industries.

In Chap. 4, Mohanty and Saha captures the role of trade in promoting manufacturing sector employment for a large economy like India which has the most diversified trade linkages both in terms of products and markets in the South Asian region. The manufacturing sector in India contributes around 15% of its GDP, a share which is significantly lower than the newly industrialised countries of Asia and that of many industrialised nations (who have a lower share now compared to the earlier industrialisation phase). Apprehensions run high that without steady expansion of the manufacturing sector, India is set to lose out on its demographic dividend where a large fraction of the workforce would be languishing in less productive farm and non-farm activities. A strategy for revival of the manufacturing sector has been in focus for the last couple of years as evident from the National Manufacturing Policy (2011) and a larger programme of 'Make in India' launched in 2015. These are supplemented with sectoral policies in many cases aimed at enhancing export competitiveness, value addition and leveraging value chains. However, the range of issues potentially hindering the manufacturing sector exports in India may be diverse and complex. Academic scrutiny on the manufacturing sector in India has focused on experiences with regard to suboptimum employment generation and therefore possible chances of deindustrialization on one hand and deeper dualism reflected in the performance indicators. After almost three decades of external sector liberalization in India, international trade is expected to have profound influence on the performance of the manufacturing sector in India–both value addition and employment generation. With significant trade integration and export orientation of the Indian industry, it is obvious that beyond the domestic market, the external sector would play an important role in enlarging and diversifying the manufacturing sector in India. However, employment absorption capacity differs from one industry to another in the domestic economy. In the context of the manufacturing sector, the chapter explores the question whether there can be a case for India to select its trading partners for preferential trading arrangements (bilateral and regional), and also sectors, in the future with the objective of maximising employment creation, both direct and indirect. Since India's composition of the export basket varies significantly from one country to another, the nature of employment creation will vary accordingly in the domestic economy. The chapter explores the spatial distribution of India's exports to partner countries with a view to examine employment intensity of export covering 165 destination countries. At the product level for each country, direct and indirect employment generation is estimated.

Chapter 5 by Joseph and Kakarlapudi once again focuses exclusively on India and makes a thorough investigation of the industry-level dynamics. The chapter presents an overview of the emerging trends in exports and employment, both in terms of its quantity and quality and locates the industries with revealed employment advantage with respect to high-quality employment and comparative advantage in terms of maximizing exports and employment. It makes an interesting case by analysing industries under four broad categories: export–employment champions, export champions–employment laggards, export laggards–employment champions and export–employment laggards, thereby indicating the scope of policy intervention. In 1990, the employment and export champions accounted for over 55% of the total manufacturing exports, which declined over the years to reach the present level of 20%. When it comes to employment, their share has shown fluctuations but has remained over 19% in 2014. While the chapter captures various facets of quality of employment, a key indicator considered is that of the measure of contractual employment. For the manufacturing sector as a whole, the share of contract labour increased almost threefold from 13% in 1990 to 35% in 2014. Encouragingly, for export-employment champions, the contract labour intensity is found out to be only 21%. Incidentally, however, it would be interesting to note that the share of contract labour intensity is found to be the highest in export and employment laggards. The contract labour intensity in such industries increased from 9% in 1992–1993 to 19% in 2000–2001 and further to 44% by 2014–2015, indicating that regardless of whether the industry is export-oriented or not, making use of contract labour presumably with a view to save on labour cost appears to have emerged as a major competence building strategy.

Chapter 6 by Javed and Suleri is focused on Pakistan. Beyond the three broad sectors of the economy and of the 15 sectors within manufacturing, textile is the most dominant. Starting 1990s, Pakistan has witnessed major changes in structure of the economy (compare this with Nepal where sector shares remain more or less unchanged). Agriculture's share in the GDP has declined substantially from 25% to around 20% in recent years, while that of mining and quarrying has increased significantly from 0.7 to 2.9%. The share of the manufacturing sector has declined from 17% to about 13%. This is contrary to trends in countries like Bangladesh and India. Most importantly, however, no major shift has been documented for employment contributions of major sectors of the economy. In the previous decade, when the share of manufacturing to GDP has been growing, its share in employment declined from 13.6% in 2005 to 13% in 2010. In fact, manufacturing's share in GDP grew double than its share in employment over the period 2000–2010. Textile and clothing outperform other subsectors in terms of value addition in manufacturing (machinery and transport equipment sector contributes the minimum). As per the last manufacturing census (which is now old by a decade), the textile industry of Pakistan contributed more than 60% of total exports and accounted for 46% of the total manufacturing value added. According to the Economic Survey of 2006–07, 38% of workers employed in manufacturing were in the textile sector. The chapter discusses in detail the structure of the textile industry in Pakistan and associated challenges of value addition and decline in exports.

In Chap. 7, Subramaniam presents the trends and composition of economic growth and industrial performance in Sri Lanka. Sri Lanka by all measures appears a special case in the South Asian context. It is expected to grow slower than the South Asian average despite higher economic development than others. It is also distinct from other South Asian countries because Sri Lanka stands on the adverse end of the demographic conditions. Arguably, Sri Lanka has already passed its peak inverse dependency ratio and is going to face the challenge of mitigating the adverse economic effects of an ageing population in the near term. This makes it difficult for Sri Lanka to continue to compete on labour cost differentials with ageing working population exerting upward pressure on wage rates. Sri Lanka's labour competitiveness can be sustained (if not improved) by an emphasis on strategies that enhance productivity above and beyond higher labour costs. The chapter captures the evolution of the manufacturing sector in Sri Lanka as well as composition, direction and trends in production and exports. The growth of the manufacturing sector in Sri Lanka has not been consistent and the momentum garnered during periods of sustained growth has been counterweighed by bouts of languid performance. "Food, Beverages and Tobacco" subsector is the largest contributor to value added in manufacturing over the past decade and half, with contribution in value added increasing steadily from 37% of the manufacturing sector in 2002 to 51% in 2014. However, the production in this segment is catered towards the domestic market. Meanwhile, export-oriented segments have experienced subdued growth in value addition. For instance, the share in value addition of the textile and garments industry, which is the largest export-oriented sector, has stagnated between 20 and 25% over the last decade. Despite higher levels of education among the youth, persistent unemployment is a matter of concern. Therefore, issues of labour force participation and skills have also been analysed in this chapter.

Chapter 8 brings us to the next part of the volume. This chapter on Economic Growth and Employment in South Asia by Ajit Ghose goes beyond industrial land-scape to revisit the economic growth paradigm, primarily from a historical and sec-toral perspective and how it compares with employment generation in South Asia. In doing so, the chapter focuses not only on employment generation but delves deeper into the question of employment conditions. While South Asian countries have expe-rienced economic growth, the quality of employment remains poor. The chapter looks into the question as to why rapid economic growth has failed to rapidly improve employment conditions. The ensuing discussion in the article highlights inappropri-ateness of the pattern of economic growth as a possible reason. Services have always been extraordinarily important (accounting for an unusually high share in GDP) in South Asian economies, which are still at early stages of development. Moreover, economic growth in South Asian countries (with the exception of Bangladesh) has also been services-led. However, the employment intensity of services has been and remains very low, contrary to the global experience. The growth process in South Asian economies did not materialize in bringing structural change in employment. The movement of workers from agriculture to non-agriculture has been low and even this small movement has often been into low-productivity informal employment in non-agriculture-driven sectors. The chapter underlines the fact that growth-as-usual will not lead to a resolution of South Asia's huge employment problem in the foresee-able future. Both the pace and the pattern of economic growth will need to change; growth will need to be significantly faster and the growth in the non-agriculture segment would have to be much more employment-intensive. Therefore, the South Asian countries should strive for rapid manufacturing-led growth along the lines of the East Asian experience.

The final Chap. 9 on competitiveness, skill formation and industrialization in the context of South Asia makes an important contribution and in a sense completes the thread of larger issues that need to be considered in tandem for a comprehensive understanding and overview of the theme of this volume. Technological competitive-ness underlies growth of industries and skill formation ushers technological momen-tum. Lakhwinder Gill in this chapter cites that although South Asian countries are undergoing steady structural transformation of their economies, they continue to host world's largest poor population having failed to promote innovation and industrial-ization. The South Asian countries are highly dependent on imported technologies.

He argues that such technologies do not suit the factor endowment character of South Asian countries that lead to limited impact in terms of technology transfer benefits. Inappropriate matchmaking between sectors and economic actors result in what the author calls low-productivity trap. Such deficiencies also promote rampant exclusion. Majority of the workforce is employed in low productive economic activities termed as disguised unemployment. On the other hand, the workforce lacks adequate skills to meet the requirements of relevant industries. Low productivity attracts low remuneration and deepens mass poverty. To overcome industrial stagnation and skill formation gaps, South Asian countries need to revamp their national innovation system for harnessing the new industrial revolution. The chapter reiterates that South Asian countries face challenges of low per capita income, low average size of firms, low productivity and low skills. The industrial sector failed to provide leadership in the transformation process in these countries. The education base, particularly of the rural workforce, is extremely low. The workforce in rural areas lacks skills to join the manufacturing sector or precision agriculture and agribusiness activities. The existing technical education is inadequate both in terms of quantity and quality. At the same time, the technical and scientific workforce is inadequate in the region and has not produced new innovations to transform low-productivity low-wage activities to high-productivity high-wage opportunities. The chapter primarily focuses on the structural factors and outlines the need for an alternative strategy of industrialisation and skill formation to address the gaps in innovation outcomes and technical skills.

References

Cooper C, Kaplinsky R (eds) (1989) Technology and development in the third industrial revolution. London, Frank Cass

Freeman C, Louçã F (2001) As time goes by: from the industrial revolutions to the information revolution. Oxford University Press, Oxford

Habib I (2006) A people's history of India: Indian economy 1858–1914, vol 28. Aligarh Historians Society and Tulika Books, New Delhi

Lall S (1992). Technological capabilities and industrialization. World Dev 20(2):165–186. Institute of Economics and Statistics, Oxford

UNCTAD (2017) World investment report 2017—Investment and the digital economy

World Bank (2017) South Asia's turn—Policies to boost competitiveness and create the next export powerhouse. In: International bank for reconstruction and development, World Bank (Conference Edition)

Job Creation in the Manufacturing Sector as a Strategy for Sustainable Economic Growth in Bangladesh

Khondaker Golam Moazzem and Faijan Bin Halim

1 Introduction

Bangladesh as an emerging South Asian economy intends to achieve considerable economic progress in order to significantly reduce its poverty and income inequality. The consistent level of economic growth maintained over the past decades has contributed to reducing Bangladesh's poverty level—from 56.7% in 1992 to 23.6% in 2016. Alternatively, this data indicates that a large section of people lives below the poverty line who needs to be taken out of the poverty trap. Over the past decades, the structural transformation experienced by Bangladesh economy led to more share of non-agriculture sector not only in GDP but also in employment. Given the persistence of a high level of poverty, job creation in the non-agriculture sector, particularly in the manufacturing sector, is still considered to be a major development strategy of Bangladesh. Besides, creating 'decent jobs' for the working population is another important aspect related to the sustainable economic growth of the country.

The present study intends to capture the nature and extent of job creation in the manufacturing sector over the last decades with a view to appreciate the major strengths and weaknesses of government strategies and initiatives of the private sector with a view to take lessons for ensuring 'sustainable' economic growth in the future. The paper analyses the growth of the manufacturing sector and its role in sustainable job creation in the previous decades by focusing on the sectoral composition of the manufacturing sector, employment trend in different sub-sectors, level of decent job creation, etc. The paper also examines the national policies related to industrial development and their impact and implications for the growth of the manufacturing sectors. Finally, the paper identifies the major challenges for the manufacturing sector and thereby put forward a set of suggestions for long term sustainable development of the manufacturing sector and employment generation in the country.

K. G. Moazzem (✉) · F. B. Halim
Centre for Policy Dialogue (CPD), Dhaka, Bangladesh
e-mail: moazzemcpd@gmail.com

© Springer Nature Singapore Pte Ltd. 2019   15
S. Chaturvedi and S. Saha (eds.), *Manufacturing and Jobs in South Asia*, South Asia Economic and Policy Studies,
https://doi.org/10.1007/978-981-10-8381-5_2

2 Literature Review

Role of Manufacturing Sector in Promoting Sustainable Economic Growth: Sustainable development is the organizational practice that ensures human development while at the same time sustaining the ability of the natural system to provide natural resources and ecosystem services upon which the economy and society depend. As the concept developed, it has shifted more on economic and social development as well as environmental protection for the future generation. The emerging concept of sustainability reflects a vital change in global thinking, which pressurizes firm to reconsider the approach in conducting their business operation. Prior researchers believe that sustainable manufacturing practice defined as a firm's intra- and inter-organizational practices that combine environmental, economic and social aspects into business activities, would lead to better firm performance (Hami et al. 2015).

Over the time period, the manufacturing sector is considered as the cornerstone of many national economies, a crucial sector to the generation of structural change, productive jobs, and sustainable economic growth. According to the research of the International Finance Group, manufacturing sectors generate the strongest forward and backward linkage across other sectors of the economy, which are important structural transmission links to growth and poverty. Literature shows that the manufacturing sector creates the largest employment multiplier. On the demand side, it creates induced jobs and on the supply side, the linkages come from knowledge and spillover effect. Empirical evidence shows that the manufacturing sector is the single most important sector in business and R&D expenditure. However, the capital intensive nature of the manufacturing sector exploits the economies of scale and achieve productivity gains through learning by doing which increases the pool of human capital—an important resource of a country in moving up to a value-added activities and services.

Manufacturing sector impacts poverty directly through the creation of jobs, which are in most cases better paid and with stable benefits. Besides, manufacturing sector plays an important role in job creation in different services through supply and distribution chains. In order to absorb a large portion of unemployed people, there is a greater need for the manufacturing sector with stable jobs and good benefits. Through this process, the manufacturing sector shares prosperity especially in the low-income countries (Rodrik 2015).

Decent Work as a Tool for Sustainable Economic Growth: The ILO and its constituents pioneered the concept of decent work to promote work as "a source of personal dignity, family stability, peace in the community, democracies that deliver for people and economic growth that expands opportunities for productive jobs and enterprise development. Job creation boosts living standard, raise productivity and social cohesion. Sustainable job creation can be defined as the process that promotes economic growth, social inclusion and environmental protection (UNCTAD 2015). Thus, jobs in any sector need to comply with four criteria in order to be considered as 'decent jobs'; which include employability, decent wage, occupational health and safety, and workers' rights.

Perspectives on the Manufacturing Sector in Bangladesh's Development Discourse: Accelerated growth and reducing poverty, income inequality and regional disparity are the overreaching goals of the current development paradigm of Bangladesh. This is reflected in different national plans (Sixth Five Year Plan (2011–15), Seventh Five Year Plan (2016–2020) and Ten Year Perspective Plan (2011–2020) and sectoral policies and initiatives such as Industrial Policy 2012 and 2015, SME Policy Strategies 2005 and The Bangladesh Economic Zones Act (BEZA) 2010, etc. The main strategy is to create productive employment in the manufacturing sector (Bakht and Basher 2015). Development of small and medium enterprises is the key concern in this regard. Enhanced micro, small and medium enterprises constitute a key component strategy to reduce poverty and overcome regional disparity (GoB 2011). To become a sustained driver of economic growth, the manufacturing sector needs to put much emphasis on diversifying its base. Side by side, it is important to support trade and industrial policies with a high focus on the supply side constraints of the manufacturing sector. Some of these constraints include lack of working capital, high-interest rate, shortage of skilled workers, lack of managerial skill, and availability of poor physical infrastructure, inefficient port, higher transport cost, week institution, poor law and order situation and invisible cost of doing business (Raihan 2015).

Overall, there is a dearth of information with regard to sectoral decomposition of employment in the manufacturing sector of Bangladesh, the extent of decent nature of those employment and level of sustainability of those jobs. The present paper intends to highlight those issues.

3 Structural Change of Bangladesh Economy and Rise of the Manufacturing Sector

3.1 Structure and Composition of the Manufacturing Sector

Bangladesh has experienced consistent economic growth over the past several decades. Since 1980, an additional one percentage point of GDP growth has been attained in every decade mainly due to double-digit growth of the industrial sector and almost unchanged growth in service sector along with slow-down of the agriculture sector. Consequently, the share of agriculture sector has declined along with a rising share of industry and services (Fig. 1). Such structural changes in the economy have contributed to a change in the composition of labour as well. Unlike changes in the composition in GDP, changes in the composition of employment in different sectors are rather slow; the agriculture sector still contributes to the highest employment share in the economy (Fig. 1). Such transformation in the economy provides two messages—first, the process of structural changes is still slow which could not adequately generate productive employment opportunities in non-agriculture sector; second, scopes for job creation in more productive sectors is still limited. Hence, it is

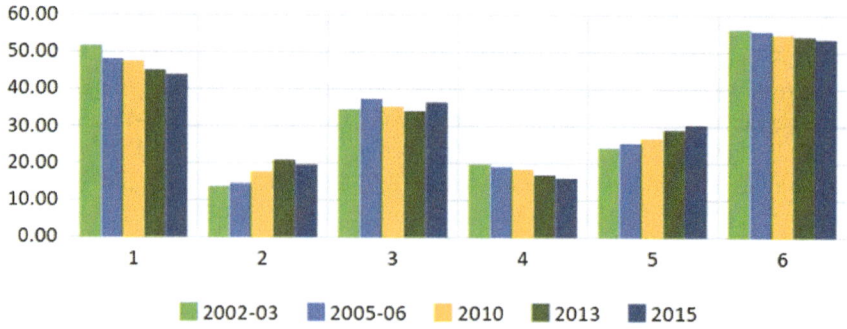

Fig. 1 Share of employment and GDP in broad economic sectors. *Source* World development indicators (WDI) database

important to explore inner weaknesses in the manufacturing sector for the sluggish growth of new jobs.

In the process of structural transformation, the industrial sector has experienced a number of changes mainly through the manufacturing sector. Over time, the manufacturing sector is dominated by few industries—both in terms of sectoral share of GDP and employment as well as an overwhelming share of large and medium scale enterprises (Fig. 2a, b). There is a growing concentration of these segments of industries. The share of top five manufacturing industries in GDP has increased from 16% in 2000 to 38% in 2012. Besides, investment in the manufacturing sector is overwhelmingly dominated by domestic private investment; foreign direct investment is largely concentrated to a few industries including textiles, apparels, agro-processing industries, etc. Lack of diversity is a major challenge in the process of growth of the manufacturing sector.

Although SMEs have less contribution to the GDP, they constitute a higher share in terms of the number of enterprises and number of employment. These enterprises

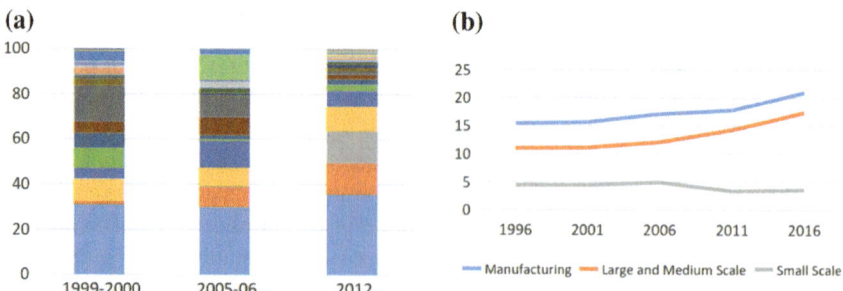

Fig. 2 **a** Changing composition of the manufacturing sector and **b** dominance of large and medium scale enterprises in manufacturing GDP. *Source* For **a** different issues of census of manufacturing industries and survey of manufacturing industries of the Government of Bangladesh and for **b** different issues of Bangladesh Economic Review (2017)

are very small in size and a part of them are self-employed and lack adequate competitiveness. Lack of formal contractual arrangement is a major attribute of a large section of these enterprises—over 87% of Bangladesh's manufacturing related activities are informal in nature which are mainly micro, small, cottage, and medium-scale industries. The weak contractual arrangement, often creates obstacles toward ensuring decent jobs. According to Moazzem (2009), a large part of these enterprises because of their low level of profitability and low level of investible surplus, have limited potentiality to grow and thereby unable to graduate to the next stage, i.e. from small to medium or medium to large enterprises.

A large part of manufacturing units have been experiencing spatial shift over time. Because of locational advantage, a major share of industrial units was earlier located in the districts such as Dhaka, Chittagong, Narayangonj, Norshingdi, Rajshahi, Bogra, Comilla, Gazipur, etc. Over the last decades, the rise of industrial clusters pushes enterprises to gradually relocate in the different regions. Consequently, industrial sector had experienced with spatial redistribution where traditional local market-based industrial enterprises such as bakery and food processing had relocated from advanced regions to relatively less advanced regions perhaps because of their low level of productivity and less profitability and also because of the rise in wage cost, rents and other costs (Moazzem 2014).[1]

Although trade openness of the country has been increasing, this has yet to ensure large-scale participation in the global value chain; only a few competitive industries have been participated in the value chain. In other words, a large section of domestic enterprises concentrates on the domestic market. Such diverge nature of market focus of major industries raise the issue of the different level of competitiveness of major manufacturing industries. Compared to its competing countries, the rate of participation in the global value chain is low—with China has the highest level of participation (59%) followed by Vietnam (48%), Pakistan (40%) and India (36%). Bangladesh has the same level of participation that of India (36%). In other words, most of the sectors are yet to be ready to participate in the global value chains.

The changes in the structure and composition of the manufacturing sector have occurred due to a number of domestic and external factors. *First*, the implementation of economic liberalization policies under which private investment has been opened up in most of the manufacturing sector in the 1980s and followed by the implementation of trade liberalization policy in late 1980s have provided domestic manufacturing sector to grow in the following decades. Unfortunately, the level of impact as anticipated through trade liberalization on employment was not found to be so strong under the following period (CPD 2011). *Second*, the preferential market access, particularly in the developed countries which initiated in late 1970s, has made a significant contribution to the growth of export-oriented industries, mainly in the RMG industry. The growth of the RMG sector has made a significant contribution to employment in the following decades. *Third*, availability of low-cost labour encourage setting up large scale labour-intensive manufacturing industries which happened in Bangladesh taking the advantage of market access facility. *Fourth*, favourable

---

[1] However, few industrial locations have observed almost no changes in the composition.

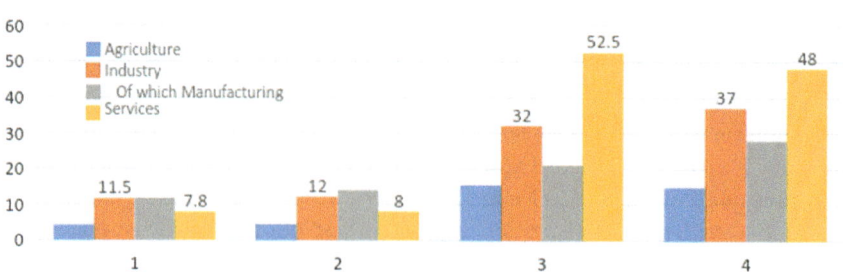

Fig. 3 Structure of Bangladesh economy in 2021. *Source* Seventh five-year plan (2016–2020), Government of Bangladesh

government policies (fiscal and budgetary) have facilitated industries to grow in the subsequent period. Despite such positive condition for the growth of industries, only a few sectors have experienced growth in the subsequent period.

As the economy progresses, the further structural transformation would shift more economic activities in the non-agriculture sectors. According to the projection of the Seventh Five-Year Plan (2016–2020), the manufacturing sector will grow further with more share in GDP in the next 5 years (Fig. 3). Such changes in the structure of the economy, as well as changes in the composition of the manufacturing sector, would impact upon changes in the composition of the labour force as well. The challenge is whether the changes in the economy would ensure enough employment opportunities in the future as well and more importantly, and the extent to which those changes in the employment structure would be sustainable.

3.2   Bangladesh's Manufacturing Sector in the Context of South Asia

Most of the South Asian economies have been passing a period which is according to Rodrik (2015) called 'premature deindustrialisation' with a declining share of the manufacturing sector in the overall share of GDP (Fig. 4a, b). Bangladesh is an exception in this regard which unlike other South Asian countries, has maintained a rising share of the manufacturing sector in GDP. However, the composition of the manufacturing sector in Bangladesh is almost similar to those in other South Asian countries. Local private investment is the major source of investment in all south Asian countries.

Except the Maldives, FDI inflow (in terms of GDP) in most of the South Asian countries is a miniscule (less than 2% of GDP) (Fig. 4c). However, India is the highest recipient of FDI in South Asia (about 87.5% of total FDI inflow in South Asia) and its share has been growing. Except India, capital market in other South Asian countries is at the nascent stage and contribute to a small share of total investment in the industrial sector. In general, entrepreneurs prefer less corporatization in terms of ownership (preferably proprietorship) of manufacturing enterprises and have a lack

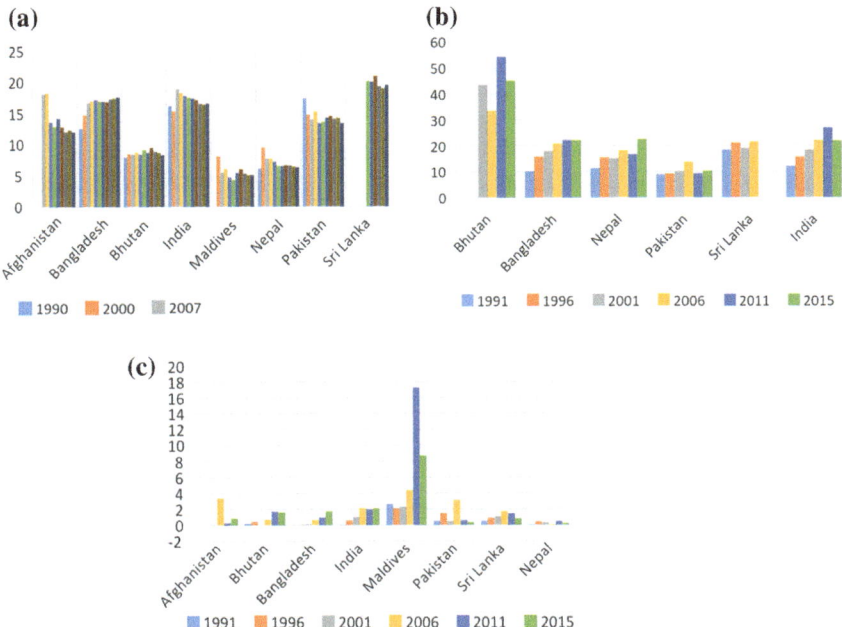

Fig. 4 a Manufacturing value added (% of GDP); **b** gross fixed capital formation in private sector (% of GDP); **c** net FDI inflow (% of GDP) in South Asian countries. *Source* World Bank (2017) World development indicators (WDI) database

of interest for the public listing of their entities. Overall, Bangladesh's manufacturing sector has a serious lack in corporate governance in all accounts including ownership, management and operation, worker-related issues, etc. Thus Bangladesh needs to take lessons from other South Asian countries in terms of corporatization, enlistment in the capital market and more FDI inflow in order to ensure better performance of the manufacturing sector.

4 Dynamics and Changes in the Manufacturing Sector: Implications for Employment

4.1 Establishments and Employment in the Manufacturing Sector

The establishments in the manufacturing sector have been increasing at a rate of 6% per annum in the past decade. According to the Survey of Manufacturing Enterprises (SME 2012), a total of 42,792 establishments were in operation in 2012 which was 31,638 in 2006 and 23,174 in 2000. Over time, compositional changes took place in terms of number of establishment; a large number of establishments related to few industries. Major manufacturing industries include textiles, RMG, food and non-metallic mineral products which comprised 73.5% of total establishments in 2012 (79.9% in 2000).

Over the past decades, non-traditional manufacturing industries have made considerable progress. These non-traditional establishments include chemical products, electrical equipment, leather products, paper products, basic metals, rubber and plastic products. In contrast, a number of industries have experienced a reduction of establishments such as textiles and pharmaceuticals. Such changes in the composition of establishments are likely to have implications on employment in respective sectors as well.

Manufacturing sector can be broadly classified as export-oriented manufacturing industry (i.e. those export over 50% of their total output) and domestic market-oriented manufacturing industry (i.e. those sell over 50% of their total output at the local market). Majority of enterprises in different sectors are domestic market oriented (Fig. 5). Industries which are fully domestic market oriented include coke and refined petroleum, machinery and equipment, motor vehicles and trainers, installation of machinery and recycling, etc. Industries which are exposed more to export market include RMG (95% of total production), transport equipment (82%), leather and leather goods (74%) and textiles products (57%). A number of industries export limited share of their products which include paper and paper products, computer, electronic and optical products, electrical equipment, etc. Lack of competitiveness, limited capacity, poor network with buyers, low quality of products and lack of competent human resources—are the major weaknesses of a large section of domestic market-oriented enterprises for not being able to become export-oriented industries. Some of the industries despite their strong potentials to be globally competitive

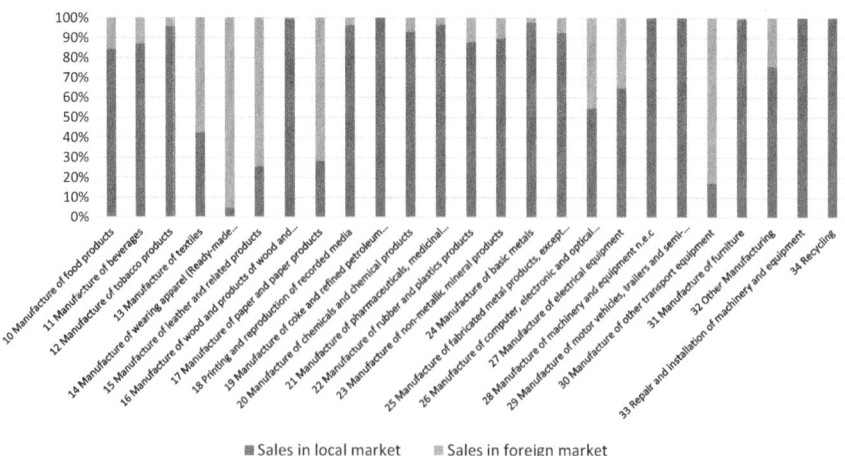

Fig. 5 Ratio of market exposure of enterprises under different manufacturing industries. *Source*: Different issues of the census of manufacturing industries and survey of manufacturing industries

are unable to do that because of the lack of 'critical minimum' number of globally competitive enterprises.

It is found that export-oriented industries are significantly higher than domestic market-oriented industries both in terms of the number of establishments (2.3 times) and number of employment (4.4 times) (Table 1). Export-oriented industries comprise 69% of total manufacturing establishments and 81% of total manufacturing employment during 2012. More importantly, the average size of establishments (in terms of employment) in export-oriented industries are larger than that of the domestic market-oriented industries and the size of the former is getting bigger while the size of the latter is getting smaller.

In terms of the number of workers employed in each enterprise, the manufacturing sector can be categorized as 'micro' (less than 9 workers), 'small' (9–49 workers), 'medium' (50–99 workers) and 'large' enterprises (100 workers and above). According to SMI 2012, over three-fourths of enterprises are either 'micro' (40.6%) or 'small' (36.6%) types of enterprises (Table 2). Sectors which comprise overwhelmingly 'small sized' firms include wood, furniture and repair of machinery. On the other hand, sectors comprise overwhelmingly 'medium sized' enterprises include paper, pharmaceuticals and electrical equipment. RMG is the lone sector which comprises 'large sized' enterprises. Over the past decade, the number of enterprises and employment in small enterprises has been growing. However, the growth of enterprises in medium and large scale industries has slowed down although the growth of employment in those enterprises is still positive and in cases considerably high.

Over the years, the average size of different types of enterprises is getting bigger which in other way indicates vertical expansion of enterprises. Enterprises under industries getting bigger include mostly export-oriented industries such as RMG, leather, pharmaceuticals and rubber except basic metals. In contrast, size of enterprises of most of the domestic market industries got smaller. Overall, there are concerns with regard to enterprises under domestic market-oriented industries particularly with regard to their level of 'competitiveness' and capacity of 'employment generation'.

Local private investment comprises the major share of investment in the manufacturing sector (Fig. 6). Industries which are fully based on domestic private investment include wood, paper, printing, chemical, basic metals, computer, electronics, furniture, etc. Few industries which endowed a part of foreign direct investment include RMG, leather and leather products, refined petroleum, etc. The ownership of most of the small-sized enterprises portrays that local private investment has limited capacity to expand their businesses. On the other hand, limited foreign investment in the manufacturing sector indicates that domestic business environment is not adequately attractive to ensure a large volume of FDI in the country.

Foreign direct investment in the manufacturing sector is overwhelmingly concentrated to a limited number of industries. Of the total stock of inward FDI of US$14.5 billion, only 26.8% has been invested in different manufacturing industries which include textiles (17.6%), food processing (2.07%), cement (1.91%), agriculture and fishing (1.87%), pharmaceuticals (1.4%), leather (1.17%) and metal products (0.79%). Most of these investments have been generated outside South Asia such as

Table 1 Number of establishment by size and major industry

Sub-sectors	No. of establishments			Share of total establishments			Av. yearly growth	
	1999–00	2005–06	2012	1999–00	2005–06	2012	2000–06	2006–12
Beverages	42	27	367	0.2	0.1	0.9	–6	209.9
Wood and cork	373	45	302	1.6	0.1	0.7	–14.7	95.2
Chemical products	43	85	563	0.2	0.3	1.3	16.3	93.7
Manufacture of motor vehicles, trailers and semi-trailers	41	30	137	0.2	0.1	0.3	–4.5	59.4
Fabricated metal	874	333	1449	3.8	1.1	3.4	–10.3	55.9
Manufacture of electrical equipment	251	251	884	1.1	0.8	2.1		42
Leather	188	283	930	0.8	0.9	2.2	8.4	38.1
Paper products	106	384	902	0.5	1.2	2.1	43.7	22.5
Manufacture of other transport equipment	197	125	276	0.9	0.4	0.7	–6.1	20.1
Tobacco products	464	242	487	2.0	0.8	1.2	–8	16.9
Other manufacturing	28	122	235	0.1	0.4	0.6	56	15.4
Basic metals	196	633	1205	0.8	2.0	2.8	37.2	15.1
RMG	2639	4532	6984	11.4	14.3	16.5	12	9
Non-metallic mineral products	2050	3063	4654	8.8	9.7	11.0	8.2	8.7
Food	5453	6081	8441	23.5	19.2	20.0	1.9	6.5

(continued)

Table 1 (continued)

Sub-sectors	No. of establishments			Share of total establishments				Av. yearly growth	
	1999–00	2005–06	2012	1999–00	2005–06	2012		2000–06	2006–12
Rubber and plastics products	305	784	1036	1.3	2.5	2.4		26.2	5.4
Petroleum products	7	15	19	0.0	0.0	0.0		19	4.4
Manufacture of furniture	462	963	1055	2.0	3.0	2.5		18.1	1.6
Textiles	8383	11,778	10,983	36.2	37.2	26.0		6.7	−1.1
Recorded media	764	1077	904	3.3	3.4	2.1		6.8	−2.7
Pharmaceuticals, medicinal chemical and botanical products	308	785	494	1.3	2.5	1.2		25.8	−6.2
Total	23,174	31,638	42,307	100.0	100.0	100.0		6.1	5.9

Source Different issues of the census of manufacturing industries and survey of manufacturing industries, Government of Bangladesh

Table 2 Size wise (no. of employment) distribution of manufacturing industry

BSCIC and description	Share in 2012			
	Micro	Small	Medium	Large
Total	40.6	36.6	14.3	8.5
Food	67.9	28.6	3.1	1.2
Beverages	43.9	51.0	3.8	1.4
Tobacco products	51.3	27.9	10.9	9.9
Textiles	49.4	37.0	10.4	3.3
RMG	10.9	15.3	34.4	39.4
Leather	57.3	29.5	10.8	2.5
Wood and cork	87.1	10.3	2.3	0.3
Paper products	23.7	71.6	4.7	0.0
Recorded media	46.2	50.3	3.4	0.0
Petroleum products	47.4	47.4	0.0	5.3
Chemical products	25.2	58.3	11.5	5.0
Pharmaceuticals, medicinal chemical and botanical products	3.0	79.4	10.1	7.5
Rubber and plastics products	51.0	44.4	3.4	1.3
Non-metallic mineral products	3.5	59.8	33.0	3.7
Basic metals	9.9	57.2	28.8	4.1
Fabricated metal	54.7	44.0	1.3	0.0
Manufacture of computer, electronic and optical products	52.3	44.3	1.3	2.0
Manufacture of electrical equipment	37.1	60.0	1.6	1.4
Manufacture of machinery and equipment	68.2	23.6	6.2	2.1
Manufacture of motor vehicles, trailers and semi-trailers	55.5	37.2	5.8	1.5
Manufacture of other transport equipment	45.7	44.6	6.9	2.9
Manufacture of furniture	75.5	22.3	1.4	0.9
Other manufacturing	79.6	14.5	3.0	3.0
Repair and installation of machinery and equipment	92.5	7.5	0.0	0.0

Source Different issues of the census of manufacturing industries and survey of manufacturing industries, Government of Bangladesh

South Korea and Hong Kong in the textile sector (29.8% and 17.7%, respectively), UK in food processing (58.6%), the Netherlands in cement (66.5%), Thailand in agriculture and fishing (60%), UK in pharmaceuticals (52.5%), Taiwan in leather and leather products (42.4%), and Canada in metal products (47.6%). According to Table 3, FDI from South Asian countries is observed in case of India mainly in textiles (2.74%), food processing (5.6%), agriculture and fishing (13.2) and pharmaceuticals (8.8%); Pakistan in case of textiles (0.19%) and metal products (18.9%); and Sri Lanka in case of textiles (1.17%), food processing (1.5%) and cement (0.1%).

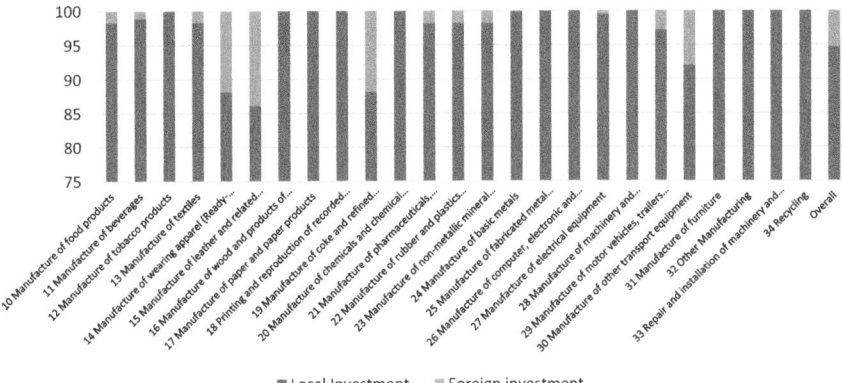

Fig. 6 Ratio of local and foreign direct investments in different industries. *Source* Different issues of the census of manufacturing industries and survey of manufacturing industries

Overall, investors of South Asian countries are yet to take part in major value chains as like those of non-South Asian countries perhaps because of limited capacity and restrictions over outward FDI.

4.2 Productivity in the Manufacturing Enterprises

The competitiveness in the manufacturing sector is largely constrained by a low level of productivity in most of the industries. Overall labour productivity (i.e. gross value added per unit of labour) in the manufacturing sector is very low (Tk. 300,000 per unit of labour per annum) (Table 4). Relatively high labour productivity is observed in case of industries such as motor vehicles, basic metals, petroleum products, electrical equipment, chemical products, beverages and computer, which are mostly capital intensive in nature, small in size and low in the number of establishments. In contrast, labour-intensive industries such as leather, RMG, furniture and recycling are less productive. Such differences in labour productivity would cause differences in returns to labour, where return to labour in the labour-intensive industries is likely to be lower. Interestingly, export-oriented industries are relatively less productive compared to that of domestic market-oriented industries. Overall, structural transformation in the economy towards more manufacturing industries somewhat led to grow low-productive labour-intensive industries which ultimately affect decent employment as well.

Table 3 Share of inward FDI stock by major South Asian and other Asian Countries in the manufacturing and non-manufacturing sectors (% of the total sectoral stock of FDI)

Sectors	South Asian countries			Other Asian countries			
	India	Pakistan	Sri Lanka	Hong Kong	China	South Korea	Singapore
Manufacturing sectors							
Textiles and wearing	2.7	0.2	1.2	17.7	3.3	29.9	2.5
Food	5.6		1.5	0.0			10.4
Cement				9.3			
Agriculture and fishing	3.5	0.0	−0.4	0.4	0.9		8.5
Pharmaceuticals and chemicals	8.8		0.1	0.0	0.2		
Leather and leather products	0.0			2.4	12.7	1.8	
Metal and machinery products	0.3	19.0	0.0	0.8	0.9	0.0	0.0
Other sectors	4.0	0.1	1.5	7.7	6.5	13.1	14.9
Non-manufacturing sectors							
Gas and petroleum		0.00					0.99
Banking	5.4	11.0	5.7	2.9		3.5	0.4
Telecommunication	0.0						22.9
Power	2.2		3.2	2.5	−0.2		35.1
Trading	5.0	0.2	0.6	2.4	3.5	10.6	34.0
Insurance	6.0						
Computer software and IT	1.8		−0.1	4.8		1.2	5.0
NBFI	1.6		7.5	0.8			
Total FDI stock							
Total FDI stock	2.3	1.7	1.5	5.0	1.7	7.7	8.6

Source Bangladesh Bank (2017)

5 Trends in Employment in the Manufacturing Sector

5.1 Composition of Employment in the Manufacturing Sector

Employment in the manufacturing sector has doubled within a period of twelve years—from 2.5 million in 2000 to 5.0 million in 2012. A major share of manufacturing employment is in export-oriented industries and over time the share has

Table 4 Gross value added per unit of labour (million Taka per annum)

	Gross value added per unit of labour 2012 (million Tk. per annum)
Motor vehicles, trailers	1.9
Basic metals	1.7
Petroleum products	0.9
Electrical equipment	0.9
Chemical products	0.7
Beverages	0.6
Computer, electronic and optical products	0.6
Food	0.6
Other transport equipment	0.5
Fabricated metal	0.5
Pharmaceuticals	0.4
Tobacco products	0.4
Rubber and plastics products	0.4
Machinery and equipment	0.4
Paper products	0.3
Other manufacturing	0.3
Manufacture of furniture	0.3
Repair and installation of machinery and equipment	0.3
Leather	0.3
Textiles	0.3
Wood and cork	0.3
Non-metallic mineral products	0.2
RMG	0.2
Recorded media	0.2
Recycling	0.1
Total	0.3

Source Different issues of the census of manufacturing industries and survey of manufacturing industries of the Government of Bangladesh

further concentrated. Employment distribution is highly concentrated to a few sectors—RMG sector alone is accounted for over 55% of total employment and the top three sectors are accounted for 80% of total manufacturing employment. Other major sectors contributing to employment include textiles (805,000 and 16% of total manufacturing employment), non-metallic minerals (471,000 and 9.4%), food processing (280,000 and 5.6%), and basic metals (120,000 and 2.4%). A large section of the manufacturing industries contributes very limited level of employment—about 16 industries have individually contributed less than 1% of total manufacturing employment.

There are two contrasting trends observed in terms of generation of employment both in export-oriented and domestic market-oriented industries (Table 5). Majority of export-oriented industries which have experienced with both rises in share and number of employment are RMG, leather, pharmaceuticals, and rubber industries. A similar type of domestic market-oriented industries include paper products, chemical products, basic metals, furniture, etc. Some of the sectors have been losing their momentum as a contributor to generate employment. For example, a number of domestic market-oriented industries such as tobacco, wood and cork, recorded media, fabricated metal, electrical equipment and few export-oriented industries such as food, beverages have lost their share in manufacturing employment. Without improving the level of competitiveness, these sectors would not grow fast and thereby would not contribute much to generate employment. Overall, employment in the manufacturing sector is still highly concentrated to few sectors.

Within a few sectors, compositional changes in employment have taken place over time. RMG sector has gradually become the major source of manufacturing employment by replacing textiles which was the major source of employment in the early 1990s (Fig. 7a). Besides, a number of other sectors though at a limited scale contributed in employment generation as their share in total manufacturing employment has been increasing over time which includes food processing non-metallic minerals, recorded media, pharmaceuticals and leather (Fig. 7b). In contrast, a number of industries are losing importance in terms of sources of employment which include textiles, tobacco, electrical equipment, fabricated metal, etc. A reduced share of employment in some of the above-mentioned sectors can be happened due to—(a) slow growth of some sectors vis-à-vis those of average growth of total manufacturing sector and/or (b) shifting of manufacturing activities (at least partly) to more capital-intensive types of activities.

Compare to other South Asian countries, the performance of Bangladesh's manufacturing sector in terms of generating employment is not so encouraging (Fig. 8). In fact, the share of employment in the manufacturing sector is behind not only those of major South Asian economies (India and Sri Lanka) but also those of other competing economies of South East Asia (e.g. Thailand, Vietnam and Indonesia) and East Asia (e.g. China). Most of Bangladesh's competing countries possess diversified manufacturing base which could absorb more employment as well as could create more opportunities for employment, unlike those in Bangladesh. Hence Bangladesh needs to expand its manufacturing base beyond few sectors with a view to enhancing the share of employment.

5.2 Nature of Job in the Manufacturing Sector

Employment in the manufacturing sector of Bangladesh comprises different types of professionals and workers which include production workers, temporary workers,

Table 5 Employment in the manufacturing sector, 2012

BSCIC and description	Total employment in 2012	Share of total manufacturing labour
Total	5,015,937	100.00
RMG	2,762,335	55.07
Textiles	805,508	16.06
Non-metallic mineral products	471,850	9.41
Food	280,257	5.59
Basic metals	120,965	2.41
Leather	75,524	1.51
Pharmaceuticals	71,380	1.42
Chemical products	52,598	1.05
Tobacco products	52,204	1.04
Electrical equipment	44,556	0.89
Fabricated metal	44,462	0.89
Paper products	42,376	0.84
Rubber and plastics products	41,139	0.82
Manufacture of furniture	33,143	0.66
Recorded media	26,667	0.53
Beverages	20,448	0.41
Other transport equipment	17,921	0.36
Computer, electronic and optical products	16,390	0.33
Machinery and equipment n.e.c.	10,001	0.20
Other manufacturing	9,471	0.19
Wood and cork	8,528	0.17
Motor vehicles, trailers and semi-trailers	4,906	0.10
Repair and installation of machinery and equipment	1,558	0.03
Petroleum products	1,417	0.03
Recycling	333	0.01

Source Different issues of census of manufacturing industries and survey of manufacturing industries of the Government of Bangladesh

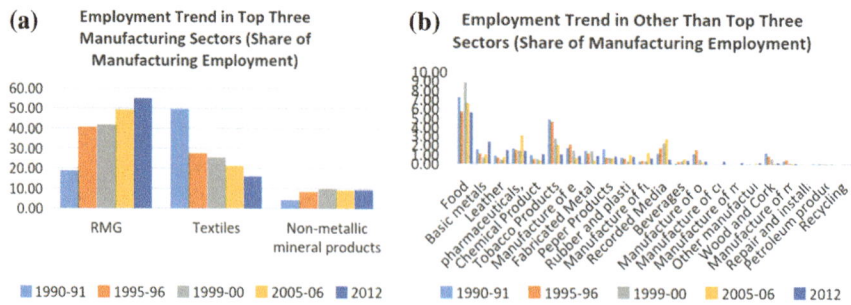

Fig. 7 a Employment share in top three manufacturing sectors and **b** employment share in rest of the manufacturing sectors. *Source* Different issues of the census of manufacturing industries and survey of manufacturing industries of the Government of Bangladesh

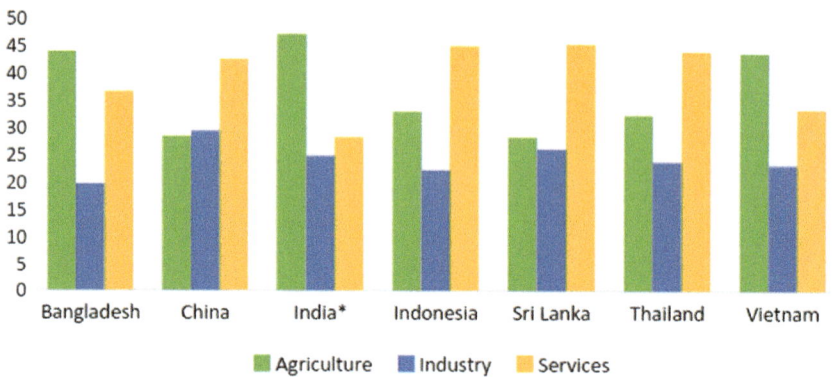

Fig. 8 Cross-country comparison of employment share in major sectors. *Source* World development indicators database

owners/proprietors, administrative and managerial professionals, clerical and sales workers and working owners/proprietors. Over 80% of the total employed person has been employed as production-related workers followed by temporary workers (8.6%); on the other hand, different categories of professionals comprise only a limited share which includes administrative and managers (4.1%), and clerical and sales workers (4.7%) (Table 6). However, the distribution of different categories of workers and professionals are disproportionately distributed among the sectors. RMG sector which is the major manufacturing sector employs 62.3% of total production workers, 42.1% of total administrative professionals and managerial professionals and 32.6% of clerical and sales workers. Textiles sector which is the second most important sector in terms of employment employed about 16.9% of production workers and 14.2% of administrative and management professionals while food processing, non-metallic and basic metal sectors employed about 3.9%, 6.2% and 1.7% of production workers respectively.

Table 6 Distribution of manufacturing employment in selected sectors (share of total employment under different categories), 2012

	Total employed person	Administrative and managerial	Clerical and sales workers	Production-related workers	Working own-ers/proprietors	Temporary labourers	Family helper
Total manufacturing (persons)	5,015,936	204,955	234,373	4,097,787	42,856	429,505	6461
Share (% of total)	100	4.1	4.7	81.6	0.85	8.56	0.12
Of which (% of total column)							
RMG	55.1	42.1	32.6	62.3	18.1	9.1	16.2
Textiles	16.1	14.2	17.2	16.9	22.7	6.4	52.9
Food	5.6	7.5	10.9	3.9	20.2	16.8	5.9
Other non-metallic mineral products	9.4	7.9	4.3	6.2	11.7	43.4	1.9
Basic metals	2.4	4.7	4.5	1.7	2.3	7.2	1.5
Others	11.4	23.6	30.5	9.0	25.0	17.1	21.6

Source Survey of Manufacturing Industries (2012), Government of Bangladesh

Other than top five sectors, employment in rest of the sectors in different types of jobs is rather limited (11.4% of total employment); only 6.2% of production workers, 7.9% of administrative and managerial professionals have been employed in other sectors. Interestingly, few sectors have experienced with an exceptionally high share of specific types of employment. For example, textiles sector has 22.7% proprietors and 52.9% family helpers. Similarly, the food processing sector has 20% of total proprietors of the manufacturing sector while non-metallic minerals sector employs 43.4% of temporary workers. In other words, the structure of employment in different industries has lots of variations which indicate nature of work of particular sectors, level of corporatization, level of investment and types of contractual arrangement with the workers, etc.

Overall gender balance in the manufacturing sector is quite encouraging. Out of 5.1 million employed, 2.79 million workers are male (55.8%) and 2.2 million workers are female (44.2%). Such a gender balance was possible because of the higher share (64% of total employment) of female workers in the most labour-intensive sector, RMG. Unlike RMG, most sector has experienced a wide gap in gender balance in employment. Similarly, unlike production workers, the gender gap is quite widespread in all other types of jobs—most importantly in management and administrative professionals (Fig. 9). Lack of gender balance in non-RMG sectors is one of the concerning issues in order to ensure decent employment.

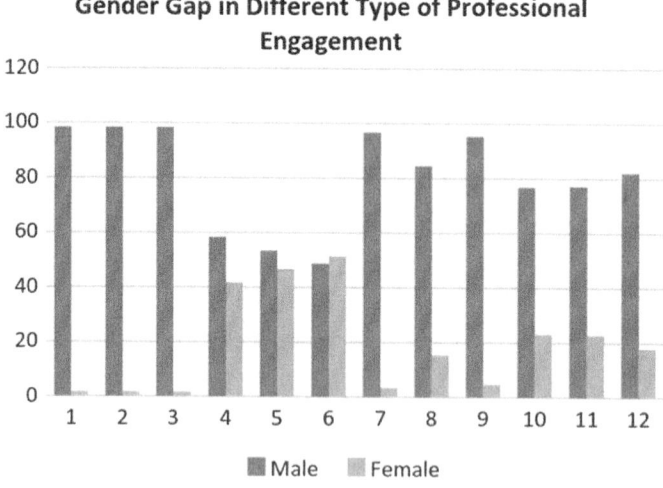

Fig. 9 Gender gap in different types of professional engagement, 2012. *Source* Survey of Manufacturing Industries (2012), Government of Bangladesh

5.3 Management Professionals

The manufacturing sector has suffered with the dearth of adequate management professionals. During 2012, a total of 204,955 administrative and managerial professionals worked in the manufacturing sector. This accounts for only 4% of total employment in the manufacturing sector. More importantly, about half (42%) of those management professionals were involved in a single sector, i.e. RMG. Worker–employee ratio is higher in tobacco products and wearing apparels (about 30), while that ratio is lower in computer electronic industry (Figs. 10 and 11). Besides, the gender gap is quite acute in the case of management professionals, as over 93% of management professionals are male. Most industries have very high female—male management professional ratio which as high as 250:1 in case of non-metallic products industry.

5.4 Future Demand for Skills in Major Manufacturing Industries

With the rise in the major manufacturing sector, demand for employment is likely to grow. The nature of future demand for employment will depend on the nature of jobs

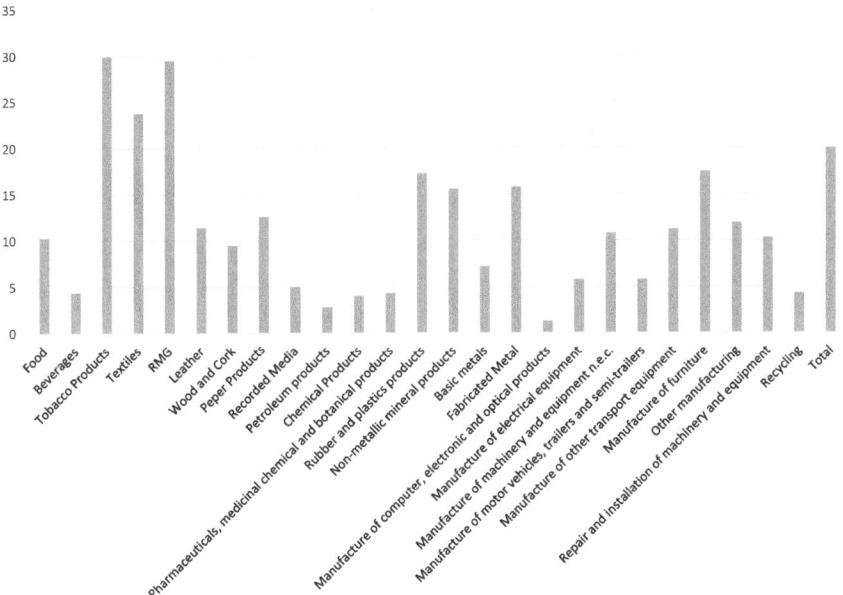

Fig. 10 Ratio of worker–employee in different manufacturing sector. *Source* Survey of Manufacturing Industries (2012), Government of Bangladesh

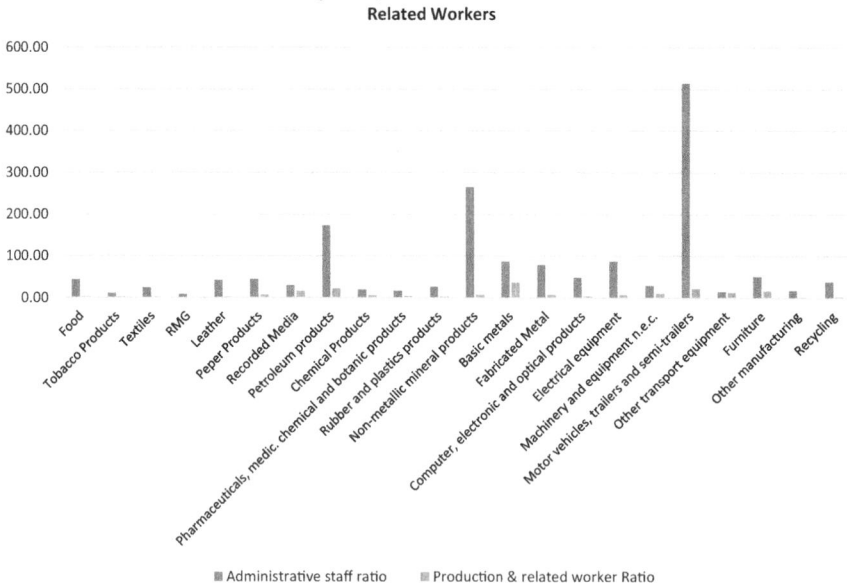

Fig. 11 Male–female ratio in management professionals and production related workers. *Source* Survey of Manufacturing Industries (2012)

as well as scope to convert some specific types of jobs through better technologies. Murshid (2016) shows that major sectors constrained with skilled, semi-skilled and unskilled professionals (Table 7). For example, agro-food processing industry has a dearth of 77% of skilled and 75% of semi-skilled professionals. The study reveals future demand for workers and training for other manufacturing sectors such as leather goods, light engineering, RMG and shipbuilding. The top manufacturing sector, RMG needs to raise its unskilled workers by 3.2%, semi-skilled workers by 48.7% and skilled workers by 122% by 2025–26; the sector needs to train over 2.1 million workers in order to cater to the future demand for workers.

6 Decent Job in the Manufacturing Sector

Decent jobs are an important component of sustainable development of the manufacturing sector. According to ILO (1999), decent jobs comprise employability, decent wages, workplace safety and security and workers' rights. Experience of decent jobs in the manufacturing sector is rather poor. While the manufacturing sector has experienced with creating employment opportunities, but the similar experience did not happen in case of other three issues—decent wages, workplace safety and security and workers' rights.

Table 7 Future demand for skills in some selected sectors

Sectors	Existing skill gap	% Increase in future labour demand (2025/26), base = 15/16	Future training needs (2025/26), base = 15/16
Agro-food	Overall: 76% Skilled: 77% Semi-Skilled: 75% Unskilled: 75%	261%	21,000
Leather goods	Unskilled: 6,935 Semi-Skilled: 6,664 Skilled: 62,246	107%	150,000
Light engineering	Overall: 35.97% Skilled: 43.3% Highly skilled: 25% Semi-skilled: 19.33%	Unskilled: 13.54% Semi-skilled: 15.02% Skilled: 58.50% Highly skilled: 76.95%	423,000
RMG	Unskilled: 8,577 Semi-skilled: 48,130 Skilled: 119,479	Unskilled: 3.17% Semi-skilled: 48.75% Skilled: 122.6%	2,117,000
Shipbuilding	NA	Unskilled: 677% Semi-skilled: 677% Skilled: 577%	53,000

Source Murshid (2016)

6.1 Employability

A major condition for ensuring decent employment is to provide a secure job for the workforce of the country. Job opportunities have improved in the manufacturing sectors but job security is remaining a major challenge. Working under informal contract, i.e. without proper registration and securing job-related documents, is a major weakness of employment. Over time, this informal nature of employment has been increasing—from 76% of total employment in 2000 to 87.5% in 2010. Although informality has increased both for male and female workers, the extent of the rise was much higher in the case of female workers. Over 92% of female workers had been working under informal labour contract while at the same time the ratio for male was 86%. The total number of casual workers has increased both among male and female workers in urban and rural areas. Unfortunately, wages of casual workers did not increase to that extent.

Child labour is still a major concern for employment in the manufacturing sector of Bangladesh. Recent data on child labour is, however, unavailable. According to a data of 2005–06, child labour in the total population was about 1.2% which declined compared to the previous survey period (2002–03). In fact, the manufacturing sector is suffering from using child labour in a different form. Similarly, most of the sectors suffer due to poor gender balance. Women have very low share in most types of

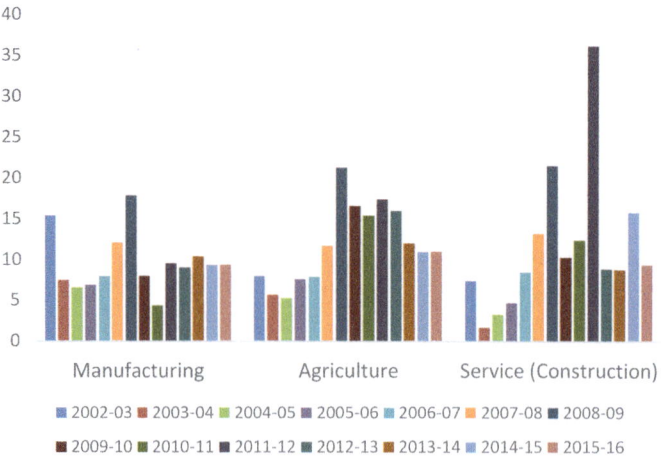

Fig. 12 Yearly changes of wage indices in major sectors. *Source* BBS (2016), Government of Bangladesh

employment—the share was lowest in case of senior officials, managers, and clerks, while the share was highest in case of trade works, professionals, etc. Ensuring gender balance in the job market should be a priority in the future.

6.2 Workers' Wages

Workers' wages in the manufacturing sector experience rather sluggish growth compared to that in agriculture and service sectors during 2000s. The growth of wage rate in the manufacturing sector has remained stagnant over the last several years (Fig. 12). The growth of wage rates in major manufacturing sectors has been influenced by the minimum wage rates revised by the Minimum Wage Board. Since the regular revision of wages did not take place in major sectors, overall wage rate indices remain at the same level.[2] According to the Labour Act (Amended) 2013, the minimum wage in different industries is supposed to be revised taking into consideration of 12 key indicators which include workers' productivity, capacity of the industry, growth of sales and profit earned by employers, etc. However, during the time of tri-partite discussion and negotiation for revision of minimum wages, often those indicators are not properly taken into consideration. Because of the lack of timely revision of minimum wages, often workers do not get a part of the benefit of increased productivity and efficiency in their activities.

---

[2]There is a long period of hibernation when minimum wages in major sectors was not revised. Between 1985 and 2005 was that period. Afterwards revision of wages started (number of sectors experienced revisions for several times).

Bangladesh's average wage/salary of employed workers/professionals is not necessarily the lowest as often projected/perceived. The average wage of the working
population, according to the Survey of Manufacturing Enterprises, 2012 was about
US$162 which is higher than that of a number of Asian economies. The average
wage/salary of Bangladesh's workers is ranged between as low as US$116 per month
in case of elementary occupations to as high as US$338 per month in case of man-
agement professionals. A large section of manufacturing workers are plant operators
who received about US$153. In general, wages in the rural areas is lower than in urban
areas (it is 77% compared to urban areas) and wages of female workers/professionals
is about 82% of that of male workers/professionals. In case of rural–urban difference,
the gap is lowest in case of elementary operations and highest in case of managers.
On the other hand gap in male–female wages is the lowest in case of managers and
the highest in case of elementary operations.

Moazzem and Raz (2014) showed that even after several revisions of minimum
wage in the RMG sector, it is still 35% less than the required minimum level. More
importantly, the minimum wage is still 62% less than the aspirational living wage.
However, weak negotiation in tri-partite wage board often slowed down the required
level of adjustment of minimum wages. Moreover, buyers and retailers who set the
price of suppliers' activities, often consider the issue of decent wages as an issue to
be dealt with by the suppliers.

6.3 Occupational Health and Safety

Occupational health and safety issues have long been neglected in major manufacturing industries. In recent years these issues have been strongly addressed in the
RMG sector particularly after the tragic incidence of Rana Plaza. According to the
data of the ILO on the situation of decent labour in Bangladesh, a large majority of
workers have to undertake excessive work against stipulated working hour. There is a
tendency to rise in excessive work in most of the jobs. According to the data of 2010,
about 51% of the total workforce had to undertake excessive work beyond stipulated
limit (48 h a week) which was 48% in 2006. In fact, excessive work is much higher
in case of male workers (65%) compared to that of female workers. Among different
types of professionals, excessive work is widely prevalent in the case of employer
(73%) and day labourers (66%). While, part of this excessive labour is related to
earn more due to subsistence pressure; however, a part of this is related to low wages
provided to workers which push them to work for more hours. However, excessive
working hours for a long period of time rather reduce the working life of workers
which is a major concern in many industries.

Poor condition of the workplace environment in terms of safety and security is
still a major concern. Over a thousand workers faced injuries every year because of
poor working condition. Of which about 30–50% are fatal injuries. The ratio of fatal
injury (over 10,000 workers) was 1.74 which was much higher compared to earlier
years. Part of the reason behind this rise in injury is the poor working condition in
the fracture owing to lack of proper inspection to be done by the inspection authority.

A limited number of factory inspectors—only 33 inspectors for 1 million registered workers in 2011 was one reason behind poor inspection record. Given the tragic accidents in the RMG sector in 2012 and 2013, a number of initiatives have been undertaken including the rise in number of inspectors and amendment of workplace safety and security clauses.

6.4 Workers' Rights

Workers' rights for organizing at the workplace and collective bargaining there are almost absent and still at a nascent stage in most of the industries. According to the data of 2010, there were only 7200 registered trade unions operated in the country with a membership of 2.2 million workers. Both the number of unions and their membership did not rise much over the years. Among those number of registered trade unions in the industrial sector is much lower.

After the tragic incidence of Rana Plaza collapse in 2013, registration of new trade unions at the factory level in the RMG sector has increased mainly because of enforcement of an agreement called the 'Sustainability Compact' signed by the government of Bangladesh, EU and the ILO. It is fact that few manufacturing sectors have practiced trade union related activities over a long period of time which include jute, pharmaceuticals, leather and leather products, etc. Trade union related activities are absent in export processing zones (EPZs), where a sizable number of manufacturing enterprises are in operation mostly owned by foreign owners. Workers are allowed to form 'workers' participation committee (WPC)' which comprise representatives of workers and employers in order to discuss workers' issues and concerns. However, the Government is now working on revising the EPZ law in order to allow forming trade unions in EPZ factories.

7 National and International Policies and Standards with Regard to Job Creation in the Manufacturing Sector

The development of the manufacturing sector over the last several decades has been significantly contributed by supporting government policies. Still, a huge gap exists between government policies and operational measures to realize those policies. Development of the manufacturing sector is the special focus in case of number of policies such as five year plans (5th, 6th and 7th Five Year Plans), Industrial Policy (2012, 2015 and 2018), Export Policy, Import Policy Order, SME Development Policy Guideline, FDI Act, BEPZA Act and SEZ Act which stipulate development of different industrial sectors, fiscal and budgetary measures, facilities for foreign investors, etc. (Table 8). Such policy measures are offered to facilitate production,

Table 8 Long-term policies on the growth of manufacturing sector and employment generation

Fifth Five-Year Plan (1997–2002)	1. Poverty alleviation and employment generation through human resource development 2. Promotion of small, cottage and rural industry as a major sector for employment generation 3. Skill development training, promotion of self-employment and foreign employment were the major activities in labour and manpower sector 4. Generation of substantial employment opportunity through an optimal choice of the traditional labour-intensive and new capital-intensive technology 5. Promotion of technology in directly productive sectors through research, diffusion and adaptations as a strategy for productive employment generation
Sixth Five-Year Plan (2011–15)	1. Government facilitate a vibrant, dynamic and competitive manufacturing sector that would contribute 30% to national income and absorb 20% of the workforce 2. To extract the true potential of the labour, total factor productivity of the labour force has to be trained 3. Set up new educational and training institute to meet the demand gap of manpower needed for rapidly expanding textile mills
Seventh Five-Year Plan (2016–20)	1. Creating good jobs for the large pool of under-employed and new labour force entrants by increasing the share of employment in the manufacturing sector from 15 to 20% 2. Economy will be creating additional jobs ranging from 2.3 million in FY 16 to 2.9 million in FY 20 3. If the projected GDP growth materializes then employment in the economy will exceed labour force each year 4. It is estimated that 12.9 million additional jobs will be available during the 5 years of Seventh Five-Year Plan including 2 million jobs for migrant workers

Source Compiled by authors from different official documents of the Government of Bangladesh

export, and investment in the manufacturing sector which would directly/indirectly contribute to generate more employment in the country.

A part of government's initiatives is linked with the development of physical infrastructural facilities such as building roads, rails and waterways, generation of electricity, supply of gas, improvement in logistic supported infrastructure especially seaports and land port facilities. Over the years, a significant amount of public investment has been targeted to develop these infrastructural facilities. Despite that, business enabling environment is still very poor—where noticeable progress is observed only in case of supply of electricity, development of key trade linked roads. Although initiatives have been taken to build special economic zones but progress is far behind in terms of ensuring availability of gas and other facilities there; further improvement is required in case of improvement of port facilities, development of railways and inland waterway connectivity, etc. Because of the absence of availability of 'full packaged' facilities, investors especially new investors found it constrained to invest in Bangladesh. Hence, the government needs to invest heavily to timely implementing infrastructural projects in order to facilitate more private investment.

Various government policies and laws have a specific target to promote decent employment in the manufacturing sector. The Labour Act (amended) 2013 is the most comprehensive law which deals with different worker-related issues including wages, working hour, use of child labour, workers' right to organize and collectively bargain, occupational health and safety, support for the injured workers, treatment benefits for injured and deceased workers, etc. While the issues of enforcement of minimum wage, working hour and abolishment of use of child labour have been maintained mainly in formal industries, there is a serious dearth of enforcement of related issues in case of informal industries. Revision of workers' minimum wages (infrequently done by the Minimum Wage Board) is part of the activity of the Ministry of Labour and Employment. Monitoring compliance standard with regard to occupational health and safety is another important job for the MoLE. Similarly ensuring workers' rights through workers' participated in different committees including trade unions is another important activity of the MoLE.

Unfortunately, the incidence of enforcement of workers' organization, collective bargaining, etc., has not yet been enforced in most of the manufacturing sectors even in formal export-oriented and domestic market-oriented industries. As a result, poor industrial relations in most of the manufacturing industries is a major concern. Lack of trust between employers and workers, government's partisan attitude towards employers, lack of understanding among workers about their rights and responsibilities, etc.—are the key issues related to slow progress in building industrial relations in the manufacturing sector.

With increasing linkages in global value chains in different manufacturing industries, market agents outside the country often play a major role in setting the terms of compliance at the factory level. Hence, buyers/brands/retailers have a direct role to play in order to ensure decent jobs in the manufacturing sector. It is important to put emphasis on effective enforcement of their code of conduct, sourcing guidelines set by government of key sourcing countries particularly in terms of better payment to the suppliers and better monitoring of their code of conduct, etc. Besides, governments and buyers of those countries should put emphasis on creating decent jobs for workers in the supplying countries.

Table 9 Changes in labour force and employment

Indicators (in lakhs)	2006–2010 (annual average)	2010–2013 (annual average)	2013–2016 (annual average)
Labour force	18.0	13.3	4.7
Employment	16.8	13.3	4.7
Overseas employment	5.8	5.2	5.2
Total employment	22.6	18.6	9.9

Source Centre for policy dialogue (CPD) (2017)

Fig. 13 Employment elasticity in terms of economic growth and investment. *Source* Centre for policy dialogue (CPD) (2017)

8 Challenges for Ensuring Sustained Growth of the Manufacturing Sector and Decent Jobs

8.1 Lack of Incremental Growth of Employment in the Manufacturing Sector

The manufacturing growth over the last several years has failed to ensure a commensurate level of growth in employment. The growth in employment has significantly declined in 2013–16 period compared to the previous period (2010–13) (Table 9). Most importantly, during 2013–16 period, net employment in the manufacturing sector declined by 0.9 million. This can be interpreted in another way—employment elasticity both in terms of economic growth and in terms of investment has significantly declined during 2013–16 period (Fig. 13). Such lowering level of employment generation, particularly in the manufacturing sector, needs thorough investigation. Part of this is related to increasing mechanization and automation in major manufacturing sectors which replace workers in some segments of the production process.

8.2 Increasing Concentration of Establishments in Few Industries

Lack of diversity in the manufacturing base is a major weakness towards developing a broad-based industrial sector and thereby to ensure a higher level of growth in employment. Over focus of public policies to specific sectors and ignoring opportunities of other potential sectors, limited capacity as per the requirement of the markets constrained developing a strong industrial base in the country. The absence of strategic policies which could facilitate intra-sectoral as well as inter-sectoral diversity in different kinds of industries and gradually becoming competitive for the global market hinders new sectors to emerge in the country. Over dependence on few sectors pose more risks towards sustainable development of the manufacturing sector as well as employment generation there.

8.3 Growing Concentration of Large Scale Enterprises

Increasingly domestic investment has been concentrated to large scale industries. Such concentration has created two different streams of employment—in one stream formal industries provide a better job with decent employment opportunities (to some extent) while informal industries provide a low paid job with the weak state of decent employment. Without diversification of the investment base by creating more investment by the medium and small investors, more investment by the foreign investors and more participation of small scale investors in the capital market, Bangladesh will continue to suffer from low base of private investment in the country.

8.4 Limited Foreign Investment

Diversification in the manufacturing base has been hampered because of the very limited inflow of FDI (only US$2.2 billion in FY2017). More importantly, the major share of FDI goes to service sector and only a limited share of FDI is targeted to different manufacturing sectors. Although the country's FDI policy appears to be liberal, however, foreign investors often face difficulty in investing in potential sectors. There are hidden barriers in case of investment by foreign companies. Bangladesh's business environment for manufacturing FDI is relatively weak compared to those of its competitors. Given the sluggish growth of private investment in the manufacturing sector, Bangladesh needs to make its policy more open and favourable towards foreign investment.

8.5 Lack of Adequate Management Professionals

Bangladesh's manufacturing sector is passing a transitional phase where a good number of entrepreneurs are interested to expand their businesses targeting bigger markets at local and global levels. However, a major challenge for them to expand their businesses is the lack of availability of skilled competent business professionals. The quality of professionals currently available is not up to the mark. Moreover, the business graduates who passed out every year from local public and private universities often lack competency in handling business-related jobs. These business graduates have serious weakness in understanding corporate management practices. As a result, large companies tend to recruit foreign professionals in those positions. A well-developed, skilled and competent business professional's base need to develop on an urgent basis in the country.

8.6 Limited Scope for Female Participation

Most of the employment in the manufacturing sector is male-dominated. Female participation is observed in few industries but only as production workers; but their participation is almost absent in managerial and administrative activities. Moreover, female workers face relatively less wage compared to that of male workers. There is an old mindset among the entrepreneurs towards recruiting male professionals for management and administrative jobs which constrain female professionals to get jobs in those positions. On the other hand, a large section of women does not put adequate emphasis on building their career in professional jobs.

8.7 Poor Deal with Buyers in GVCs

Local entrepreneurs working with foreign companies often complain about low price rates for their work. This constrains the entrepreneurs to earn the required level of profit for reinvestment for expansion of their enterprises as well as for improvement of various facilities required for decent jobs. Moreover, sluggish growth in global demand for Bangladesh's major manufacturing products creates adverse pressure both in volume and price of the product ('volume effect' and 'price effect') which ultimately reduce the production orders over the years. The price of products exported by Bangladesh has been declining at a higher rate (compared to its competing countries) in most of the major markets. As a result, margin received by manufacturers is found to be difficult to ensure own profit as well as to ensure decent wage and other benefits. Moreover, new investment has slowed down which also reduce opportunities for creating new employment.

8.8 Weak Institutional Performance in Managing Social Compliance

The size of the public institutions which are directly related with facilitation, monitoring and enforcement of national rules and public policies, unfortunately, did not improve much at the same pace as that of the growth of production of the manufacturing industries. Consequently, the private sector has been deprived of getting the required level of facilities from the public agencies. Similarly, workers have suffered due to weak enforcement of national rules and regulations. Public institutions such as MoLE (DIFE, DoL), BIDA, BSCIC, SME Foundation, DIFE and DoL—need to be strengthened in order to facilitate sustainable development of the manufacturing sector in Bangladesh.

8.9 Less-Focused Public Policy

Public policies are in most cases non-binding in nature which often discourage investors from taking long term investment decisions. Most of the public policies and various kinds of fiscal and budgetary instruments mentioned in those policies are mostly non-binding nature in terms of timeline, nature of benefits and requirement of unforeseen conditionalities. As a result investors' long term investment decisions face problem under such a situation. The government has yet to set strategies taking into account strategic interest of different sectors including lack of sectoral policies is a major weakness in this regard.

9 Suggestions for Sustainable Development of Manufacturing Sector by Creating Decent Jobs

9.1 Need Strategic Industrial and Trade Policies

Targeting potential industries having the capacity to generate adequate employment and thereby promote them for the long term by providing them adequate fiscal and budgetary support is urgently needed. Apart from sectoral support measures, more and more non-conventional support measures such as support to the entrepreneurs (irrespective of sectors) need to be expedited. In the long run, the government should refocus its stance towards more sectoral policies as well as entrepreneur/product/service specific policies to encourage potential investors across sectors to invest in the country.

9.2 Need to Promote Backward-Linkage Industries

Firms producing raw materials, intermediate products and capital machineries can also be encouraged to invest more in the country which would improve the competitiveness of the sector. Given the limited competitiveness of domestic entrepreneurs in investing in backward-linkage industries, the government should promote more and more foreign investment in establishing backward-linkage industries. Products of those industries would cater to the need of both domestic market as well as global market especially in the market where Bangladesh enjoys preferential market access facility. In this connection, FDI related facilities need to be extended at pre-establishment phases in order to provide facilities for taking credible investment decision (by providing market-related information including market players, market shares, market-related risks, size of market and amount of import, etc.).

9.3 Need to Develop Well Participated Production Chains

Small and medium sized firms should be promoted to take part in globally competitive production chains. The scope of participation of SMEs in the GVCs needs to be extended considering their limited capacity, competitiveness in a certain activity and limited exposure to the buyers' market. Taking the successful example of linkages between large and small enterprises in case of participation in global value chains as observed in developed and developing countries, government and private sector should promote such large-small enterprises linkages in a different segment of the value chains by assuring the global standards.

9.4 Develop Skilled Professionals Particularly Management Professionals

Ensuring the availability of competent professionals for industries is critically important. In this context, the government should put pressure through university grants commission to improve the quality of professionals of the private universities. The private university should consider thorough revision of their curriculum including case study based exercises, changes in examination systems and recruitment of competent teachers/trainers in order to improve the quality of their graduates. The private sector should collaborate with internationally renowned management schools to set up their franchises in Bangladesh with a view to develop skilled management professionals in the country. Besides, private universities should introduce short-term courses, lectures and, seminars (both online and in presence) to be taught by renowned professionals and academia in order to acquaint local students on global issues and practices.

9.5 Focused Initiative Targeting Female Workers and Professionals

Government should increasingly focus on improving the gender parity in the job market. More women should be encouraged to take part in the job market. In this context, necessary training should be provided to female professionals in order to encourage them to take more responsible jobs including management and administrative positions. More demonstration will be required at the factory level with the participation of female workers in equally competent higher level positions.

9.6 Foreign Investment in the Manufacturing Sector

Foreign direct investment should be facilitated by providing due facilities and incentives for setting up their establishments. It is important to provide pre-establishment facilities to potential investors in order to ensure better understanding by them about the market risks, opportunities and challenges. Given the increasing demand for raw materials, capital machineries and intermediate products, foreign companies specialized in those products could be approached to invest in Bangladesh.

9.7 Global Players of the GVCs Should Take More Positive Role

Instead of simply placing production order through fierce price deal, brands/retailers/buyers should take a more favourable role in ensuring decent jobs with regard to decent jobs in the supply chain. In this connection, they should follow 'open accounting' system to provide a better understanding about receipts vis-à-vis those of suppliers in order to be transparent whether market players participating in the production process get an adequate return for their contribution. Besides it, the participation of the manufacturing industry in the global value chain (GVC) can help to increase industrial upgrading and economic performance (Gereffi 2002).

9.8 Efficient and Capable Public Agencies

There need to have capable public agencies to oversee good business practices and thereby to ensure compliance standards. In this connection, public agencies should be equipped through adequate human and financial resources. Given the huge requirement of monitoring activities in order to ensure decent jobs, a part of their activities could be done through outsourcing part of inspection related activities to the private sector (e.g. public–private partnership model).

9.9 Development of 'Full-Packaged' Infrastructural Facilities for Setting up Industries

Public investment for infrastructure development should ensure full-packaged facilities for the private sector in order to do business in the country. These infrastructure include the development of roads, rails, inland waterways, seaports, inland terminals, land ports, special economic zones with all kinds of facilities including the supply of gas, electricity, water supply, ETP facilities, availability of trained workers, etc. The timely delivery of those facilities is urgently needed in order to assure the private sector about enabling a business environment in the country.

References

Bakht Z, Basher A (2015) Strategy for development of the SME sector in Bangladesh, vol 131. Bangladesh Institute of Development Studies, Dhaka, pp 1–39

Bangladesh Bank (2017). Foreign Direct Investment in Bangladesh Survey Report July–December, 2017. Statistics Division, Bangladesh Bank, Dhaka. https://www.bb.org.bd/pub/halfyearly/fdisurvey/fdisurveyjuldec2017.pdf

Bangladesh Economic Review (2017) Finance division, ministry of finance. https://mof.gov.bd/en/index.php?option=com_content&view=article&id=403&Itemid=1. Accessed 10 June 2017

BBS (2016) Statistical bulletin 2009–16. Bangladesh Bureau of Statistics, Dhaka

Centre for Policy Dialogue (CPD) (2011) Bangladesh labour and social trends report 2010. CPD and ILO, Dhaka

Centre for Policy Dialogue (CPD) (2017) Bangladesh economy in FY 2016–17. Interim review of macroeconomic performance. Centre for Policy Dialogue, Dhaka

Gereffi G (2002) Outsourcing and changing patterns of international competition in the apparel commodity chain. Paper presented at the conference on responding to globalization: societies, groups, and individuals, on 4–7 April 2002, in Colorado. http://www.colorado.edu/IBS/PEC/gadconf/papers/gereffi.pdf. Accessed 23 May 2017

GoB (2011) 6th five year plan. General Economic Division, Planning Commission. http://www.plancomm.gov.bd/sixth-five-year-plan/. Accessed 22 May 2017

Hami N, Muhamad RM, Ebrahim Z (2015) The impact of sustainable manufacturing practices and innovation performance on economic sustainability. Procedia CIRP 26:190–195

ILO (1999) Decent work. https://en.wikipedia.org/wiki/Decent_work. Accessed 22 May 2017

Moazzem KG (2009) Micro, small and medium enterprises in Bangladesh: are they scaling up?. https://www.cmi.no/publications/file/4261-micro-small-and-medium-enterprises-in-bangladesh.pdf

Moazzem KG (2014) Strategies for industrialisation in the next decade. A presentation made in a discussion meeting on Industrialisation Strategies for the next decade organised by the Ministry of Industries and Bangladesh Chamber of Industries

Moazzem KG, Raz S (2014) Minimum wage in the RMG sector of Bangladesh: definition, determination method and levels. CPD working paper 106, Dhaka

Murshid KAS (2016) Skill gap analysis for selected sectors. Bangladesh Institute of Development Studies. http://bids.org.bd/uploads/events/TS_1_KAS%20Murshid.pdf. Accessed 20 June 2017

Raihan S (2015) The manufacturing sector in Bangladesh: is it a sustained driver of economic growth and employment creation? The Daily Star. http://www.thedailystar.net/op-ed/economics/it-sustained-driver-economic-growth-and-employment-creation-81206. Accessed 22 May 2017

Rodrik D (2015) Premature deindustrialisation. Economics working paper 107, School of Social Science, Princeton

Survey of Manufacturing Industries (2012) Statistics and informatics division, ministry of planning, Government People's Republic of Bangladesh. http://203.112.218.65/WebTestApplication/userfiles/Image/LatestReports/SMI-%202012.pdf. Accessed 21 May 2017

The Seventh Five Year Plan (2016–20) Planning commission, ministry of planning, Government People's Republic of Bangladesh. http://www.plancomm.gov.bd/7th-five-year-plan-2/. Accessed 22 May 2017

UNCTAD (2015) Extractive industries and sustainable job creation. In: Oil gas mine trade and finance conference and exhibition. http://unctad.org/meetings/en/SessionalDocuments/suc_OilGasMine2015_bgNote_en.pdf. Accessed 24 May 2017

World Bank (2017) World development indicators. http://data.worldbank.org/data-catalog/world-development-indicators. Accessed 23 May 2017

Role of Manufacturing in Employment Generation in Nepal: Experiences and Lessons for the Future

Dilli Raj Khanal and Posh Raj Pandey

1 Introduction

1.1 General Background

South Asia faces uneven and transformative growth problems, despite excellent average growth performance. The threat of secular stagnation and prolonged crisis in today's global economic system are adding complexities to these economies. It is evidently clear that even after many years of the global financial crisis countries are confroned with both cyclical and structural predicaments, emanating from, among others, declining trade flows, stagnating investment, diminishing productivity growth, and above all aggravating unemployment and underemployment (UNDESA 2016). Such a phenomenon by raising questions on the efficacy of neo-liberal policy regimes indicate the need for devolving alternatives for overcoming from such deepening problems (Ocampo 2011; Korz 2015; Khanal 2017). Grounded on empirical evidence, recent literature emphasizes on the need of reviving, among others, the manufacturing sector for revitalizing the real sector to generate productive employment, key toward inclusive growth and sustained development (UNIDO 2013; Salazar-Xirinachs et al. 2014). Equally noticeably, inclusive and sustainable industrialization forms one of the main ingredients of the Sustainable Development Goals (SDGs).

D. R. Khanal (✉)
National Planning Commission, Kathmandu, Nepal
e-mail: drkhanal10@gmail.com

Institute for Policy Research and Development (IPRAD), Kathmandu, Nepal

P. R. Pandey
South Asia Watch on Trade Economics and Environment (SAWTEE), Kathmandu, Nepal

© Springer Nature Singapore Pte Ltd. 2019
S. Chaturvedi and S. Saha (eds.), *Manufacturing and Jobs in South Asia*, South Asia Economic and Policy Studies,
https://doi.org/10.1007/978-981-10-8381-5_3

It is worth noting that compared to many other South Asian countries Nepal faces more challenges in both growth and employment fronts. The growth trend indicates that in the last four decades the average growth rate was hardly 4.0% (Khanal et al. 2012). Such a growth rate further slowed down to 3.7% during the latest period of 2001/02–2015/16 with very meager manufacturing value-added growth rate at 1.4% on the average amidst almost stagnating trend in the largest agricultural sector (MoC 2016). Largely, urban-centric capital-intensive sectors have contributed to the low but poor quality growth with very adverse implications, among others, on the employment front amidst around 0.5 million working population entering into the labor market each year (CBS 2012a; Khanal 2015).

Although the unemployment rate is estimated to be only 2.2%, it conceals some unique structurally driven unemployment and underemployment problems. In addition to time-related overall underemployment at 6.7%, underemployment rate among the age group of 20–29 is estimated to be high at 8.1%. Noticeably, labor underutilization rate among the age group of 20–24 is derived to be 46% (CBS 2012b). A labor force survey further shows that out of 30% of the total economically active population classified as underutilized, 49.9% in urban and 26.9% in rural areas are underutilized (CBS 2009). Furthermore, the inter-census economically active population data shows a sharp deceleration in overall employment growth in recent years, from 2.7% during the period of 1991–2001 to 0.6% during the period of 2001–2011. During the period of 2001–2011, sectors like electricity, manufacturing, and trade registered a negative employment growth at 16, 3.7 and 1.3%, respectively. Out of the total economically active population, the share of manufacturing employment reached 8.8% in 1991 from 2% in 1981. Such a ratio reduced to 5.5% in 2011 (Khanal 2015). On the other hand, despite moderate value-added growth, the rest of the sectors also could not absorb growing labor force on large scale (CBS 2012a). The manufacturing sector has had the most dampening impact on employment due to little or no spillover effect through forward and backward linkages. The manufacturing censuses result reinforcing such a possibility.

Manufacturing data shows that there was a decline of employment by 20.5% during the period of 1991/92–2006/07 from a level of 2.14 lakhs in 1991/92. Although some pick up was there with 14.8% growth during the period of 2006/07–2011/12, the expansion, however, could not catch up even to the level of 1991/92. Close down of labor-intensive or domestic resource-based industries had a detrimental impact on employment (CBS 2014).

Such a phenomenon perpetuated despite implementation of industrial policy since long. Back in the 1986, a new industrial policy was introduced allowing foreign direct investment in the manufacturing sector. Industrial policy received priority even in the aftermath of economic liberalization drive which started in the early 1990s. An Industrial Enterprise Act was enacted in 1992. An Act on Foreign Investment and Technology Transfer Act was introduced besides a new Labor Law in the same year. For attracting foreign investment and promoting export promoting and other industries through the rule-based trading system, Nepal became the member of WTO in 2004 apart from being the member of regional free trade block under the SAFTA and BIMSTEC. Membership of Multilateral Investment Guarantee Agency and completion of Bilateral Investment Protection and Promotion Agreement (BIPPA) with some countries have been other parallel moves. In this fiscal year 2016/17, all three Acts noted above have either been revised or are in the process of revision.

Apparently, all such initiatives have been taken with the aim of enhancing rapid industrialization in the country through, among others, boosting investment including foreign investment and trade for augmenting higher growth and employment in a more sustained way. However, the miserable performance of the manufacturing sector with very adverse employment implication indicates that there is a need of closer review of industrial and other related policies from the standpoint of future policy directions in the changing policy context. As an offshoot, exploring the prospect of promoting regional integration for boosting the manufacturing sector having a positive impact on employment would be equally imperative from the future policy viewpoint.

1.2 Significance of the Study

Historically, a shift from agriculture to manufacturing and drive toward industrialization has been the key for rapid socioeconomic transformation and economic prosperity of the nations. Structural changes have contributed to accelerating fast-growing activities in areas with higher value added and productivity as well as increasing returns to scale (Szirmai 2011; UNIDO 2013). Importantly, manufacturing sector by augmenting domestic market has immensely contributed to generate employment, raise wages, and income levels of working population simultaneously leading to sustained self-reliant development (UNIDO 2003; Salazar-Xirinachs et al. 2014).

Despite such crucial roles of the manufacturing sector, a rethinking on its role started after the breakdown of the Keynesianism in the early 1970s which led to the reintroduction of market-oriented liberal policies. Poor growth performance, rising income inequality, widening balance of payments and debt problems along with increased rent-seeking practices in countries pursuing import substitution industrialization created added ground to push such a liberal policy discourse globally. For the same purpose, the Structural Adjustment and the Enhanced Structural Adjustment Facility (ESAF) programs were introduced in the developing countries in the mid-1980s and early 1990s, respectively, which focus on the policies of liberalization, privatization, and deregulation. For intensifying the liberal and open up policies further globally, the Washington Consensus (WC) was evolved and launched by the World Bank and the International Monetary Fund (IMF) jointly in 1995. The WC further downplayed the role of the industrial policy in the economies. Even the Poverty Reduction Strategy Paper (PRSP) advanced in the late 1990s after worldwide criticism of the WC was termed as augmented WC based on the policy agenda laid down in it (Rodrik 2004). The financialization policy route intensified by the developed countries in general and US in particular amidst frequent but deepening crisis has had added influence on the policies of the developing countries (Shafaeddin 2010; Khanal 2014).

The bigger problem, however, was such that they were introduced in a homogeneous fashion without reference to particular country context and above all they were neither favorable to enhance productive capacity of the economies nor to augment broad-based growth (UNCTAD 2011). Instead, people in most of the African and other poor economies driven by urbanization and decades of neglected agriculture were compelled to move to the informal services sectors having low productivity and low income leading to the deterioration in living standards. More broadly, many poor country's patterns of structural changes were serving to reduce rather than increase economic growth since the 1990s emanating from premature de-industrialization with lowered income levels compared to the experience of early industrializers (Rodrik 2015).

With compounding economic problems emanating largely from the policies of market fundamentalism, there is now increased realization that like in the period of rapid economic transformation in the East Asian countries (Adelman 1999; Robinson 2009), there is a need of revival of more robust industrial policies in which a balanced role of the state and market is ensured. The recent thrust on reactivating the industrial policy is also due to the experience that the shift towards market fundamentalism grounded on "structural adjustment" helped very little to bring about changes in the production structure of the countries in a way that could help in promoting sustained growth and enhancing productive employment simultaneously.[1] Grounded on different country experiences, it is now strongly argued that rebalancing of economies of developing countries towards higher value-added and more employment generating sectors is possible through the revival of the manufacturing sector (UNIDO 2013).

In the Nepalese context, one recent study is found to be examining the manufacturing sector performance in terms of value-added growth and employment generation (CBS 2014). Another has concentrated on estimating employment elasticity and labor productivity growth in different industries (Khanal 2015). Similarly, a study has attempted to identify constrains faced by the selected industries of the private sector in integrating their products in the global value chain system (Basnett and Pandey 2014). Thus, in the Nepalese context, the role of the manufacturing sector in employment generation has yet to be reviewed more exclusively taking economic integration aspects into special account. The proposed study aims to fulfill such a gap.

1.3 Objectives

The overall objective of the study is to critically review the role of the industrial and other related policies in the development of the manufacturing sector and thereby

---

[1] For a detailed discussion on such lines of reasoning see Ocampo et al. (2009) and Salazar-Xirinachs et al. (2014), among others. See also UNCTAD (2007) in which reasons for rethinking on the industrial policy in the context of developing countries has been pointed out more distinctly.

augment employment generation and identify the better policy options. The specific objectives are:

1. Critically review the role of industrial and other related policies in promoting manufacturing sector development in Nepal,
2. Examine the role and contribution of manufacturing sector in employment generation,
3. Identify the major policy, structural and institutional constraints including external constraints in manufacturing growth in Nepal, and
4. Explore some important policy options for promoting manufacturing sector development led employment generation including such a prospect through economic and value chain integration in South Asia.

1.4 Methodology and Data Sources

In the study the qualitative methodological approach has mainly been followed. For the purpose of verification or substantiation, some quantitative analysis has also been made. The study is based on secondary data sources. For the analytical purposes, published and unpublished government documents and also findings of the national and international studies have been used.

1.5 Structure of the Paper

In the next section below, the main features of the industrial and other related policies since the 1990s is reviewed. This is followed by the discussion on the structural changes and performance of the manufacturing sector in which its role in employment generation has been examined more exclusively. The role of economic integration in the development of export promoting industries including inducement to Nepal's participation in regional and global value chains is also briefly examined there. Major policies, structural and institutional constraints impeding the growth of the manufacturing sector are discussed in the fourth section. In the fifth section, some policy options are presented. The last section is devoted to providing the conclusions very briefly.

2 Main Features of Industrial and Other Related Area Policy Reforms Since 1990

2.1 Overall Policy Reforms and Changes: The Context

Prior to the mid-1980s, Nepal had followed the import substitution industrialization discourse through state-led protectionist policies under the banner of the mixed economic system. As such, a system of direct price controls, import licensing, high import tariffs with numerous slabs, overvaluing of currency, quota, and quantitative restrictions was introduced and strengthened. Such a policy regime, however, prevented rapid industrialization including technological upgrading by encouraging unproductive activities such as smuggling, lobbying, and evasion of tariffs and building of plants with excess capacity for obtaining import licenses (Sharma and Bajracharya 1996). Consequently, the policies became highly detrimental to promote high value-added industries and exploit Nepal's comparative advantages in the international markets (Maxwell 1990). Anti-export biases and deliberate policy of trade deflection for political expediency purposes hindered genuine development of both manufacturing and trade sectors leading to triggering of at first economic crisis followed by the political crisis (Panday 1999; Blaikie et al. 2001). However, along with referendum in 1979 aimed at diffusing the political crisis, the financial indiscipline and anarchism heightened leading to an unprecedented rise in the deficit financing. Such a practice by fuelling excess liquidity in the economy raised imports massively and thereby widened balance of payments deficits markedly leading to the emergence of foreign exchange crisis by the mid-1980s. In such a situation, Nepal had to make standby credit arrangement with the International Monetary Fund (IMF) under the Economic Stabilization program which took place in 1984/85. This was followed by the implementation of three years Structural Adjustment Program (SAP) of the World Bank and the IMF. Thus, Nepal through these programs embarked on the path to market-oriented economy in the mid-1980s.

Although these policies helped to contain budgetary deficit, liberalize trade and industry to some extent with certain inducement to the private sector, they were neither adequate nor effective in promoting market orientation and enhancing efficiency (Cohen 1995). It was recognized that, besides administrative structure being inefficient, fragile and excessive rent seeking, the legal system was also too archaic, unpredictable and unreliable (Dixit 1995). Both tariffs on output and other non-tariff measures including quantitative restrictions were still counterproductive from the standpoint of promoting export-oriented industries (Maxwell 1990). In a situation of continuity of the autocratic system through riggings in the referendum of 1979, the economy fuelling the economic hardship of the people again contributed to aggravating the political crisis. Ultimately, democracy was restored in the country in 1990 with a marked rise in the people's expectation. This was a period when drive toward liberalization was mounted by both multilateral and bilateral donors globally. India had also started pursuing economic liberalization policies with which Nepal had very close economic and trade relations. All these prompted the democratic governments to embark on the path to a liberal economic system. Noticeably, Nepal's liberalization drive has broadly driven by the conditional aid programs which Nepal so far has implemented almost in their entirety (Khanal et al. 2005; Khanal 2014).

With big bang reforms in some critical areas, today Nepal stands as one of the highly liberalized countries in the South Asian region (GoN 2004; Khanal 2009). Except in small and cottage industries, 100% foreign equity participation is allowed. This is true in insurance and wholesale banking sector also. Out of hundred, about three fourth foreign equity participation has been granted in some private banks since long. The services sectors including tourism have been opened with priority. There are also moves to initiate capital account liberalization. Now institutional investment in the secondary market through the listed companies has been granted. Beyond WTO obligations, no subsidy or quantitative restrictions are applicable in both exports and imports. The market has been entrusted the key role toward augmenting export-led industrialization. A brief review of industrial and other related policies will clear this.

2.2 Main Features of Industrial and Other Related Area Policy Reforms and Changes

As a part of economic policy reform, a new industrial policy was bought out in 1992. Deregulation and competition were the major focus of the policy. It emphasized on the need for promoting market forces to induce more resources allocation for the development of the manufacturing sector. Under the same premises, a new Industrial Enterprise Act was introduced in the same year in which various institutional and regulatory arrangements facilitating market forces were provisioned. As such, a catalyst role was provided to the private sector in establishing and expanding manufacturing industries in the country.

In parallel, the privatization program was launched massively through the Privatization act of 1994 for withdrawing government's involvement from the business and industry and providing such a role more exclusively to the private sector. With privatization of many profit-making industries or enterprises in the beginning, the program became highly controversial leading to halting of privatization for some years. With the beginning of the twenty-first century, it was restarted.

Grounded on the industrial policy and act, various steps were taken aimed at promoting manufacturing industries. Industries establishing in remote or backward areas were provided tax exemptions and other facilities. The registration process was simplified. Policies also allowed a higher rate of depreciation to the industries using machinery and equipment. Exports were exempted from domestic indirect taxes. Reimbursement of customs duties and VAT was granted to the imported inputs with certain conditions. The policies also guaranteed no nationalization of industries.

In the institutional fronts, an Industrial Promotion Board was constituted under the chairmanship of the Minister of Industry for coordinating the formulation and implementation of policies, rules, and regulations related to the industrial sector. In the Board, various government agencies, the private sector, and the experts were represented. At the Department level, a One-Window Committee under the coordination of the Director General of the Department of Industry was constituted to provide facilities and concessions through a single service point.

In the same year 1992, the Foreign Investment and Technology Transfer Act was also enacted. Through this act, Nepal took a number of steps to attract foreign direct investment. Except in cottage industries, industries producing arms, ammunition and explosive materials and few other service industries, 100% foreign equity investment were allowed. Repatriation of the sales proceeds from FDI, as well as dividends, was permitted in convertible currency. Similarly, foreign exchange for payment of principal and interest on foreign loans was guaranteed. National treatment with regard to facilities and incentives were provided to foreign investors. All required information and facilities were provided from a single point, a one-window system to the foreign direct investment. Nepal also joined the Multilateral Investment Guarantee Agency (MIGA), which provides guarantees to foreign investors against noncommercial risks like currency transfer, expropriation, breach of contract, and war and civil disturbance in the host country.

In the same year 1992, a new labor law was introduced which provided employment guarantee of the workers and also provisioned tripartite arrangement to determine wage level and fix other facilities of the workers. This law, however, was confined to cover the workers in the organized sector. Because of employment guarantee provision, it was opposed by the private sector from the very beginning by pointing out that such a rigid law has hampered investment environment by adversely affecting product diversification and productivity growth in industries, the key for enhancing competitiveness.

To bring certain complementary with the industrial sector and augment trade liberalization, bold reforms were initiated in the trade front. A new trade policy was introduced in 1992. Apart from rationalization in the structure, a drastic reduction in the tariff rates was made. Restriction in imports was abolished. Export procedures were simplified, with facilities for duty-drawback, bonded warehousing, and simpler documentation requirements. Export duties were exempt. The current account balance was made fully convertible. After joining the World Trade Organization (WTO) in 2004, trade liberalization was further accentuated for making Nepal as one of the highly liberalized countries in South Asia in the trade front (Khanal 2009). Certain moves through South Asia Free Trade Agreement (SAFTA) also facilitated that process. As a least developed country, Nepal also enjoys duty-free and quotas free market access facilities in Europe and other selected developed and developing countries.

After lapses of almost two decades or more, a number of policy reforms in the areas of trade, foreign direct investment and industry were initiated recently aimed at reviving and boosting the industries and promoting exports through exportable industries. The Trade Policy drafted in 2009 was revised and implemented in 2015. Similarly, a Nepal Trade Integration Strategy developed in 2010 (MoCS 2010) was updated in 2016 (MoC 2016). A New Industrial Enterprise Act has also been introduced recently incorporating various policies laid down in the Industrial Policy of

2010. The Special Economic Zone Act of 2016 has also been enacted separately. Similarly, a new Foreign Investment and Technology Transfer Act, incorporating various policies laid down in the Foreign Investment Policy of 2014, is under discussion. Equally important, an Investment Board under the Chairmanship of the Prime Minister has been established through Gathan Aadesh in 2011 for mobilizing and promoting larger investment in mega projects in the areas of industry and infrastructure. Now the labor law has also been revised with certain hiring and firing rights to the Employers. It also emphasizes on the need of enhancing labor productivity through various facilities to the workers. This has resolved the major concern of the private sector.

The Nepal Trade Integration Strategy introduced in 2010 has been replaced by the new one in 2016. Based on the past experience, it focuses some specific measures to overcome the outstanding problem of trade creation, diversification and competitiveness challenges faced by the country's export sector. It emphasizes on strategic measures to build institutional capacity for trade including trade negotiations besides focusing on creating a business environment for investment and trade, enhancing trade and transport facilitation, improving standards and technical regulations, strengthening intellectual property rights and augmenting trade in services. It has identified certain export competitive agro, forestry and other manufacturing products (MoC 2016). To attract FDI, provisions like income tax waiver against foreign loans and exports are in place; while 15% tax is levied on royalty income and other such sources of revenues. FDI in the infrastructure sector that directly benefits the industry like electricity qualifies for additional incentives. Standard incentives like tax waivers for machinery and equipment, raw materials, etc., in the export-processing zone are also applicable. Nepal has investment related treaties with ten countries and Bilateral Investment Protection and Promotion Agreements (BIPPA) with six countries.

Changes in tax structure and reforms in tax administration were carried out in tandem considering, among others, that they have an important bearing on the development or boosting of the manufacturing sector. A system of VAT was introduced in 1997 by replacing sales tax. This was followed by the implementation of a new Income Tax Act in 2002 which tapped services income as well. It introduced personal income tax brackets at 15 and 25% added by corporate and banks and other financial institutions tax rate at 25 and 30%, respectively. Since then, a number of reforms and changes in the tax have been made to promote investment in industry and augment exports broadly in line with the policies in these areas as pointed out above. Tax rebates and tax exemption are given to the industries that provide large employment or are established in the underdeveloped areas. Industries established in the 'Special Economic Zone' also get both income tax rebate and exemption facilities. The foreign investors are provided especial rebates and exemption. Similarly, a special industry as categorized, industry based in agriculture and tourism is additionally granted the facility of capitalizing the profit for the purpose of capacity expansion. Now exporters are provided cash incentives as well.[2]

Thus, various policy initiatives, institutional reforms or new institutional arrangements and other measures proposed or implemented apparently indicate that concerted efforts are there to promote manufacturing industries including exportable industries, especially so in more recent years. Various policy and institution-related measures perused to attract foreign investment are the most noticeable developments in recent years apart from priority to promote regional trade through SAFTA. As an offshoot, the importance of integrating trade with global and regional value chains has also been recognized as the trading strategy of 2016 reveals.

3 Structure of Manufacturing Sector and Industry Wise Performance with Special Reference to Employment Generation

A closer examination on the changed structure of the manufacturing sector and its industry wise performance, as well as employment generation in this sector, gives a broad idea on the underlying reasons for Nepal's poor performance in both fronts.

3.1 Structure of Manufacturing Sector and Industry Wise Performance Since 1990

A typical phenomenon of the manufacturing sector is that a decline in the establishments' number took place during the period 1991/92–2011/12, from 4271 in 1991/92 to 4076 by 2011/12. Although number matters less if there is more specialization in particular products added by increased economies of scale, the changed structure entails a different story.

As shown in Table 2, despite industrial policy offering various facilities to the industries, the most sufferers during the liberal economic regime have been the textile industries. In terms of both numbers and share in total industries, they have gone down considerably. Similarly, closing down of the number of establishments in the paper, wearing apparel and leather industries has taken place during the period 1995/96–2011/12. On the other hand, there has been albeit fast rise in non-metallic, food and food-related industries in the period under consideration. Some expansion in fabricating, wood and furniture and printing establishments has also taken place during the same period. Notwithstanding that during the period prior to 2005 industries were affected by the conflict, the erosion in competitiveness amidst rising cost of production and transaction cost and marketing problem due to the overflow

---

[2]For review of the industrial policy see in different phases see Khanal et al. (2005) and Basnett and Pandey (2014). Brief discussion is also found in CBS (2014).

of imported goods has had an adverse effect on the survival or growth of many manufacturing establishments. Many industries had to operate below the capacity utilization level that also raised unit cost (Basnett and Pandey 2014). Problem of technological up gradating and management capability enhancement also eroded the competitiveness problem of many industries. More broadly, the pattern shows that industries having more domestic resource content have been the sufferer most.

3.1.1 Changes in Value Add Contribution and Structural Pattern of Industries

Along with rise or decline in the manufacturing establishments in different sub-groups, changes in the value add composition also took place at a faster pace. During the period 1996/97–2011/12, a major increase in the value-added share of food and beverages took place, from 22.8 to 34.0%. Likewise, value added of non-metallic industries rose to 14% in 2011/12 from 7.2% in 1995/96 to 34.0% in 2011. However, a drastic reduction in the value-added share of textiles took place during 1996/97–2011/12, from 25.9 to 3.8%. In 1995/96, the value-added share from textiles was the highest. Similarly, the share of wearing apparel has gone down to just 0.5% from 6.3% during the same period (Table 3). Noticeably, increased food industry predominance in the value added at the cost of other important sectors depicts that there is some reversal from the standpoint of the move toward more dynamic or sustained path to industrialization. Noticeably, the food industry has a feature of very low-value addition as a result of excessive use of agricultural inputs. This phenomenon is apparent in the Nepalese context as well.

More broadly, apart from food and beverages and non-metallic mineral products, wood products, rubber and plastic products, chemicals and chemicals products, furniture, manufacturing n.e.c. and fabricated metal products expanded steadily between the period 1996/97 and 2011/12. However, estimated integral coefficients of structural change suggested that no significant overall structural change has taken place over the years although the structural change in value added (0.415) has been albeit faster compared to the manufacturing industries themselves (0.233) during these periods. Similarly, the high degree of rank correlation coefficient derived for different periods suggested that the sector shares are highly correlated without major structural changes between the two periods (i.e., 1995/96–2011/12 and 2006/07–2011/12) indicating that emergence of any leading sector in the manufacturing industry is yet to take place in Nepal. Moreover, the estimated coefficient of diversification over the manufacturing census years further depicted that together with very low structural change, the industrial sector remained largely stagnant over the years with almost evenly spread across sectors in a situation of low value-added and lack of any leading sectors (CBS 2014).

3.1.2 Total Factor Productivity Growth in the Industries

Total factor productivity (TFP) is a critical indicator on the extent of probably sustained growth in the manufacturing sector which, in turn, is affected by important factors such as technology, entrepreneurial capability, institutional quality of enterprises and skilled manpower besides infrastructure facilities and macroeconomic policy environment, among others.

A quick review of the estimated TFP in the manufacturing sector by the UNDP covering the period of 1996/97–2006/07 shows that there is a large variation in the TFP among different industries with negative TFP in some industries added by wider fluctuation from one period to another (UNDP 2014).

The estimates show that compared to 1996/97, a steady reduction in the overall TFP took place in the manufacturing sector up to 2001/02. Among others, the conflict might have adversely affected the TFP. In 1996/97, TFP in the manufacturing sector was 0.69 which reduced to 0.43 in 2001/02. Thereafter, an improvement took place with TFP reaching at 0.72 in 2011/12. In 1996/97, chemicals and chemical products, electrical machinery and apparatus, and wood and wood products had higher than one TFP. In 2001/02, publishing, printing, and reproduction of recorded media had registered albeit higher TFP. In 2006/07, jute, carpet, pashmina and textile factories, sawmills and plywood factories, lube oil and lubricant industries, electronics manufacturers and producers of medical instruments had recorded a TFP of more than one (UNDP 2014). But the problem is that despite more industries recording relatively higher TFP lately, no continuity in higher growth could be maintained among most of those which had recorded higher TFP in the earlier period. Amidst low overall TFP, such a trend resembles poor conducive environment to the industries for their sustainability in a growing competitive situation.

3.1.3 Economic Integration and Export Performance of the Manufacturing Industries

Trade liberalization and open up policies are justified on the ground that they by helping to reduce barriers and costs to trade and create conducive investment climate can boost both intra-regional trade and investment through both backward and forward linkages (Rahman et al. 2012). Experiences show that many countries have benefitted not only from vertical integration but also from horizontal integration through complementarities following dynamic policy approach. The East Asian countries have particularly benefitted in the ongoing process of global production sharing and global value chains by reaping gains from the new form of production (international production fragmentation) and exchange (Athukorala 2013). They portray the complementarities between the liberalized trade, FDI and value chains, both regionally and globally.

It is, however, ironical that in terms of both intra-regional trade and FDI flows the SAARC is least integrated. Not only trade expansion within the member countries is very low at below 5% of the total trade of SAARC member countries but also progress in regional integration is very slow and discouraging. Regional integration through value chains is also minuscule and not encouraging. Amidst such an adverse environment regionally, Nepal faces more adverse atmosphere in promoting manufacturing industries driven trade expansion with South Asian and other countries. Promotion to export-oriented industries has been particularly problematic leading to widening of the trade deficit in an unsustainable way. Despite liberalization and open up drive, Nepal has also succeeded very little to attract FDI satisfactorily. Expansion of trade through Global or regional value chains is even more challenging (Basnett and Pandey 2014).

From the point of view of economic integration with other countries in general and South Asian countries in particular, there are some unique phenomenon in the Nepali context. As a share of GDP, total trade in goods and services reached 53.1% in 2014/15 with a slight reduction in 2015/16 due to the devastating earthquake and trade blockade. This means that Nepal is more liberal and integrated with the rest of the economies. More interestingly, however, such trade integration is predominantly with single country SAARC country India. Despite intra-regional trade among SAARC countries remaining below 5% of total merchandise trade, Nepal's trade with India is in the neighborhood of 65% (NRB 2016). But the most worrisome phenomenon is that the ratio of exports to imports has reduced to 11.4% in 2014/15. As an offshoot, the share of total commodity export was 12.6% of GDP in 2001/02 and reduced to as low as 4.6% of GDP in 2014/15 with further reduction in the ratio in 2015/16. On the other hand, merchandize commodity import went up to 36.1% of GDP from 24.2% during the same period. As a result, the deficit of goods and services trade reached almost 30.0% of GDP in 2014/15 from 10.8% in 2001/02 (NRB 2016). Had there not been continuous inflows of remittances of almost the same magnitude, this would have created havoc in the economy. It is also worth noting that the rise in imports is not due to a rise in the imports of inputs and capital goods, a symptom of developmental momentum including industrialization in the country but primarily due to the phenomenal rise in imports of petroleum products, essential consumable and other luxurious goods.

Although after 2000 there has been some improvement in the share of manufacturing exports in total exports despite a sharp reduction in total commodity exports, the share of manufacturing exports stood at 70.1% in 2012 from as high as 83.7% in 1995 (Table 1). A sharp reduction in other manufacturing products contributed to such a phenomenon. Like in many other low country's experiences, immediately after the liberalization drive including trade, some jump in exports took place which reached at peak by the mid-1990s and thereafter, a declining trend manifested which is continuing even today. Noticeably, most of the exports are directed to India, accounting for more than 50%. In the exports besides a few light manufacturing products such as textiles and fabrics, iron and steel, ready-made garments, non-ferrous metals, agriculture products such cardamom, tea, and ginger constitute the predominant share in the export baskets (NRB 2016). The most annoying phenomenon is that both degrees of product specialization and existing export capabilities are dwindling or evaporat-

Table 1 Exports of manufactured Products (% of total export value)

Descriptions	1995	2000	2012
Chemical products	1.2	7.8	5.4
Machinery and transport equipment	0.1	0.5	1.4
Other manufactured goods	82.4	60.0	63.3
Total	83.7	68.3	70.1

Source UNCTAD (2013)

ing. The estimation based on manufacturing survey reveals that the export of major manufacturing products in total exports has a very dismal trend (Table 4). In almost all industries ranging from food and machinery, textile, leather, chemicals, rubber, electric, paper to basic metals, the export share in total output has reduced sharply more so during the period 2006/07–2011/12.

Inability to attract foreign direct investment despite tax rebates, concessions, and various facilities provisioned in the Foreign Investment and Technology Transfer Act has additionally constrained the growth and development of manufacturing sector in terms of output, productivity, and exports. The data on foreign direct investment inflows indicate that the total FDI inflow in 2014 and 2015 was in the order of US $30 and $51 million, respectively (UNCTAD 2016). Although FDI commitment through registered industries has been relatively high (MoC 2016), the actual inflow has always been extremely low. In the total inflow, the share of Indian Investment has been above 40% followed by China and other countries.

Similarly, GVC participation index shows that the backward index is 15.5 compared to forward index of 8.8 indicating an inability to be tapped into value chains (De and Rahman 2017). The Enterprise Survey of World Bank (2013) shows[3] that apart from very limited firms with foreign investment (only 0.1% foreign owned), only 8.2% of firms were found to be receiving internationally recognized quality certification, essential for participation in GVCs. Similarly, survey depicts that out of total sales, 97.0% was found to be domestic, 1.8% direct exports and 1.2% indirect exports during the survey. Although a sizeable proportion of firms were using inputs of foreign origin (44.9%), as a proportion of total inputs, domestic input share was very high at 72.3% compared to foreign inputs at 27.6%. These corroborated that Nepal's participation in GVC is low. Importantly, Nepal's experience shows that unless the export and import composition and their pattern is closely examined, simple measures like trade share in GDP cannot be used as a yardstick of advantages or gains through trade or economic integration.

---

[3]For more details see http://www.enterprisesurveys.org.

3.2 Role of Manufacturing in Employment Generation

Employment is regarded to be a prerequisite for inclusive growth and sustainable development. With rising discontent globally resulting from a steep rise in inequality and jobless growth, the creation of productive employment through the revitalization of the manufacturing sector has received high priority in policy agenda in recent years as already pointed out. How manufacturing sector is contributing to generate employment, thus, becomes extremely important. Moreover, the changes in employment structure additionally portraying the extent on the use of productive forces indicate to what extent the shared prosperity has been enhanced over time.

3.2.1 Growth and Changes in Employment Structure in Manufacturing Industries

A quick review of the manufacturing censuses indicates that growth in employment has taken place almost similarly to the pattern observed in the growth of manufacturing establishments. As already indicated, employment level never reached the level of 1991/92 in the post-liberalization period despite a trend in average employment per firm being slightly different. In 1991/92 the average employment per firm was 50 which after some upswing went down and reduced to 48 in 2011/12 (CBS 2014).

As the detailed analysis shows, during 1996/97 and 2006/07, in several industries such as tobacco, textile, and leather there was a sharp fall in employment. Only in wood related, chemical, rubber and plastic, basic metal and electrical industries, there was some rise in employment during this period. In terms of numbers, food, textile and cement, and ceramic industries were hiring relatively more workers. The textile industry, which is more labor intensive, was hiring 75,283 workers in 1996/97. It could hire only 40,500 workers in 2006/07 due to the closure of many such industries after the end of quota to the USA in 2005. In apparel industries also, there was a substantial fall in employment between 2001/02 and 2006/07 amidst growing competition from similar imported goods. The adverse employment effect accumulated due to decade long armed conflict, often unreasonable demand of labor and phasing out of quota to the apparel industries. On the whole, more recent economically active population data show that the performance of the manufacturing sector employment has been miserable with negative growth of 3.7% during the period 2001–2011 (Khanal 2015).

3.2.2 Employment Elasticity in Manufacturing Industries

The employment elasticity gives an idea on the relationship between the growth in output and employment with some statistical precision. A rigorous exercise carried out by a recent study shows how the manufacturing industries have performed in relation to the output during the period 1996/97–2011/2 (Khanal 2015). The estimates made based on a cross-sectional basis (at a point of time) are presented in Table 5.

As shown in Table 5, the employment elasticity of manufacturing industries ranges from minimum 0.25 to maximum 0.70 with no firm trend across industries. As a result of low elasticity of many industries except textile, apparel and some other light manufacturing industries, the overall elasticity is relatively low. The employment elasticity computed for the two periods, viz. 1996/97–2001/02 and 2001/02–2006/07 taking a ratio of proportionate change in employment to proportionate change in the output shows a different pattern. During the period 2001/02 and 2006/07 food industries had the highest employment elasticity whereas tobacco had the negative elasticity in both periods (Table 6). On the other hand, employment elasticity of textile, chemical and cement, and ceramic industries turned into negative in the second period. But industries such as sawmills, leather, paper, fabricated metal, and electrical converted negative employment elasticity into positive during the later period. During the same period, publishing and printing, and furniture industries recorded very low employment elasticity. Thus, consistent with the findings in the previous section, either employment is predominant in traditional and low productive industries or there is a move toward that direction rather than toward modern and high productive industries.

3.2.3   Labor Productivity in Manufacturing Industries

Labor productivity calculated at 1990/91 prices for the period 1996/97–2006/07 followed by indexing of labor productivity in different industries shows that on the whole there is some increment in the growth of labor productivity over time. However, across industries, no uniform pattern is found (Table 7). For instance, in tobacco industries labor productivity remained relatively high and increased over time. In paper, rubber, and plastic, basic and fabricated metal industries also some increment in labor productivity took place. In contrast, labor productivity in food, apparel, publishing and printing, and chemical industries slowed down from one period to another. The estimates showed that industries like apparel, cement and ceramic and furniture industries have the lowest productivity. A moderate productivity level was maintained by industries like textile, wood, publishing and printing industries remained moderate. In general, industries employing more people faced low productivity, indicating the persistence of some tradeoff problems.

Interestingly, a correlation analysis between the labor productivity and change in employment share shows that both can move in the positive direction if inter-industrial restructuring is made leading to positive spillover effects in both fronts. For instance, during 1996/97–2001/02, textile industry witnessed a substantial fall in employment amidst low productivity (Fig. 1a). The removal of the textile industry makes the trend line below negative reflecting that this industry has growth reducing effect (Fig. 1b). During 2002–2007, the apparel industry also faced a similar problem (Fig. 1c). Removal of it lowered the slope of the trend line, showing a tardy pace of industrial transformation which could lead to augment high productivity industries having a positive employment effect (Fig. 1d). The correlation analysis clearly shows that there are only a very few industries like chemical, rubber, plastic, and a few others that are contributing to increase employment and maintain labor productivity above the average level simultaneously.

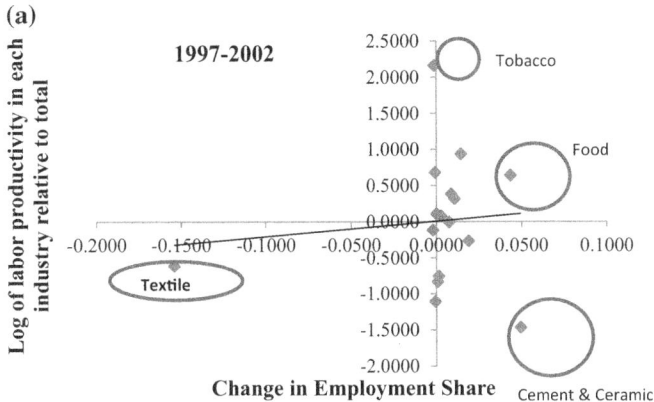

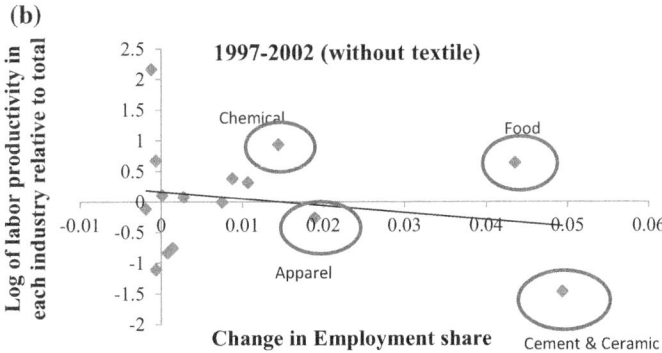

Fig. 1 Correlation between labor productivity and change in employment share within manufacturing industries. *Source* Khanal (2015)

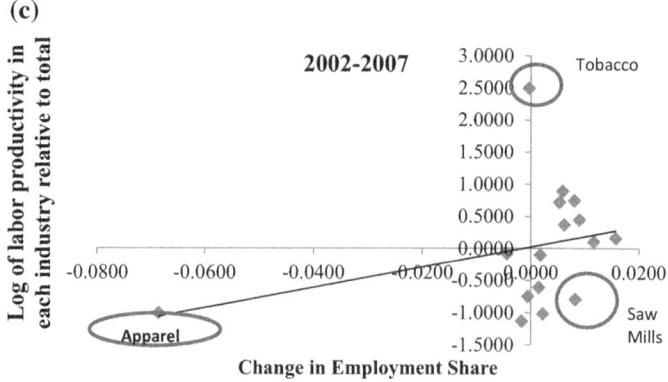

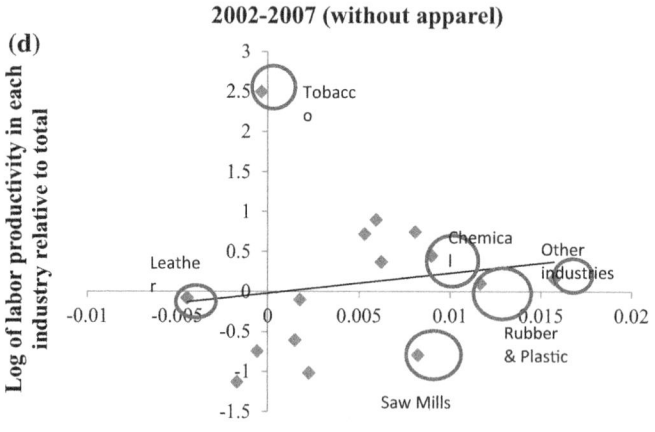

Fig. 1 (continued)

4 Major Constraints in the Growth of Manufacturing Industries

Today the manufacturing sector is in a serious crisis with very severe adverse spillover effects, among others, on external trade and employment front. Despite worsening of manufacturing sector performance in the late-1990s, no bold moves to address the problems were taken for almost two decades. Notwithstanding the adverse effect of almost one decade long conflict, even after the bigger change of 2006, no drastic reforms in the economic front were made. Continuity to business as usual practices worsened the situation further in critical fronts of the economy. Since last few years only, there have been some new initiatives to bring about policy reforms in industrial and other related areas such as trade, foreign investment, and technology transfer and labor. New acts have either been introduced recently or are in the process of enactment in these areas by replacing the old ones and hence their impact is yet to be felt or seen. However, based on the above analysis, some of the major policy, institutional and structural constraints together with some serious external impediments faced by Nepal affecting the growth of manufacturing sector with added adverse implications on employment can be highlighted in the following way.

4.1 Asymmetries in Overall, Industrial, and Other Related Areas Policy Direction

Despite the introduction of new industrial and other related policies in the early 1990s followed by recent reforms and changes, the neo-liberal thinking is still predominant in the overall policy setting and direction. Macroeconomic stabilization induced free market and open policies are the core of the policy directions. The problem of market failures amidst weak market institutions and ineffective regulatory system is yet to be explicitly recognized or internalized in the overall policy frame. This is the reason why despite industrial and other related polices provisioning various tax concessions, incentives, and facilities, they either could not be implemented or made effective. More broadly, clarity on the balancing role of the state and market key for the revival of the industrial sector is yet to be made from the standpoint of correcting both market distorting and state capturing practices.

Past experience shows that amidst tight fiscal policy for macroeconomic stabilization with little attention on structural and institutional constraints, more liberal policy stand was taken by the monetary authorities to induce investment in non-tradable areas including durable luxurious consumable goods through low-interest policy, among others. With growing inflows of remittances, such a policy contributed to the proliferation of banking and financial institutions which, in turn, enhanced their capacity to lend in consumption and real estate related areas and activities for quick profits. Though the priority sector lending has been revived recently, the withdrawal in the past additionally enhanced their lending capacity in such areas at the cost of industrial sector lending. Amidst privatization of profitable industries or enterprises unsuccessfully, a shift in economic discourse augmented with increased concentration of investment and lending in finance, trade and other services activities. Thus, trade and finance led economic activities flourished overtime with a gradual erosion of production base of the economy in the absence of investment in productive areas. Such a discourse bypassed needed transformational development discourse despite such a thrust after the political change of 2006. This not only constrained productivity induced diversification in agriculture as a base for industrialization but also inhibited a process of restructuring of industries driven by high productivity and comparative advantages considerations. Though there is some emphasis on import substitution recently, hardy such a necessity figured in the policy agenda in the past.

Nepal's experience, therefore, exhibits that unless a more balanced policy discourse with a focus on correcting policy mistakes is perused, revival and development of manufacturing sector will be hardly possible.

4.2   Infrastructural Bottlenecks and Supply Side Constraints

The supply-side constraint is a serious problem in the development of manufacturing industries in the country. One of the pervasive problems is inadequate and low-quality infrastructure which is hindering not only promotion of industries but also inhibiting the scope of augmenting internal domestic market for produced goods. In terms of both stock and quality of infrastructure, Nepal is far behind compared to many other South Asian countries. Similarly, despite abundant water resources, energy shortage has remained a big problem in the past for fostering manufacturing industries. Industry's development is equally constrained by the shortages of high-quality manpower as well as weak entrepreneurial skills and capabilities. Organizational capacity of the industries is also a problem. In general, entrepreneur and business environment are poor. Lack of compliance in delivering committed facilities and cumbersome tax procedures are adding both production and transaction costs (Basnett and Pandey 2014; MoC 2016).

The low saving rate is also an additional problem from the supply side consideration. The domestic saving rate which was albeit high during the 1990s is now below 10% of GDP. Amidst banking sector investment largely concentrating on non-tradable and other non-productive activities, this has constrained meeting the demand for investment in the industrial sector.

4.3   Absence of Restructuring and Continued Erosion in the Competitiveness of Industries

Along with enhanced integration of the economy with the neighboring countries and others, maintenance and strengthening of comparative advantages in industries would have been the foremost priority. This, in turn, required upscaling and restructuring of industries based on the competitive strength and market conditions. This would have helped to restructure industries toward high value-added and employment generating labor-intensive industries. As country experiences suggest, comparative advantages only enables industries to be competitive, reap high returns, augment capital accumulation and capture both internal and external market. In view of relative prices and their movements in factor and product market playing a decisive role in maintaining the competitiveness, it gives enough space to correct likely misalignment of prices in these markets. In the absence of such considerations carefully on the assumption of automatic correction of likely distortion or anomalies through market forces industry's competitiveness eroded markedly leading to augmentation of deindustrialization in the country. Expansion of informal economy added by market capturing practices through cartels and syndicate system adding competitiveness problems fuelled that process further.

The worsening of labor productivity amidst poor skills and rising wages also affected the comparative advantages of the industries. The rigid labor policy also had some adverse impact. In addition, Nepal's fixed exchange rate regime with India drastically eroded the competitive edge of Nepalese industries because of misalignment of prices between the two countries. In recent years, the inflation rate in Nepal has been high compared to India.

The instruments chosen at the sector level including partial exemptions, rebates on taxes and other concessions were highly unable to address adequately the market failures and boost industrial development. In addition, industrial policy turned into a pseudo investment policy because of strategic thrusts provided by periodical planned documents and annual budgetary policies sometimes became incompatible with the announced industrial policy. For example, the facilities and concessions, in terms of tax rebates and exemptions provided by the industrial policy, were quite often repealed by the income tax law and the annual budgets. Moreover, other sector policies—for example, monetary and financial, agriculture development, trade, energy, tourism, foreign investment, etc.—rarely established strong linkages with industrial policy (Basnett and Pandey 2014).

4.4 Low FDI, Least Participation in GVCs and Sallow Regional Integration

Despite relatively high integration with SAARC countries, Nepal is deprived of or unable to reap expected benefits as the dwindling of exports of manufacturing products indicates. Internally, no adequate attention were given to expand and diversify exportable industries for ensuring access to a competitive export market. The cascading tariff structure by hampering domestic resource based high value-added and employment generating industries further constrained the growth of exportable industries. In the process of industrial and trade policy liberalization, no proper attention was given in bringing policy coherency, strengthening market institutions, maintaining efficient incentive structures and providing other support systems in a broader way. As an offshoot, no care was given to ensure that in the process there is need of promoting exportable manufacturing industries through selective policy interventions and other means including judicious resource allocation decisions, which is recognized to be critical (Lin and Treichel 2014).

Although there are some positive signs of increased FDI in sectors such as energy recently, still the manufacturing industry is highly disadvantaged. Apart from internal factors, regional barriers have worked as major constraints in promoting more genuine regional integration so that Nepal could reap maximum benefits. There is no any incentive mechanism that could promote both intra-regional FDI and value chains. No preferential investment policy added by a negative list, high tariffs and non-tariff barriers, high cost of trading, regulatory and other factors preventing intra-regional services trade expansion have worked very adversely (De and Rahman 2017). Internally, legal, institutional and policy factors discouraging investment from abroad added by supply-side constraints are working very adversely in attracting large FDI inflows (Adhikari 2013). Long political transition and policy uncertainty also adversely affected the FDI inflows as in many instances even the pledged and committed FDI could not come.

As an offshoot, no policy attention was given in the past to tap the opportunities emanating from the global value chains. Even the bigger challenges coming from the GVCs with likely adverse effect on Nepal's industrial development was hardly foreseen. Amid these, weak and ineffective industrial policy, reduced productive capacity of the economy added by high cost of transport and energy, inadequate provision of public goods and low levels of investment reduced country's ability to participate in the global value chains (Basnett and Pandey 2014). As a land-locked country, Nepal faced additional global market problems due to regional barriers.

4.5 Transit and Trade Facilitation a Big Problem

Lengthy export and import times and cost escalation in the transits are the most pressing problems for Nepal from both export promotion and import substitution industrialization perspectives. In many raw material imports to be used for exportable or import substitution industries as well as final imports, the cost becomes more than double of the price at seaport (MoCS 2010; MoC 2016). Apart from very cumbersome procedures in the trade routes, poor infrastructure, weak support services and governance system at the custom points have remained big problems in making trade facilitation as a means of enhancing competiveness and promoting trade to be advantageous for Nepal. Despite commitments in Bali to ensure trade facilitation more exclusively to the land-locked countries like Nepal, Nepal is still deprived of such committed benefits. Therefore, with ongoing impediments, Nepal's reindustrialization drive will be highly jeopardized.

4.6 Coordination and Implementation Failures

As partly indicated above also, one of the most serious problems in the policy and implementation front is that coordination is a big bottleneck with no built-in system in place that could ensure compliance as a binding. This is the reflection of a very weak governance and accountability system. It is not that there is no provision to make decisions in a coordinated way or through consensus to ensure the ownership of the decisions by all concerned. For instance, the high-level investment board in the

Ministry of Industry is represented by both concerned ministries and private sector agencies. But the irony is that the decisions are hardly enforced or implemented. Probably hundreds of decisions are pending related to tax rebates and concession or guaranteeing the smooth supply of energy to the industries. There is indeed a common tendency of refusing to comply with the decisions. Needless to add, in the absence of a system ensuring compliance, implementation failure will be most challenging in the future too.

5   Some Suggestive Policy Options to Revitalize Manufacturing Sector for Sustained Higher Growth and Employment Generation

5.1   Adaptation of Transformational Approach in Development Discourse

Nepal's experience clearly indicates that there is a need for revamping the production structure and raising the productive capacity of the economy. For both trade creation and accompanying changes in trade pattern also this is essential. This, however, will require a big shift in the development discourse grounded on transformational approach at the first place. The structural and institutional reforms and changes should form an integral part of it. Under such a paradigm shift, revitalization of the agriculture sector through intra-sectoral restructuring for product diversification and productivity enhancement is a must. This has to be accompanied by the highest priority to the development of the manufacturing sector and industrialization in which both expansion and restructuring of industries grounded on comparative advantages will be necessary. At the same time, such a strategic shift requires investments in social and physical infrastructure including investment in new technologies, know-how and innovation simultaneously which, in turn, creates productive synergies within and between sectors of the economy for enhancing exports as well in a more sustainable way through diversification, upgrade and changes in the structure of production and trade, among others. This will create a strong ground for a broad-based growth and sustained development.

More fundamentally, this will require rebalancing the role of the state and the market for ensuring their catalyst, complementary and facilitating role. For correcting market imperfections or distortions of different forms and controlling state captured practices also, their balanced role will be essential.

5.2 Restructuring of Macroeconomic Policy with Development Focus

The strategic shift focused on changing dynamics of production structure with assurance to distributional gains to the large section of the population will require major reforms in macroeconomic policies. More specifically, there is a need for replacing pro-cyclical macroeconomic policy rules of neo-liberalism by a well-designed macroeconomic policy for development with a mix of sound countercyclical policies and policies of diversifying production structures. The macroeconomic policies have to be revamped in a way that discourages speculative and other quick yielding business activities and instead enables them to play a catalyst role in minimizing or resolving supply side bottlenecks constraining accumulation of productive capital, enhancing the productivity of inputs (i.e., land, labor, and capital) and augmenting factor productivity growth. This will require changes in both composition and pattern of the state as well as private investment. In a balanced way, there is also a need for revisiting the fiscal consolidation and macroeconomic stability centric macro policy orthodoxy by looking into the likely ramification on the aggregate demand side of the economy. In this context, macroeconomic policies affecting wages, consumption and distributional gains will be important particularly from the standpoint of enhancing internal domestic demand led market expansion and growth which would have huge employment implications. In summary, there is a need of bringing about compatibility among fiscal, monetary, trade and labor policies with a primary focus on development.

5.3 Industrial Policy Reforms and Rebalancing to Promote Both Import Substituting and Export Promoting Industries

Grounded on the transformational approach, a new policy discourse has to be evolved with a focus on both export based and import substitution industrialization. This requires some sweeping changes in the policies pursued in the areas of taxation, tariff structure, credit system and institutional arrangements added by a built-in effective incentive structures. Apart from domestic resource based, imported raw material based industries to be competitive due to location, labor, and other hosts of factors could be strategically advanced. In such a course, the strategy of restructuring and technology-based upgrading of industries with assurance to both productivity enhancement and employment generation has to be pursued effectively. Enhancing organizational and managerial capacity of industries for improved efficiency has to go side by side. More specifically, large and strategic industries could be promoted with the help of foreign investment which would help technology transfer, improve management skill, raise competitive strength and promote exports as well. Domestic investors could be particularly encouraged to engage in medium to small industries. More incentive/marketing facilities to the agro, forestry, mining and other labor-intensive industries will be necessary. Priority to skill development led labor productivity enhancement should go side by side. From the employment perspectives, focus on micro, small and medium enterprises will be particularly necessary with a focus on women's entrepreneurship development by facilitating women's access to finance, credit and skills including business, accounting skills, etc. All in all, effectiveness in one-window system through better coordination must be there. There is also a need for institutional support that provides regular feedbacks on the changing pattern of the market both internally and externally. Initiatives to promote and expand free economic and export-processing zone must be guided by the aim of importing new technology and retaining high value added in the country. Duty and quota-free facility must be tapped linking with the development of exportable industries in a more effective way.

Regulatory reform should also form the part and parcel of overall industrial policy reform. There is also a need for improving industrial relations by containing over politicization of trade unions and strengthening a mechanism that helps to resolve labor disputes quickly. Although new labor law has addressed the concern of employers to a greater extent, it is necessary that various means including social security means are employed and strengthened to improve the labor productivity which is one of the lowest in South Asian region, critical for enhancing the competitiveness of both export-oriented and import-substituting industries.

5.4 Removing Supply Side Bottlenecks

Considering structural and institutional aspects as major constraints, there is a need for high priority to minimize and remove supply side bottlenecks. Removal of power shortages and improvement in connectivity will be the key to reduce cost, increase market access and the opening of markets to exports. Such steps have to be accompanied by rationalization of taxes, improved delivery of services and other support systems to reduce production as well as transaction costs which are very high in Nepal. All these require huge investment. Leaving other areas to the private sector, government has to limit its investment in areas where the private sector may not come. In this respect, the FDI inflows from South Asian countries could be important especially in the areas linked to connectivity and energy development from SAARC regional cooperation for greater integration perspectives.

5.5 Attracting Foreign Direct Investment and New Technology in Strategic Manufacturing Industries

As noted above Nepal in order to attract foreign investment, a high level investment board was constituted a few years before. Recently, legislation on the special economic zone (SEZ) has also been passed with several facilities and added incentives. Still FDI is not forthcoming, particularly in the manufacturing sector. Therefore, further review of FDI policy may be needed with a focus on institutional reforms. It is necessary to ensure that investment in Nepal is more attractive in comparison to others. Duty and quota-free facilities and other preferential treatments need tapping more aggressively which has not been the case so far. At the same time, there is a need for banning frequent strikes and bandhs. Main attention has to be given for a sustained improvement in the investment climate. New initiatives can be taken to establish an economic corridor between the two countries or sub-region by attracting intra-regional FDI.

5.6 Promoting Manufacturing Exports Through Regional Cooperation and Supply Chains

For countries like Nepal to benefit from the regional integration, there is a need for reviewing overall regional cooperation policies including investment and trade policies. Problems of tax, non-tax and other barriers constraining, among others, manufacturing development and eroding export competitiveness have to be addressed. In the process, trade facilitation through infrastructure and other governance-related facilities for the market will be the key. Equally important is strengthening of confidence-building both bilaterally and regionally.

In order to cope with the challenges posed by the global value chains, new initiatives would be needed to promote intra-regional value chains following some complementary approach for augmenting production processes in a more integrated way. Most important is that at first various bottlenecks pointed out above may need due attention. This may help to revitalize manufacturing industries in countries like Nepal to some extent.

5.7 Obtaining Assured Freedom of Transit and Trade Facilitation

For enhancing competitiveness in manufacturing industries, minimizing external vulnerability and augmenting employment inducing sustained growth, freedom of transit and other trade facilitating measures are very critical Nepal. For genuine economic integration ensuring the fair benefits to the member countries, fulfillment of such freedom is a must. It is needless to add that there is an also added benefit of promoting transit trade which among others may improve investment climate as well.

5.8 Enhancing Coordination and Improving Delivery and Governance

In the Nepalese context, substantial improvement in the coordination at both policy and institutional level is a must. Coordination at both levels may ensure not only policy consistency through minimizing overlaps and conflicts but also implementing policy decisions effectively. Therefore, assurance of declared facilities and incentives in a time bound manner is necessary through effective one-window policy in which a parallel compliance mechanism could be evolved and implemented.

The system of transparency and accountability should also go side by side for containing corruption and improving governance and delivery. Weak delivery and lack of transparency in public institutions have been one of the primary deterrents to doing business and attracting foreign investments. Right-to-information law also needs strengthening. Anti-corruption agencies including the judiciary need autonomy to check the influence of the government as well as political elites. Civil society, the media, and other non-state stakeholders must have strong say in enhancing sustainable accountability in society and thereby minimize democratic deficits.

Regulatory reforms must form the important ingredient of governance reform for improving business, investments, and trade crucial for manufacturing sector development and enhance competitiveness. Higher levels of regulation lead to inefficiency, and South Asia is an important example. New initiatives may be necessary to make business and its processes much easier through, among others, automated systems for removing unnecessary procedural and administrative regulations that lead to delays and increased transaction costs. Processes must be streamlined to save time, and overall costs.

6 Conclusions

The paper after analyzing the process of structural change in the Nepalese economy concludes that neo-classical economic premises based weak industrial policy has not succeeded to put the economy into the trajectory of dynamic path of industrial growth and development. Instead of profound structural transformation, the economy today faces the problem of declining share of manufacturing in output, export, and employment. The paper also derives the conclusion that despite economic integration with SAARC countries to a greater extent, Nepal has also not been able to take expected benefits from this. Both challenges and opportunities of global value and supply chain have not adequately been internalized in the policy-making so that manufacturing industries by attracting both domestic and foreign investment could flourish with an added contribution to sustained high growth and employment.

At first, therefore, it is imperative that a new approach on industrial policy is adopted which addresses market, government and coordination failures more effectively which in addition to enhancing growth could contribute to create jobs in tandem along with the growth of labor force. As an offshoot, there is a need of right balance between the role of the state and market in building productive capacity of the economy in which state should work as a facilitator, guide and catalytic agent of rapid industrialization and employment generation. Since raising the demand for labor is not sufficient to create jobs, the focus should equally be on increasing the supply of skilled labor.

In a new policy setting, there is also a need for reviewing the overall regional cooperation policies including investment and trade policies for ensuring benefits for Nepal from the regional integration. In such a new policy discourse, the priority should be given on promoting manufacturing industries in the country by addressing both internal and external impediments more exclusively for ensuring accelerated growth and rapid employment generation simultaneously. Promotion to the intra-regional value chains following some complementary approach should form an integral part of it. Confidence building both bilaterally and regionally will equally be the key to the successes.

Positively, with the promulgation of the new constitution after prolonged political conflict and transition, some consensus are emerging among the political parties on the imperatives of rapid economic transformation and job creation. The new industrial policy discourse could be equally an important ingredient of such an essential national consensus.

Appendix

See Tables 2, 3, 4, 5, 6 and 7.

Table 2 Growth of manufacturing industries by ISIC group during 1996–2011

ISIC	Description	1996/97		2006/07		2011/12	
		Num	% share	Num	% share	Num	% share
15	Food related	661	18.6	863	25.1	1071	26.3
16	Tobacco product	38	1.1	28	0.8	30	0.7
17	Textiles	828	23.3	519	15.1	288	7.1
18	Wearing apparel	136	3.8	36	1.0	71	1.7
19	Leather and leather products	77	2.2	36	1.0	50	1.2

(continued)

Table 2 (continued)

ISIC	Description	1996/97		2006/07		2011/12	
		Num	% share	Num	% share	Num	% share
20	Wood product	198	5.6	271	7.9	319	7.8
21	Paper and paper products	118	3.3	91	2.6	92	2.3
22	Printing and publishing	79	2.2	105	3.1	94	2.3
23	Coke, refined petrol	3	0.1	7	0.2	6	0.1
24	Chemicals and chemical products		2.6	109	3.2	131	3.2
25	Rubber plastics		92	162	4.7	237	5.8
26	Non-metallic mineral	623	14.6	657	19.1	928	22.8
27	Basic metals	22	0.6	67	1.9	43	1.1
28	Fabricated metal	183	5.1	124	3.6	229	5.6
29	Machine n.e.c.	19	0.5	18	0.5	26	0.6
31	Electrical machine	29	0.8	33	1.0	33	0.8
32	Radio, television	5	0.1	5	0.1	5	0.1
34	Motor vehicles	5	0.1	5	0.1	14	0.3
36	Furniture n.e.c.	295	8.3	306	8.9	409	10
Total		3557	100	3442	100	4076	100

Source CBS (2014)

Table 3 Composition and changes in value add pattern by industries

ISIC	Description	1996/97		2006/07		2011/12	
		VA	% share	VA	% share	VA	% share
15	Food products	4996	22.8	12,907	27.0	30,865	34.0
16	Tobacco products	2624	12.0	8164	17.1	11,921	13.1
17	Textiles products	5673	25.9	4873	10.2	3425	3.8
18	Wearing apparel	1376	6.3	668	1.4	486	0.5
19	Leather and leather products	288	1.3	293	0.6	771	0.8
20	Wood product	309	1.4	615	1.3	1798	2.0
21	Paper and paper products	370	1.7	2007	4.2	904	1.0
22	Printing and publishing	316	1.4	541	1.1	571	0.6
23	Coke, petrol	33	0.2	942	2.0	366	0.4
24	Chemical	1318	6.0	3897	8.1	6976	7.7
25	Rubber plastic	649	3.0	2004	4.2	4225	4.7
26	Non-metallic	1584	7.2	3758	7.9	12,716	14.0

(continued)

Table 3 (continued)

ISIC	Description	1996/97		2006/07		2011/12	
		VA	% share	VA	% share	VA	% share
27	Basic metals	386	1.8	2418	5.1	4903	5.4
28	Fabricated metal products	1095	5.0	3409	7.1	8117	8.9
29	Machine n.e.c.	18	0.1	132	0.3	270	0.3
31	Electrical machine	483	2.2	547	1.1	772	0.8
32	Radio, television	59	0.3	188	0.4	492	0.5
34	Motor vehicles	5	0.0	23	0.0	82	0.1
36	Furniture n.e.c.	292	1.3	449	0.9	1169	1.3
Total		21,874	100	47,835	100	90,829	100

Source CBS (2014)

Table 4 Export share of manufacturing industries in their total output

ISIC3	Description	Export as percent of output			
		1996	2001	2006	2011
15	Food and beverages	7.1	27.2	17.4	5.7
16	Tobacco products	0.0	0.0	0.0	1.5
17	Textiles	56.1	67.1	64.9	59.7
18	Wearing apparel, furniture	96.3	95.2	73.1	45.0
19	Leather, leather products and footwear	58.0	54.8	54.2	44.3
20	Wood products (excluding furniture)	0.3	0.3	10.8	4.2
21	Paper and paper products	5.0	17.6	5.6	0.6
22	Printing and publishing	0.0	1.6	2.6	0.5
23	Coke, refined petroleum products, nuclear fuel	0.0	0.0	8.4	0.0
24	Chemicals and chemical products	41.9	56.0	29.2	9.7
25	Rubber and plastics products	1.5	24.6	48.9	28.8
26	Non-metallic mineral products	1.4	1.3	3.3	2.6
27	Basic metals	1.2	39.4	34.5	23.8
28	Fabricated metal products	2.2	22.0	33.2	2.7
29	Machinery and equipment n.e.c.	0.3	0.0	0.0	0.0
31	Electrical machinery and apparatus	7.8	42.4	10.8	5.7
32	Radio, television and communication equipment	0.5	0.1	0.2	0.0
33	Medical, precision and optical instruments				
34	Motor vehicles, trailers, semi-trailers	0.0	0.0	0.0	0.0
35	Other transport equipment			59.3	0.0
36	Furniture; manufacturing n.e.c.	0.5	6.7	2.5	0.3
Total		25.7	35.2	25.9	10.7

Source CBS (2014)

Table 5 Employment elasticity (cross-sectional at a point of time)

Industry	1997	2002	2007
Food industry	0.37	0.38	0.37
Tobacco industry	0.40	0.41	0.33
Textile industry	0.57	0.52	0.50
Apparel industry	0.56	0.57	0.70
Leather industry	0.35	0.25	0.44
Saw mills (wood related industries)	0.25	0.28	0.25
Paper industry	0.30	0.40	0.41
Publishing and printing	0.51	0.51	0.45
Chemical industries	0.43	0.47	0.44
Rubber and plastic industries	0.26	0.33	0.35
Cement and ceramic industries	0.49	0.55	0.37
Basic metal industries		0.40	0.45
Fabricated metal industries	0.40	0.42	0.45
Electrical industries		0.53	0.54
Furniture industries	0.30	0.34	0.28

Source Khanal (2015)

Table 6 Employment elasticity of manufacturing industries

Industry	1997–2002	2002–2007
Food industry	0.46	7.31
Tobacco industry	−0.28	−0.13
Textile industry	1.02	−0.79
Apparel industry	0.48	0.89
Leather industry	−0.07	1.19
Sawmills (wood-related industries)	−0.07	0.36
Paper industry	−3.46	0.08
Publishing and printing	0.68	0.03
Chemical industries	0.47	−2.3
Rubber and plastic industry	0.92	0.71
Cement and ceramic industries	2.56	−0.11
Basic metal industries	2.46	0.15
Fabricated metal industries	−0.18	0.28
Electrical industries	−0.91	0.33
Furniture industries	0.24	0.01

Source Khanal (2015)

Table 7 Labor productivity in manufacturing industries

Manufacturing industries	Labor productivity @ 1990/91 price in '000			Labor productivity index (average = 100)		
	1997	2002	2007	1997	2002	2007
Food industries	118.9	153.4	149.2	186	189	144
Tobacco industries	468.5	702.6	1252.3	734	868	1212
Textile industries	43.2	43.8	48.9	68	54	47
Apparel industries	52.2	62.1	37.5	82	77	36
Leather industries	77.5	90.1	95.3	121	111	92
Saw mills (wood related industries)	47.5	35.1	46.6	75	43	45
Paper industries	60.3	71.8	211.8	94	89	205
Publishing and printing	69.2	80.4	56.1	108	99	54
Chemical industries	148	205.8	161.1	232	254	156
Rubber and plastic industries	107.6	111.2	114.4	169	137	111
Cement and ceramic industries	20.7	18.7	33.3	32	23	32
Basic metal industries	179.6	118.5	252.3	282	146	244
Fabricated metal industries	120	159.2	217.1	188	197	210
Electrical industries	171.9	87.5	93.3	269	108	90
Furniture industries	31.8	26.7	37.3	50	33	36
Other industries	59.1	37.9	121.3	93	47	117
Total	63.8	81	103.3	100	100	100

Source Khanal (2015)

References

Adelman I (1999) The role of government in economic development. Working paper no. 890, California Agricultural Experiment Station, California

Adhikari R (2013) Foreign direct investment in Nepal: current status, prospects and challenges. Working paper no. 01/13, SAWTEE, Kathmandu

Alcorta L (2012) Industrial structural change, growth patterns and industrial policy. Paper presented to the International Economic Association Pretoria, UNIDO, Vienna, 3–4 July 2012

Athukorala P (2013) Intra-regional FDI and economic integration in South Asia: trends, patterns and prospects. Background paper no. RVC 7, UNCTAD, Geneva

Basnett Y, Pandey PR (2014) Industrialization and global value chain participation: an examination of constraints faced by the private sector in Nepal. Economics working paper no. 410, Asian Development Bank, Manila. http://www.adb.org/publications/industrialization-and-global-value-chain-participationexamination-constraints-Nepal

Blaikie et al (2001) Nepal in crisis: growth and stagnation at the periphery (revised and enlarged edition). Adroit Publishers, Delhi

CBS (2009) Nepal labor force survey report. Kathmandu, Nepal

CBS (2012a) Population census results of 2011. Central Bureau of Statistics, Kathmandu

CBS (2012b) Nepal living standard survey 2010/11. Central Bureau of Statistics, Kathmandu

CBS (2014) Development of manufacturing industry in Nepal: current state and future challenge. Central Bureau of Statistics, Kathmandu

Cohen NP (1995) Why does economic liberalization make sense? EconNews, USAID, Kathmandu

De P, Rahman M (eds) (2017) Regional integration in South Asia. KW Publishers Pvt Ltd, New Delhi

Dixit PM (1995) Economic policymaking: the Nepal experience. Kathmandu, Nepal

GDI (2011) Industrial policy in developing countries: overview and lessons from seven countries cases. Discussion paper 4/2011, German Development Institute

GON (2004) Nepal: trade and competitiveness study: a study conducted with donor's assistance as a part of the integrated framework for trade related assistance for government of Nepal. Kathmandu, Nepal

Khanal DR (2009) Public finance implications of trade policy reforms in Nepal. A report submitted to UNDP Regional Centre, Sri Lanka

Khanal DR (2014) Contemporary issues on global and Nepalese economy: mainstreaming the real policy agenda. Adroit Publishers, New Delhi

Khanal DR (2015) Employment challenges in Nepal: trends, characteristics and policy options for inclusive growth and development. ESCAP-SSWA, New Delhi

Khanal DR (2017) Political economy of self-reliant development: theories and practices in Nepal. In: Gyanwaly RP (ed) Political economy of Nepal. Central Department of Economics, TU and Friedrich Ebert Stiftung, Kathmandu

Khanal DR, Rajkarnikar P, Aharya K, Upreti D (2005) Understanding reforms in Nepal: political economy and institutional perspective. Institute for Policy Research and Development, Kathmandu, Nepal

Khanal DR et al (2012) Sources of growth, factor returns and sustained growth: a comparative study of primary, secondary and tertiary sectors in Nepal. ESCAP/ARTNeT, Bangkok

Korz DM (2015) Neo-liberalism, globalization, financialization: understanding post-1980 capitalism. University of Massachusetts (Department of Economics), UK

Lin JY (2012) A new structural economics: a framework for rethinking development and policy. The World Bank, Washington

Lin JY, Treichel V (2014) Making industrial policy work for development. In: Salazar-Xirinachs JM, Nubler I, Kozul-Wright R (eds) Transforming economies: making industrial policy work for growth, jobs and development. ILO, Geneva

Maxwell S (1990) Second industrial sector study Nepal. Report prepared for the ADB and GOV, Kathmandu, Nepal

MoC (2016) Nepal trade integration strategy 2016. Ministry of Commerce, Kathmandu

MoCS (2010) Nepal trade integration strategy 2010. Ministry of Commerce and Supplies, Kathmandu

MoF (2001 and 2016) Economic survey of 2000/01 and 2015/16. Ministry of Finance, Kathmandu

NRB (2016) Economic situation of Nepal 2015/16. Nepal Rastra Bank, Kathmandu

Ocampo JA, Rada C, Taylor L (2009) Growth and policy in developing countries: a structuralist approach. Columbia University Press, New York

Ocampo JA (2011) Macroeconomy for development: countercyclical policies and production sector transformation. Capital review 104, Santiago

Panday DR (1999) Nepal's failed development (reflections on the mission and the maladies). Nepal South Asian Center, Kathmandu, Nepal

Rahman SH, Khatri S, Brunner H-P (eds) (2012) Regional integration and economic development in South Asia. Asian Development Bank, Manila

Robinson JA (2009) Industrial policy and development: a political economy perspective. Paper presented to the World Bank ABCDE conference, Seoul, 22–24 June 2009

Rodrik D (2004) Rethinking growth policies in the developing world. Harvard University, USA

Rodrik D (2015) Premature industrialization. School of Social Science Institute for Advanced Study, Princeton

Rowthorn R, Ramaswamy R (1997) Deindustrialization—its causes and implications. IMF (Economic Issues 10), Washington

Salazar-Xirinachs JM, Nubler I, Kozul-Wright R (eds) (2014) Transforming economies: making industrial policy work for growth, jobs and development. ILO, Geneva

Sapkota C (2014) In-depth analysis of Nepal's export competitiveness, Kathmandu. Sapkota's blog: www.google.com

Shafaeddin M (2010) Trade liberalization, industrialization and development: experience of recent decades. Keynote speech delivered at the fourth ACDC (annual conference on development and change), University of Witwatersrand, Johannesburg, South Africa, April 2010

Shafaeddin M (2011) The impact of the global economic crisis on industrialization of least developed countries. South Centre, Geneva

Sharma S, Bajracharya P (1996) Impact of economic liberalization in Nepal. IIDS, Kathmandu, Nepal

Szirmai A (2011) Manufacturing and economic development. Working paper no. 2011/75, UNU-Wider, Helsinki

UNCTAD (2007) Rethinking industrial policy. Discussion paper no. 183, UNCTAD, Geneva

UNCTAD (2011) Development-led globalization: towards sustainable and inclusive development paths. Report of the Secretary-General of UNCTAD to UNCTAD XIII, UNCTAD, Geneva

UNCTAD (2013) Handbook of statistics 2013. UNCTAD, Geneva

UNCTAD (2016) World investment report 2016. UNCTAD, Geneva

UNDESA (2016) World economic situation and prospects 2015. UN Department of Economic and Social Welfare, New York

UNDP (2014) Nepal human development report 2014. United Nations Development Program, Kathmandu

UNIDO (2003) The role of industrial development in the achievement of the millennium development goals. United Nations Industrial Development Organization, Vienna

UNIDO (2013) Industrial development report 2013: sustaining employment growth: the role of manufacturing and structural change. United Nations Industrial Development Organization, Vienna

Wade RH (2007) Rethinking industrial policy for low income countries. Paper presented to the African economic conference organized by African Development Bank and UN Economic Commission for Africa, 15 Nov 2007

World Bank (2013) Enterprise surveys: Nepal country profile 2013. The World Bank, Washington

Manufacturing Trade and Employment Linkages in India

S. K. Mohanty and Sabyasachi Saha

1 Introduction

The manufacturing sector in India contributes around 15% of its GDP, a share which is significantly lower than the newly industrialised countries of Asia and those of many industrialised nations (who have a lower share now compared to the earlier industrialisation phase). Apprehensions run high that without steady expansion of the manufacturing sector, India is set to lose out on its demographic dividend where a large fraction of the workforce would be languishing in less productive farm and non-farm activities. The share of manufacturing in total employment increased to 12.2% in the first-half of the last decade and declined to 11% in the second-half of the decade indicating higher capital intensity.[1] The approach to inclusive prosperity and sustainable economic growth is centred on faster expansion of economic opportunities, tied with minimum or higher wages and desirably additional social security benefits. The industry is expected to potentially offer more jobs that fall in this category.

A strategy for revival of the manufacturing sector has been in focus for the last couple of years as evident from the National Manufacturing Policy (2011) and a larger programme of 'Make in India' launched in 2015. These are supplemented with sectoral policies in many cases aimed at enhancing export competitiveness, value addition and leveraging value chains. However, the range of issues potentially hindering the manufacturing sector in India may be diverse and complex. India's post independence inward-looking development strategy based on controls and import substitution had been faulted more often for technological backwardness of the Indian industry. Yet, industrial policies of that period were also credited for laying the

---

[1] Twelfth Five-Year Plan (2012–17) Document.

S. K. Mohanty (✉) · S. Saha
Research and Information System for Developing Countries (RIS), New Delhi, India
e-mail: skmohanty@ris.org.in

© Springer Nature Singapore Pte Ltd. 2019   85
S. Chaturvedi and S. Saha (eds.), *Manufacturing and Jobs in South Asia*, South Asia Economic and Policy Studies,
https://doi.org/10.1007/978-981-10-8381-5_4

foundation of some of the knowledge-based industries which proved beneficial to the Indian growth story in the later years. However, more puzzling has been the experience of the manufacturing sector in the recent decades when many of the alleged bottlenecks arising out of the extended presence of the government in India's industrial production were progressively removed and the competition was fostered through the opening up of the economy for trade and foreign investment. Such policies encouraged greater integration of the domestic economy with the world economy and ushered productivity growth in some of the sectors. However, the failure of the manufacturing sector to expand and employ most from the working age group has been attributed to the same set of policies (Chaudhuri 2015).

India is a booming economy with its global openness hovering around 50% since 2011, but started declining after 2015. In the last decade, the contribution of trade in services to GDP was between 11 and 12% per annum, but mercantile sector remained the most dominant segment in the external trade. Despite having a large export sector, India continued to have a large trade deficit with the rest of the world over a long period. India's export sector expanded with robust growth, but slowed down with the onset of recession. Deepening of recession with the 'Euro Zone Crisis' brought down the growth rate of the domestic export sector, despite surging real growth rate of the economy. This could be the outcome of India's immediate policy response to adopt the 'Domestic Demand Led' strategy to counter the adverse effect of the global recession (Mohanty 2012).

The temporary sliding of the trade sector got corrected, and Indian exports started growing during the last several months in a row.[2] The relationship between the manufacturing trade and employment was not in a healthy state as was argued by a few studies (Revenga 1997; Gaston and Trefler 1997; Moreira and Najberg 2000; Trefler 2004; Baldwin and Brown 2004). RIS study (2006) concluded with empirical evidences that the export sector contributed positively to generate employment in the domestic economy and made a headway in reversing the trends of rising unemployment in the manufacturing sector in India. Similar conclusions have also been observed by recent studies (Veeramani 2016).

Industrial policy for the promotion of the manufacturing sector often responds to sectoral needs and hence, assessment of static and dynamic comparative advantages in the context of international trade becomes important at the industry level. This, in turn, has significant implications for growth in employment linked to trade at the sectoral level as well as the nature of such employment was broadly categorised as blue collar and white collar. The impact of trade on employment is intensely debated in the world economy, and more recently in South Asia. The experiences of countries in regard to the debate are diverse. While importing manufactured goods from developing country, industrialised countries experienced a small negative effect of employment, but it did not have any impact on wages (Ghose 2000). Developing countries have a similar perspective with respect to the trade employment debate. On account of trade liberalisation, growth in the export-oriented sector in the developing

---

[2]Ministry of Commerce and Industries, October, 2018, http://commerce-app.gov.in/meidb/comq.asp?ie=i.

countries has stimulated activities in other sectors, which further lead to demand for skilled and unskilled labour in the domestic economy. It was observed that trade liberalisation in developing countries recorded a positive effect on both manufacturing employment, and wages in export-oriented sectors as well as import-competing industries (Ghose 2000).

The manufacturing sector's contribution to India's merchandise exports has significantly expanded over time. The structure and composition of India's manufacturing exports and their destinations may have undergone significant diversification. This is a reflection of the greater integration with the world economy. This may also be an outcome of India's increasing strategic engagement with its trading partners through regional and bilateral arrangements. In this paper, we have initiated an exercise to probe the link between evolving directions of India's trade in manufactured goods and the potential in terms of employment creation. We are, in fact, prompted by the question whether there can be a case for India to select its trading partners for FTAs (bilateral and regional), and also sectors, in the future with the objective of maximising employment creation, both direct and indirect, particularly in the manufacturing sector. We have analysed whether trade policy can play a major role in creating more jobs in the country by choosing a set of economies for economic partnership which can create more employment in India with export competitiveness. This would ensure appropriate policy action to promote trade and employment in the domestic economy. We have focused on the creation of economic opportunities/gainful employment in the manufacturing industry across firm sizes. The nature of employment in terms of formal provisions characterised by social security benefits, however, are not the concern in this study as we investigate employment creation in the manufacturing sector and evolving trends in the mix of blue- and white-collar employment. In this paper, we have explored trends in the real wage rate in the manufacturing sector, value of output and net value added. Accounting for the difference in production functions according to the size of firms within a particular industry, at the product level, we have proposed to estimate direct and indirect employment to be generated from India's exports, especially covering 84 RTAs. In this exercise, we have attempted analysis-based understanding of changing patterns noticed in the composition of jobs linked with the demand for goods in the domestic economy, mostly driven by the trade sector.

After the introductory Sect. 1, Sect. 2 discusses the recent debates on the performance of the manufacturing sector in India covering debates on jobless growth, deindustrialisation and dualism. In Sect. 3, we present the literature review on the global experience of manufacturing trade and employment linkages. The empirical methodology is presented in Sect. 4 followed by empirical findings in Sect. 5. The key conclusions are presented in the final section.

2   Debates on the Manufacturing Sector in India

2.1   *Whether Jobless Growth?*

As per the NSS 68th Round (2011–12), the unemployment rate (UR) remained at 2% in rural areas combined for both the genders and was 3% among males and 5 per among females in the cities. The unemployment rate for the youth was found to be significantly higher. Further, as per the Report on 5th Annual Employment —Unemployment Survey (2015–16), the unemployment rate (principal status) was 5.0% at the country level. On the other hand, the Sixth Economic Census (2013–14) found that the growth in employment since 2005 was 38.13%. While looking at the coverage of the census, out of 58.5 million establishments, the largest employer was the manufacturing sector (23.1%). However, there was strong evidence that informal sector created the bulk of employment in India given that 55.71% establishments hired at least one worker and 44.29% were own account establishments.

The micro, small and medium enterprises (MSME) sector, often to a large extent is identified with the informal sector, information is generally available periodically. The 4th MSME Census (2006–07), however, provided detailed information on employment generated in the sector. The time period of the MSME Census continued to be of relevance, due to its overlap with the years that were associated with the pre-recessionary high economic growth phase in India and hence could generate important insights on growth–employment linkages. This sector is almost made up of the micro-units, in both registered and unregistered categories with a slightly higher incidence in the unregistered segment. Within the registered segment manufacturing activities comprised nearly 67%, with only 26% in the unregistered segment. Between the Third Census (2000–01) and the Fourth (2006–07), in the registered segment, the per unit employment went up marginally from 4.48 to 5.93, and, declined significantly as a ratio of investment in this sector.

We encountered accumulating evidence around economic growth in India not translating into productive employment despite rapid structural transformation. It has been argued that the policy paradigm failed to take care of concerns about decent job creation–the dominant service sector selectively benefitted high skill and the large informal economy offered bleak prospects to the workforce. The missed bus on manufacturing continues to trigger panic in this regard. The National Commission for Enterprises in the Unorganised Sector (NCEUS 2009) pointed out that growth in employment during 1993–94 and 2004–05 had fallen to 1.85% from 2.03% for 1983 to 1993–94, despite high growth in the corresponding period.

Estimates of the earlier Planning Commission suggest that employment in manufacturing declined in absolute terms from 55 to 50 mn between 2004 and 2005 and 2009–10, after having grown by 25% between 1999 and 2000 (44 mn) to 2004–05 (55 mn). According to Chaudhuri (2015), there was a steady growth in manufacturing employment from 4.8 million in 1970–71 to 7.1 million in 1996–97 and thereafter, it declined to about 5.8 million in 2006–07. The study also found that manufacturing employment had fallen from 27% in 1970–71 to 21% in 2005–06. EXIM Bank (2016) finds that export-oriented employment (direct plus indirect) in the manufacturing sector increased from 26.2% in 1999–2000 to 38.5% in 2012–13.

Respective share of employment in the industrial and services sector remained low, at 22.7 and 24.4% in 2009–10 despite increase in the share of output for both the sectors, most notably the services sector, in the preceding two decades (Mehrotra et al. 2012). In this light, the authors argue that increasing employment outside agriculture must be a desirable goal in itself. Goldar (2011) noted that between 2003–04 and 2008–09, the growth in real value added for manufacturing (organised) was about 10%. Also, between 2003–04 and 2008–09, the employment in this sector increased at 7.5% per annum. The growth rate of employment for total ASI (coverage slightly greater than manufacturing) was marginally higher at about 7.6% per annum. This was interesting as from 1995–96 to 2003–04, employment in the organised manufacturing had fallen at the rate of about 1.5% per annum. This data clearly refutes the often reiterated 'jobless' growth pattern for India.

For the high growth years, Basu and Maertens (2009) observed: 'China's labour force growth rate is 0.83%; the figure for India is 1.85%. In China, 53% of employment is classified as informal sector employment; the corresponding figure for India is 94%. As the unemployment rate in India is only around 4%, the high employment growth is just a reflection of the underlying higher population growth and population structure (32% of the population is under age 15 in India, compared to 21% in China). The majority of these entrants are absorbed by the informal economy'. Ohara and Lin (2011) also present a comparative picture of employment absorption in the manufacturing sector between China and India in the recent decades. In 1985, the Chinese firms on an average employed 1.6–4 times more employees than firms in India, but the sales was lower than the Indian counterparts in many subsectors. However, the size of Chinese firms increased significantly during the subsequent decades.

It was reported that both labour force participation rate (LFPR) and workforce participation rate (WFPR) during 1993 and 2009–10 had declined (Mehrotra et al. 2012). One possible reason for this was access to education at higher levels. The increase in the workforce between 1999–2000 and 2004–05 was 60 million. However, during the following five years, employment creation was just 2 million. There were some indications that quality of employment improved during this period with a declining share of subsidiary status, notwithstanding the increase in informal employment within the organised sector. This is what is known as the rising informalisation of the labour force. Other studies also indicate rising informalisation in employment in India (Himanshu 2011). The rise in employment in India was actually in the informal sector in the self-employed category. Employment growth slowed to 0.17% between 2004–05 and 2007–08. IHD (2014) reflect that "most important challenge is the large number of 'working poor' and under-employed engaged in low-productivity activities in the unorganized sectors. By the current poverty line (equivalent to about US $1.25 per day in terms of purchasing power parity or PPP), one-fourth of all workers-about 118 million—are poor. The low earnings are compounded by deplorable conditions of work in many informal-sector enterprises, as well as in the work premises of self-employed workers engaged in petty activities either at home or on the streets. They suffer from high health risks as well as lack of safety standards".

2.2 Is India Facing Deindustrialisation?

One persistent concern for the Indian economy has been its stagnating manufacturing sector. In the recent years, several studies (Rodrik 2015; Amirapu and Subramanium 2015; Dasgupta and Singh 2006; Felipe et al. 2014; Kumar 2017) have hinted at chances of de-industrialisation in India (declining contribution of the manufacturing sector and suboptimum labour absorption).[3] Manufacturing sector's contribution to the GDP in India has stagnated at less than 15%. The figure for China is slightly over 30%, for Thailand it is ~35% and for South Korea slightly less than 30%. However, the advanced economies maintain smaller manufacturing sectors (around 20% in Germany and Japan, both considered leaders in manufacturing). Clearly, manufacturing has moved out of the developed countries to the developing and the newly industrialised countries. India has so far been unable to exploit the opportunity in a meaningful way. Amirapu and Subramanium (2015) in highlighting recent international experience suggested that in the face of symptoms of de-industrialisation globally, the Indian experience was more challenging since India could be facing premature non-industrialisation as India has so far not industrialised sufficiently. Through detailed analysis of state-level performances, the study concluded that Indian manufacturing may not be growing and probably would be shrinking, but not as a consequence of poor productivity performance. Kumar (2017) concluded that the rising share of imports in final consumption or import dependence corroborates de-industrialisation in India in select sectors. Rao and Dhar (2011) reported that between 2005 and 2008 share of manufacturing in total FDI inflow came down from 41.41 to 20.35% (it is well acknowledged that services, together with sectors like construction and real estate attract substantially more FDI than the manufacturing sector in India). Our own estimates for the later years indicate that on this count, manufacturing have registered a comeback during 2011–2015 (refer Annexure).

The manufacturing sector in India had registered significant output growth post 1980 (barring periodic slackening) when reforms were first initiated. Although the

---

[3]Kumar (2017) explained that the share of manufacturing began to decline after a certain level of per capita income was reached as services began to attain a greater prominence, as happened in most of the industrialised countries. However, de-industrialisation happening in developing countries is an issue that warrants attention. Agarwal (2015) summarised that the share in the middle-income countries had increased before 1990s but has tended to decline since then. The exact timing of the reversal from an increasing share of manufacturing in GDP to a decreasing share varied between the regions. In East Asia Pacific (EAP) and Sub-Saharan Africa (SSA), it started decreasing after the period 1974–82, whereas in the Latin America and Caribbean (LAC), the decline has been particularly sharp since the 1983–90 period. There is a further difference in the performance of the sector in more recent years. Its share has declined continuously in LAC and Sub-Saharan Africa (SSA), whereas in East Asia and Pacific (EAP) it has been almost constant and in South Asia (SA), there has been an overall increase though with fluctuations.

decade of the 1980s was known for piecemeal reforms, more drastic changes were introduced after 1991. As reported in Virmani and Hashim (2011), the manufacturing output grew by 7.7% per annum during 1981–82 to 1990–91, which improved to 8.2% in the period 1991–92 to 2007–08. During the period in between 1991–92 and 2007–08, the growth in manufacturing output showed a high degree of variability across sub-periods from 7.4% between 1991–92 and 1997–98 to 2.7% between 1998–99 and 2001–02 and 12.9% between 2002–03 and 2007–08. Nagraj (2017) broadly concluded the following: 'over a quarter century of market-oriented (or liberal, or free market) reforms (1991–2016), the manufacturing (or industrial) sector has grown annually between 7 and 8% on a trend basis (depending upon the data series chosen). The growth rate after the reforms is higher than in the preceding quarter century, but it is roughly the same as in the 1980s, when the early reforms were initiated'. Goldar (2011) noted that between 2003–04 and 2008–09, the rate of growth in real value added in organised manufacturing was 10%.

Rajakumar (2011) arrived at the following conclusions pertaining to the growth of the corporate segment of the manufacturing sector. The manufacturing GDP of the corporate sector accounted for 6.7% of the GDP in 1998–99, which gradually rose up to 8.9% in 2007–08. The manufacturing GDP of the corporate sector registered a phenomenal growth, as compared to the total GDP of the economy. In particular, between 1999–2000 and 2002–03, it grew at an average rate of 8.3%, as against 5.1% of the country's manufacturing GDP. Among BRICS, as reported in Agarwal (2015), the share of the manufacturing sector that exported (between 1995 and 2011) increased for all the countries except Russia where it steadily declined from its peak in 1999. The increase has been the greatest and the steadiest for India; India exports a larger share of its manufacturing output than the other three. The peak export share for China was in 2005 and for Brazil in 2004. Nagraj (2017) summarised that 'India has avoided deindustrialisation—defined as a decline in the manufacturing (industrial) sector's share in GDP, or share in workforce but confronts a quarter century of stagnation, in contrast to many Asian economies that have moved up the technology ladder with a rising share of manufacturing in domestic output and global trade'.

The apparent decline in the manufacturing sector in terms of growth rate could be more recent. The Index of Industrial Production (IIP)-based manufacturing sector growth index (2004–05 base prices) shows that the sector grew at 8.95% in 2010–11. This dropped to 3% in 2011–12, and slid further to a mere 1.3% in 2012–13. Alarmingly, by this very same measure, the manufacturing sector in India contracted by 0.8% in 2013–14 (Economic Surveys, various years). Between April and October 2014, the manufacturing grew barely (0.7%) compared to the corresponding period of the previous year. IIP-based growth of the manufacturing sector had fallen from 2.3% in 2014–15 to 2% in 2015–16. During April–February 2016–17, as per estimates, the sector experienced contraction. The government announced a revision of the base year to 2011–12, and the new series showed higher growth rates of industrial production in most months in the period April 2012 to March 2017.

We also note that the manufacturing sector slowed in the emerging economies of Asia (Malaysia, South Korea and Thailand), as well over the period 2010–2013.

Reports suggested that the manufacturing sector in China must have experienced very low growth (close to contraction) over the recent months. As percentage of economy-wide GDP at factor cost, manufacturing GVA, as per NAS, showed a marginal decline between 2008–09 and 2011–12 from 15.4% in 2008–09 to 14.1% in 2012–13 (Rajakumar 2017). Commenting on the new methodology, the study concluded that the trend and magnitude of manufacturing output growth rates, be based on NAS or ASI data sets, were at variance with IIP-based growth rates, which remained lower.

However, Rodrik (2015) placed India along with Sub-Saharan Africa where countries appeared to have reached their peak manufacturing employment shares at income levels of $700. Taking the dual parameters into account (1) contribution of the manufacturing sector and (2) share of employment, India was placed along with countries like Bangladesh, Bolivia, Botswana, Chile, Colombia, Honduras, Pakistan, Panama, Peru, Syria (Felipe et al. 2014). Ohara and Lin (2011) captured a broad comparison of characters between Chinese and Indian model of industrialisation. Apparently, two generic distinctions are proposed. One, Chinese firm management is volume oriented, whereas in India, the profit motives drive firms. It is highlighted that Chinese firms operate on 'low profit, high turnover' principle, compared to Indian counterparts. Second, Chinese firms operate in competitive environments with numerous homogeneous firms, while India has heterogenous firms characterised by oligopolistic modern sector vis-a-vis traditional industries that are under 'perfect competition'. The authors conclude, that Chinese manufacturers had benefitted from labour-intensive activities, followed by rapid technological catchup leading to transformation into superior producers.

2.3 Is Dualism (in Manufacturing) a Challenge?

Productivity and efficiency differentials between firms (of different sizes) often spells lessons on duality within the manufacturing sector. Dualism has been a prominent characteristic of the Indian manufacturing industry; dominated by a very large number of small and medium firms. Total Factor Productivity Growth (TFPG) has been the most dominant conceptual and methodological approach to measuring productivity. However, this has primarily been applied to measure the productivity in the organised sector manufacturing; for which time series data is available with certain generality. As elaborated below, distinct movement of the production frontier captured by TFPG has contributed only modestly to the process of technological catch-up of the Indian industry. This may seem to suggest that there may not exist apparent differences between large and small firms with regard to productivity. But, beyond productivity, efficiency (in terms of resource use and cost) and technological competence (in terms of achieving value addition) of firms are equally a function of other factors including access to finance, physical infrastructure, connectivity (also, digital), human resources, knowledge, etc. Larger firms have stronger command over such resources leading to dualism. The Indian experience is no different.[4]

Ahluwalia (1991) concluded that long-term TFPG for the Indian industry was negligible up to mid-1980s. Balakrishnan and Pushpangadan (1994) calculated TFPG for the Indian industry at 3.3 during 1970–71 to 1988–89. Both these studies covered periods prior to the introduction of the new industrial policy in 1991. Ray and Bhaduri (2001) estimated that between 1975–76 and 1994–95, 8 out of 29 industries recorded positive TFPG with the maximum attained by the electrical and electronics industry. The KLEMS India Project Report suggests that the median TFP growth increased for 26 industries from 0.13% for 1980–99 to 0.63% during 2000–08. Capturing more recent trends Goldar (2014) reports that TFPG of the Indian industry was 3.04 for the period 1999–00 to 2007–08. However, it dived into negative territory (−0.98) during 2007–08 to 2011–12. The recent World Bank estimates indicate overall TFPG lately declining in India, Kathuria et al. (2010) reports the improvement in TFP growth in organised manufacturing in 2000s at the State level. Decline in TFP and increase in capital intensity in the unorganised sector, has been noted in this study.

Kathuria et al. (2013) examined the effects of economic reforms on manufacturing dualism, captured in terms of productivity differentials between informal and formal manufacturing firms covering measures of technical efficiency. They found that economic reforms, perhaps, had an pronounced positive effect on absolute levels of technical efficiency in the entire manufacturing sector. While average efficiency increased for both informal and formal sector manufacturing, the increase was higher for the formal firms. Kumar (2007) concluded that irrespective of ownership, higher export intensity is evident in the case of low-technology segment of manufacturing that was also labour intensive. However, in terms of exports, larger firms enjoyed definite advantages over small ones. It also suggested that Indian affiliates of MNEs appeared to have performed better than their local counterparts in terms of export orientation.

Mazumdar and Sarkar (2009) characterised the manufacturing sector dualism in India in terms of the 'missing middle' after the adoption of the so-called economic liberalisation. They suggest that there was a bi-modal distribution in employment with a high concentration of employment at the level of small- and large-size firms with a conspicuous 'missing middle'. This was true even when the household micro-enterprises in manufacturing were left out of consideration. Also, the productivity (and wage) gap between these two groups was significantly wider in India than of other Asian economies. Finally, employment intensity was inversely related to the size of the firms even as export intensity was mostly uniform (RIS 2006). Thus smaller firms may have had higher employment potential.

---

[4]The recent World Bank study on South Asia and Manufacturing arrives at similar conclusions.

3 Global Experience: Manufacturing Trade and Employment Nexus

There has been no consensus with regard to the impact of trade on employment. Studies done for various countries (Revenga 1997; Gaston and Trefler 1997; Moreira and Najberg 2000; Trefler 2004; Baldwin and Brown 2004), reveal that trade reforms had a negative impact on employment. On the other hand, findings of Milner and Wright (1998), Raihan (2008), Athukorala and Rajapatirana (2000) indicated that there was a positive impact of trade on the manufacturing employment in several economies. McMillan and Verduzco (2011) presented a mixed perspective for developing countries. Empirical evidences indicate that the level of employment has increased in East Asia and East Europe, whereas the manufacturing employment has declined in Latin America, the Middle East, North Africa and Sub-Saharan Africa. However, there are studies which have found no significant impact of trade on employment Currie and Harrison (1997), Lang (1998) and Sen (2008).

India has a plethora of studies, examining the critical linkages between trade and employment. Similar to the evidences received from the global economy, Indian experience has not been very conclusive about whether trade improves employment or not in the country. Some studies observe that trade did not have any significant effect on employment in the manufacturing sector (Sen 2009; Raj and Sen 2012; Raj and Sasidharan 2015), whereas others concluded that trade liberalisation led to a decline in the manufacturing employment (Nambiar et al. 1999; Asghar et al. 2014).

Some studies observed that the impact of trade liberalisation was different in diverse labour markets. In encapsulating the debate, some studies observed that decline in employment in organised and unorganised manufacturing sectors is inversely related to trade, but reforms had a differential impact on various groups and sub-groups at the industry level (Rani and Unni 2004; Kakarlapudi 2010; Jadhav and Husain 2016). Krishna et al. (2016) explained the situation by arguing that lower growth in employment was due to the use of high capital intensive technology in the manufacturing sector, leading to low labour intensity and declining of labour force participation.

There are many evidences in the literature supporting that trade improved employment generation capacity in the country. There are studies analysing the impact of trade on employment in India that found a positive impact of trade on employment (UNCTAD 2013; Ramaswamy 2003; and Deshpande 2004). In another study (RIS 2006), it was found that the declining trend of labour employment in the Indian manufacturing sector, including both organised and unorganised sectors, was somewhat arrested due to the export sector. Pradhan (2006) observed that trade had been neutral for contractual and regular workers Exports had become a major reason of generating employment for women and unskilled labour in India's manufacturing sector.

The impact of economic reforms on employment was reinforced by certain studies. Goldar (2000) found that employment in the organised manufacturing sector increased in India during the period 1990–96. In another study, Goldar (2002) observed that after the liberalisation, employment elasticity for the export in the organised manufacturing sector increased, but import-competing sectors witnessed a fall in this regard. Labour policy also played a vital role in furthering the impact of trade on employment in India. A flexible labour policy tends to increase the positive impact of trade on employment (Hasan et al. 2007).

For explaining the relationship between trade and employment, many discussions hovered around blue- and white-collar employment. Several studies observed that trade liberalisation increased the wage rates of skilled labour while not impacting unskilled labour wages to that extent, resulting in rising inequality in the wages of these two sub-groups of labour (Bhagwati and Dehejia 1994; Greenaway et al. 2002; Salvanes and Førre 2003; Hoekman and Winters 2005; Janiak 2006; Brooks and Go 2012; UNCTAD 2013). On the contrary, Mishra and Kumar (2005) showed that liberalisation in trade led to reduction in wage inequality in India due to reduction of tariff rates, particularly in those sectors which were dominated by unskilled workers. Therefore, liberalisation has increased the wages of unskilled workers more than skilled workers.

The preceding discussion indicates that (1) use of skilled and unskilled workers is influenced by the trade sector, (2) the tilt towards wage differences between the two is directed by trade and (3) trade policy has a role to play in shaping the demand pattern of skilled and unskilled workers in India.

4 Model

India has data constraints relating to the availability of consistent manufacturing employment data across disaggregated industries and different forms of industries over a period of time. It is relatively easier to access formal sectoral employment data than getting informal employment data. Annual Survey of India (ASI), reported time series data from 2000 to 2014 in NIC 1998 nomenclature, based on ISIC revision 3. In another format, ASI data was also available from 2008 to 2014 in NIC 2008 nomenclature, using ISIC revision four industrial classifications. The Ministry of Small and Medium Enterprises (MSME) provides registered and unregistered manufacturing data at the industrial level based on the national census. MSME industrial census is conducted, based on a benchmark survey which is often conducted once in every five years. Like ASI, the MSME collects data at 5-digit industry level, but they are available for the years 2001–02 and 2006–07.

Combining these two sources of data, one can avail manufacturing employment data at three tiers for India—(1) corporate sector, (2) small-scale industries (SSI) and (3) cottage industries. It is assumed that production function differs from corporate to small-scale industries and from SSI to cottage industries. For a specific industry, we have estimated three separate production functions for each of these groups separately using panel data.

Since industry-level data is available at 4 digit and 5 digit level, production functions are estimated at 3-digit ISIC level of industry, using most disaggregated data. It is assumed that the output of an industry is shared by domestic consumption and exports. It means the export sector doesn't have a separate production function and takes into account only domestic production functions. We found that 63 industries are enumerated in India and for each industry, and three types of industries, namely corporate, small-scale industries and cottage industries are coexisting. For each industry, production function differs across corporate, small-scale industries and cottage industries. However, production capacity would differ significantly across these three types of industries. For a better understanding about the structural dynamics of the industrial structure, employment has been further divided into direct and indirect employment. For estimating direct and indirect employment at the sectoral level, we have used input–output table technique to decompose the employment effect. For correlating production output with trade, input–output table is linked with NIC/ISIC database, and again linking NIC/ISIC with HS classification. We have established a technical relationship between employment and exports at 6-digit HS level. The detailed methodology can be seen in RIS (2007).

The following assumptions are undertaken to carry out the empirical analysis:

1. In the Indian manufacturing sector, three different types of firms coexist in a specific industry, namely corporate firms, small-scale industries and cottage industries.
2. In a specific industry, production functions differ across three different types of firms, indicating variations in factor elasticity.
3. From total production in an industry, part of it is consumed in the domestic economy and rest is exported to the world. There is no separate production function for the export sector. Therefore, the technical relationship between exports and inputs is determined by domestic production functions.
4. The capital–labour ratio is considered constant in the short run.

Employment absorption capacity differs from one industry to another in the domestic economy. Output drawn from these industries for exports also demonstrate similar tendencies in terms of employment generation in the country. There are two factors governing this trend. First, industries are classified into primary, resource based, low technology and high technology, based on technology embodied in products which are produced by these industries. Over the last three decades, studies in the trade sector classified disaggregated products into the above categories based on their technology intensities (Pavitt 1984; OECD 1995; Lall 2000 and Mohanty 2003b). As the products differ in their technology intensity, labour requirement for their production varies. It is observed that high-technology industry absorbs less labour than primary and low-technology-intensive industries. Second, many industries use blue- and white-collared employment for undertaking the production process. Because of wage rate difference and nature of the industrial requirement, the composition of labour intake varies between white- and blue-collared jobs. Often substitution effect of labour is not unity meaning thereby more blue jobs are substituted for less white-collared jobs. With increasing demand for technology-intensive products, high level of atomisation and robotisation is taking place in medium and high-technology-intensive industries, and therefore, more white-collared jobs are generated as compared to blue-collared jobs. It is a critical question to answer that why demand structure is such that there is high demand for technology-intensive products, leading to continuous replacement of blue-collared jobs by white-collared jobs, and eventually decline in the absolute number of employment in the formal sector. This trend is very much evident from various studies across the globe.[5]

4.1 Implications

Demand for labour in the domestic economy from the export sector depends upon demand for a specific set of products from abroad. As substantial trade takes place through regional groupings, the pattern of employment to be generated (composition of white- and blue-collared employment) in the domestic economy would depend upon the basket of commodities that are demanded by the RTAs with which the exporting countries have trade agreements. It is presumed that in a situation where trade ties of the exporting is more towards developed and emerging countries, the likely pattern of demand for employment would be in favour of white-collar employment and it would be for blue-collar employment in case of developing countries. The exact nature of export demand from various sections of the global economy is a critical question which needs empirical examination.

Apart from the demand factor, the nature of labour absorption is very much contingent upon the type of production functions existing in the exporting country, and the kind of RTAs negotiated for exports. As discussed earlier, the generation of employment from the export sector can be estimated with the assumption that the capital–labour ratio remains unchanged in the short run. With liberalisation, Indian manufacturing sector experienced rise in imported inputs, replacing domestic inputs in the production system. The use of imported inputs improved manufacturing productivity at the cost of domestic inputs in large corporate firms.

Such substitution of domestic inputs by imported inputs replaces labour due to the introduction of atomization in the production process, making production function more capital intensive. With the changed technical relationship in production functions, employment generating capacity in the economy would decline. As a result, output would grow much faster than labour absorption in the country. The use of imported raw materials in the production process has its implications for generating demand for white-collar employment. Increasing practice of the use of imported inputs has its inhibiting effects on the generation of blue-collared employment in the manufacturing sector. In such a situation, the rate of growth of employment will decline with increased imported intermediates, and will promote opportunities for white-collared jobs. The necessity for creating opportunities for white-collar jobs is an issue, which needs to be debated in the context of an emerging industrial economy.

Over the years, the gradual replacement of imported raw material for domestic factors is glaring and substitutability of the white collar for blue-collared employment

---

[5]https://www.seeker.com/ai-threatens-to-replace-millions-of-white-collar-workers-2201607545.html.

is increasingly felt. In the process, the rise of white-collar employment dampens the prospects of blue-collar employment in the Indian economy. Therefore, with the rise of output, employment growth is low due to lack of absorption of blue-collared employment in the economy. As the size on blue-collar unemployment is larger than white-collar unemployment, a disproportionate rise in white-collar employment is not contributing significantly to overall employment growth scenario in the Indian economy.

4.2 Export Sector and RTAs

Demand for manufacturing goods is rising in the developed countries, but a substantial part of their manufacturing imports is capital intensive products. Looking at nature of their pattern of import demand, more engagement with the developed countries through various regional arrangements may end up with the creation of white-collared employment in the domestic economy and vice versa in the case of developing countries.

Conventional wisdom suggests that within a product group (i.e. HS section or chapters or HS heading), there are several products which are not of the same nature so far as employment intensity is concerned. Some products are more employment-intensive than others. Therefore, the employment intensity of manufacturing sector has to be understood at the product level rather than at the industry level. The dynamism of employment intensity loses its relevance when we move from micro level to a more aggregated level of product grouping. Therefore, employment effects are to be examined at the product level rather than at the industry level.

In a broad sense, labour-intensive products create more blue-collar jobs, whereas capital-intensive products generate more white-collar jobs. Depending upon the nature of export demand and labour conditions existing in the industry, including labour laws and regulation, choice of production function to use imported inputs is decided by firms. In each domestic industry, there is simultaneous existence of corporate, small and cottage firms and their production functions are different. With the expanding export sector, domestic opportunities for production across these sectors grow. With varying demand pattern for production in different categories of firms within an industry, the demand pattern for labour for white and blue collar would be different. The pattern of production of output in the domestic economy is possibly supporting absorption of white-collar employment with imported inputs. Particularly, in the corporate firms, there is a greater possibility of substitution of white-collar employment for blue-collar employment. On the contrary, the employment of white-collar employment has led to a rise in the wage bill of the manufacturing sector.

There is a rise in the proportion of technology-intensive products in India's export basket, and manufacturing wage bill is increasing faster than employment generated. These spotty evidences lead us to infer that substitution of white-collar employment for blue-collar employment by the corporate sector might have resulted in the decline of growth rate of employment as compared to domestic output and exports.

5 Empirical Findings

There are many unresolved issues relating to the current debate on trade and employment which need to be examined in the context of India. Despite the persistence of global recession, some countries are posting robust performance in manufacturing export as compared to India. As the global demand for imports is shrinking, high-export-performing countries are adopting inward-oriented strategies for promoting their domestic absorption and also continuing with the export sector to employment in the domestic economy. However, the extent of employment generation depends upon commodity structure demanded by importers. As some studies (Pavitt 1981; OECD 1996; Lall 2000; and Mohanty 2003a) stipulate, certain commodities are more labour intensive than others. Bundle of commodities in the import basket of a country would determine the nature of employment to be created in the exporting country. As commodity composition in import basket differs from one country to another, therefore, employment effects caused by importing countries would be different in the market of the exporting country, depending upon the nature of the commodities commanded by the importers.

Selection of countries/RTAs for trade partnership has been undertaken in such a manner that it would optimise national objective of employment generation with high-technology-intensive trade. In this context, trade policy is important in choosing countries/RTAs in which substantial employment and trade can be generated in the domestic economy. In a labour abundant economy, the trade strategy need to be evolved in such a manner that external demand for imports from India should optimise both high-technology-intensive trade and employment in the domestic economy. For an emerging country like India, there should be simultaneous growth of employment in the external sector and switching of export towards technology-intensive exports. Therefore, two alternative strategies are to be adopted to focus on these alternative goals of trade policy. The objective of each agreement (BFTA/FTA/CECA/CEPA) is to pursue employment generation or promotion of high-technology trade. Trade policy has to make a balance between these two strategies to optimise the national objective of employment with exporter of high-technology-intensive trade. Under the trade policy, the choice of trade partners for BFTA/FTA/CECA/CEPA, has important implications for the nature of trade and employment generation in the domestic economy.

5.1 Trade and Employment Trend in India

As discussed earlier, the literature on the debate between trade and employment presents no conclusive view on the debate. Empirical studies argue from both sides, emphasising that trade does not promote employment whereas others argue from the opposite side. In the context of India, two issues are important relating to the debate: (a) considering the present trend in trade and employment in the manufacturing sector, is it going in the same way as experienced by more matured economies? (b) Can trade policy play a major role in creating more jobs in the country by choosing a set of economies for economic partnership which can create more employment in India with export competitiveness? This would ensure appropriate policy action to promote trade and employment in the domestic economy.

India passed through a phase of industrial restructuring where the real wage rate was rising with phases of fluctuations during 2006–16. Using ASI time series data on wages to workers and inflation deflator for the period 2000–14, real wage bill for the Indian manufacturing sector was estimated. Taking the generated series along with the number of workers in the manufacturing sector, the average real wage rate in INR was estimated with the base year 2012. Using the same base year index, the real wage rate was estimated for the period 2000–16 as shown in Fig. 1. It is important to note that the real wage rate index declined steadily during the period of global buoyancy and started rising with the onset of recession by the end of 2007. The rising trend in real wage rate index continued till 2015; though certain changes occurred as the world economy shifted from first to the second episode of the recession in 2013. That policy switching experienced in India in the form of deepening of real wage index was observed for a brief period. India experienced a rising real wage rate in the manufacturing sector during 2006–16, particularly in the organised sector.

The relationship between output/value added, manufacturing value added and employment in the manufacturing sector is complex in India. Growth performance of these variables during different trade policy regimes in the 2000s has been presented in Table 1. During the period of global buoyancy, particularly during the period 2003–07, CAGR of the value of output, net value added, total inputs wages to workers and number of workers expanded rapidly in the manufacturing sector. With the onslaught of recession in 2008, the course of economic activities changed significantly in India, including in the manufacturing sector. The pace of growth remained subdued in case of total inputs, value of output, net value added and number of workers during 2008–14; reflecting strong presence of recession in India. Despite declining growth of labour absorption and output value added, wage bill of the manufacturing sector increased rapidly. The growth rate of wage bill during recession surpassed than that of buoyancy.

The surge in wage bill and real wage rate reflect the transition of the labour market. This could be the outcome of gradual substitution of white-collar employment for blue-collar employment in the manufacturing sector. As less number of white-collar employment was engaged for large number of blue-collar employment, CAGR of number of workers declined during 2008–14. This change occurred despite the persistence of recession in the world economy including India. This development entails two inferences about the employment situation in the country. First, gradual substitution of white-collar employment is taking place because of India's graduation from low income to middle-income group, reflected in upsurge of real wage rate. In order to sustain high real wage rate, industrial restructuring would take place, leading to the transition of certain manufacturing sectors to more productive sectors within the economy. In the past, many countries passed through the similar phase of industrial restructuring, leading to 'flying geese' pattern of migration of industries in Asia and other parts of the world. This is likely to happen in India where low

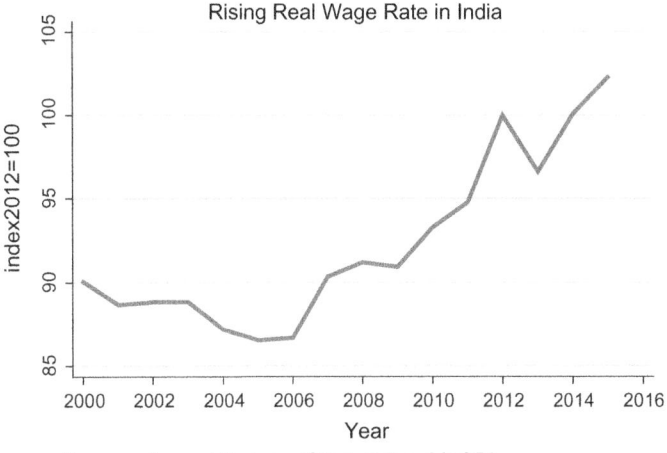

Source: Annual Survey of Industries, MoSPI

Fig. 1 Growth of real wage in the Indian industry

Table 1 Growth of rising wage rate with a declining number of employment

Sl	Variables	CAGR (%)			Value (Lakh)	
		2003–07	2008–14	2003–14	2003	2014
1	Number of factories	3.1	6.8	5.8	1.2	2.3
2	Fixed capital*	14.7	15.2	16.6	457.8	2474.5
3	Number of workers	7.7	3.4	5.5	60.0	107.6
4	Wages to workers*	13.7	15.3	15.0	30.1	140.5
5	Total inputs*	20.8	13.6	17.1	1011.7	5719.1
6	Value of output*	21.0	13.2	16.7	1254.0	6883.8
7	Net value added*	23.9	10.8	15.6	198.8	975.2
8	Gross capital formation*	37.0	4.7	15.2	72.8	344.6
9	Gross value added*	22.0	11.3	15.3	242.3	1164.7

Note *denotes value in thousand crores
Source Annual Survey of Industry, MoSPI

productive sectors are to be restructured because of rising wage conditions. Second, the possibility of creating production opportunities in the domestic economy by
opening up new markets outside the country through BTAs/FTAs/CECA/CEPA, can
generate more employment opportunities in the domestic economy. Job opportunities for blue-collar and white-collar employment would depend upon the nature of
BFTA/FTA/CECA/CEPA, which is to be undertaken by India in future.

The nature of employment creation by the export sector in the domestic economy depends upon India's bilateral export basket with different trade destinations in
the world. Since India's composition of export basket varies significantly from one
country to another, the nature of employment creation will vary accordingly in the
domestic economy. We have tried to examine the spatial distribution of India's exports
to partner countries with a view to examine the employment intensity of export in
2016. For this purpose, we chose 165 top export destinations of India in 2016. For each
country, we have examined employment embodied in each exported product from
India separately to consider a country to be relevant for India to generate employment
in the domestic economy. High employment intensity of exports is defined as one
in which more employment is created in the domestic economy with the given level
of exports. On the basis of this criterion, countries were scaled in terms of their
employment creating capacity in India through their import demand.

At the product level for each country, we have estimated direct and indirect
employment to be generated from India's exports. On the basis of India's exports
to each country, total employment created was estimated by considering both direct
and indirect employment together in India. As discussed earlier, direct employment
is created by the labour force which is engaged in the production of output. On
the other hand, indirect employment is related to post-production activities. While
direct employment was estimated by using industry-wise production functions for
corporate, SMEs and cottage industry, indirect employment were estimated by using
input–output analysis. These methodological issues are discussed in Sect. 3. The
spread of India's employment intensity to exports in different countries, based on
India's bilateral exports in 2016 is shown in Fig. 2.

The results show that employment intensity of exports is significant for India in
certain regions of the world. In the empirical analysis, we had chosen India's bilateral
export engagement with selected countries with product-wise trade in 2016. Countries with green shades show high employment creating partners, whereas purple colour
indicates low employment intensity trading partners in Fig. 2. The green area shows
India's export interest from the point of view of high employment effect at home.
India's strong export linkage with Asia is important since it serves India's export
and employment interest. India's employment interest through export is seen in the
selected region such as Asia, North and West Africa, Canada and the Oceania. India's
future trade engagement in the form of BFTA/FTA/CEPA/CECA with these countries
can give leverage to India in generating large employment at home.

It is evident from the global trade that substantial trade takes place through the
regional route since trade flows are mostly guided by the preferential trade practices.
For promoting trade, India needs to engage in the process of regionalism as an
emerging economy, aspiring to reach the level of $5 billion economy by 2025. Export

India's Employment Intensity in Exports: 2016

Fig. 2 India's employment intensity in exports in 2016. *Note* Low employment intensity of exports refers to relatively low level of labour employment to high exports. *Source* Based on estimation of authors

activities in trade destinations are subdued due to prolongation of the global recession, but the return of buoyancy to the world economy may spur export activities in those countries. If India is to enter into the exclusive club of top five economies by 2025, export has to take the driving seat to steer growth. In this context, India is likely to sign the number of RTAs to strengthen its external sector engagement.

In fact, the choice of RTA for BFTA/FTA/CECPA/CECA would be important for the kind of policy mix India has to undertake to duel ensure employment creation in the domestic economy and promotion of high tech exports. Trade policy is likely to play a major role to generate and to make a balance between both white and blue-collared employment in India. In this study, 84 important RTAs from Africa, Asia, Europe, Latin America and Caribbean and Oceania were considered to examine India's employment interest through its exports as shown in Table 2. In each continent, the study tries to identify RTAs based on their potential to generate high/medium/low level of employment in the Indian economy, based on the structure of bilateral import basket that each of the export destination is having with India in 2016.

The spatial distribution of selected RTAs indicates that except for Oceania, in all other broad regions, the number of RTAs chosen were in double digits. In most of the broad regions, RTAs are divided into high/medium/low in terms of their employment intensity of exports. It is evident from the empirical analysis that in each continent, specific RTAs have the potential to generate different levels of employment in India,

Table 2 Employment prospects of India from the export sector: by RTAs in 2016

RTAs	Number of RTAs	Employment intensity of exports	Distribution of RTAs (H/M/L)
Africa	20	High	14/3/3
Asia	18	Medium	5/12/1
Europe	15	Medium, High	7/8/0
LAC	14	Low	0/1/13
Oceania	6	Medium	0/6/0
Trans continental	11	Medium	2/7/2
Total	84	Medium, High	28/37/19

Note Low employment intensity of exports refers to relatively low level of labour employment to high exports

Source Based on estimation of authors

based on their bilateral import demand. India's trade policy has to capture appropriate RTAs for BFTA/CEPA/CECA/FTA in order to meet its national objectives.

The results show that 28 RTAs from a total of 84 RTAs, can generate high employment in India. About 37 of them would ensure a moderate level and 19 of them would have low level of employment in the domestic economy. While referring to large employment generation in India, it is indicating to large number of employment creation for blue-collared employment. Similarly, low employment generation refers to import demand of high-technology-intensive products, which may create less number of employment in the country, but mostly, white-collared employment in the manufacturing sector.

In terms of employment generation in India, the RTAs across the globe are clearly regionalized in terms of their employment generation capacity in India. From this perspective, RTAs from African can generate high level of employment, followed by Asia with medium level, Europe with the mix of medium and high level, LAC with low and Oceania with medium level of employment in India. In terms of levels of employment intensity of exports, specific RTAs in particular regions can be identified for BFTA/CEPA/CECA/FTA negotiations. If ECOWAS can generate more employment, particularly, blue-collared employment in India, based on its bilateral import structure, Indian bilateral negotiation should focus on deeper level of liberalisation on those specific commodities which can create more of blue-collar employment at home. Therefore, trade policy may be used effectively to create more economic opportunities at the domestic economy to create jobs without compromising with exports of technology-intensive goods.

6 Conclusions

Analytical studies on the Indian manufacturing sector have been limited to a few dimensions, viz. productivity, employment–wage linkages, exports and investment albeit with important lessons. The debates on the manufacturing sector in India primarily point towards economy level jobless growth and suboptimum labour absorption by the manufacturing sector; apprehensions on de-industrialisation; and dualism primarily with respect to productivity, efficiency and export competitiveness between large and small firms. Many of these studies also looked into the impact of India's external sector liberalisation on the performance of the manufacturing sector.[6] Nevertheless, we feel, that policymaking for the promotion of deeper industrialisation has been much less informed through academic research and has been more dependent on stakeholder feedbacks, overwhelmingly from the industry alone. Nonetheless, the negative impact of structural bottlenecks (physical infrastructure, power, land, labour and skills) and policy dilemmas (zoning, tax laws, structural reforms, dispute settlement) are more or less well founded. In other words, a combination of hardware and software issues may be at work hindering manufacturing sector performance in India.

There is structural transformation taking place in India in the manufacturing sector and also in the labour market. Rising share of the external sector is evident since the last three decades, particularly in the manufacturing sector relating to trade with employment. The share of technology-intensive trade in the total trade is growing persistently during the same period. Wage rates are increasing while the rate of growth of output, value added and number of employment are declining. There is a surge of imported raw materials, replacing domestically available intermediates.

India's real wage rate is rising while the number of employment in the manufacturing sector is declining, thus, reflecting the incidence of industrial transition in the economy. Indian economy witnessed a decline in wage rate during buoyancy, whereas the reverse trend of rising wage rate continued during the last two decades. With rising wage rate and declining size of employment happening during the last two decades, the share of high technology trade in the total trade has risen. These phenomena are partially pointing towards gradual substitution of more of blue-collar jobs by less number of white-collar jobs in India. However, SME and cottage industry sectors have more employment–output ratio than corporate sectors. For generating more employment in the economy, SME and cottage industries are to be promoted.

Such a changing pattern noticed in the composition of jobs can be due to change in the demand for goods in the domestic economy, mostly driven by the trade sector. In fact, trade has a major role in determining the composition and size of labour employment in the domestic economy, and trade policy can play a key role in shaping

---

[6]Research on opportunities of market access, value addition, competitiveness, agglomeration, innovation, integration and challenges of market competition, industrial structure, capacity gaps, etc. has been less frequent and prominent. These factors along with others highlighted above affect performance of the manufacturing at the sectoral level. These also define the scope of firm level analysis for policy design, regulation and organisational innovations.

the composition of labour employment in the domestic economy. In recent years, the global trade is governed by preferential trade through RTAs. Export sector being the growth driver, India needs to sign a number of FTAs in future to maintain export-led growth strategy during the period of the global buoyancy. In this context, the choice of RTAs for BFTA/CEPA/CECA/FTA is important.

Considering employment creation at the backdrop, India has to pursue two-prong strategy in its trade policy to promote employment and high-tech exports. With one strategy, India can have RTAs with those countries/RTAs which may create more of blue-collar employment at home. In another strategy, selected number of RTAs may involve imports demand for those commodities which can promote technology-intensive exports and demand for white-collar employment in the domestic economy. Combination of both the strategies would identify a set of RTAs which can fulfil the desired objectives of India's trade policies of promoting employment and high-tech exports.

Empirical findings suggest that some countries/RTAs can generate more labour-intensive jobs, particularly, blue-collar employment than others, based on their import demand from India. Similarly, some other RTAs would demand more of technology-intensive products from India, thus, having the potential to create white-collar employment in India. The analysis has identified 84 major RTAs in different continents with potential for forming BFTA/CEPA/CECA/FTA with India. From the total of 84 RTAs, 28 of them have high employment generating capacity, whereas 19 of them have the capacity to import high-technology products from India. 37 RTAs have a mix of products where they can import products, which can generate employment like skilled, unskilled and semi-skilled jobs in the country. India's trade policy has to prioritize its regional grouping for BFTA/CEPA/CECA/FTA to meet its short- and medium-term objectives of employment generation in the domestic economy.

Annexure

See Table 3.

Table 3 Sector-wise distribution of FDI inflows (USD Millions)

Years	Values (USD Million)						Shares (%)				
	Manufacturing	Mining	Construction	Services	Others	Total FDI	Manufacturing	Mining	Construction	Services	Others
2006–07	1641	42	967	6395	262	9,307	17.63	0.45	10.39	68.71	2.82
2007–08	3726	461	2551	11803	884	19,425	19.18	2.37	13.13	60.76	4.55
2008–09	4777	105	2237	14481	1097	22,697	21.05	0.46	9.86	63.80	4.83
2009–10	5143	268	3516	13150	384	22,461	22.90	1.19	15.65	58.55	1.71
2010–11	4793	592	1599	7449	506	14,939	32.08	3.96	10.70	49.86	3.39
2011–12	9337	204	2634	10879	419	23,473	39.78	0.87	11.22	46.35	1.79
2012–13	6528	69	1319	10327	43	18,286	35.70	0.38	7.21	56.47	0.24
2013–14	6381	24	1276	8081	292	16,054	39.75	0.15	7.95	50.34	1.82
2014–15	9613	129	1640	13134	232	24,748	38.84	0.52	6.63	53.07	0.94
2015–16P	8439	596	4141	22677	215	36,068	23.40	1.65	11.48	62.87	0.60
CAGR	19.96	34.28	17.54	15.10	−2.17	16.24					

Source RBI various year annual reports
P stands for Provisional

References

Agarwal M (2015) Make in India: state of manufacturing in India. RIS policy brief no. 73

Ahluwalia I (1991) Productivity and growth in Indian manufacturing. Oxford University Press, New Delhi

Amirapu A, Subramanium A (2015) Manufacturing or services? An Indian illustration of a development Dilemma. Centre for Global Development, Working paper no. 409

Asghar M, Yousuf MU, Ali S (2014) Impact of trade liberalization on employment: review of SAARC countries

Athukorala PC, Rajapatirana S (2000) Liberalization and industrial transformation: lessons from the Sri Lankan experience. Econ Dev Cult Change 48(3):543–572

Balakrishnan P, Pushpangadan K (1994) Total factor-productivity growth in manufacturing industry—A fresh look. Econ Political Wkly 29(31)

Baldwin JR, Brown WM (2004) Regional manufacturing employment volatility in Canada: the effects of specialisation and trade. Pap Reg Sci 83(3):519–541

Basu K, Maertens A (2009) The growth of industry and services in South Asia. In: Ghani E, Ahmed S (eds) Accelerating growth and job creation in South Asia. Oxford University Press, pp 91–140

Bhagwati J, Dehejia VH (1994) Freer Trade and Wages of the Unskilled-Is Marx Striking Again? In Bhagwati, Kosters, pp 36–75

Brooks DH, Go EC (2012) Trade, employment and inclusive growth in Asia. In: Policy priorities for international trade and jobs, p 327

Chaudhuri S (2015) Premature deindustrialization in India and re thinking the role of government. Fondation Maison des sciences de l'homme Working Paper Series FMSH-WP-2015-91

Currie J, Harrison A (1997) Sharing the costs: the impact of trade reform on capital and labor in Morocco. J Labor Econ 15(S3):S44–S71

Dasgupta S, Singh A (2006) Manufacturing, services and premature deindustrialization in developing countries—A Kaldorian analysis. UNU-WIDER research paper no. 2006/49

Deshpande LK (2004) Liberalisation and labour: labour flexibility in Indian manufacturing. Institute for Human Development

EXIM Bank (2016) Inter-linkages between exports and employment in India. Occasional paper no. 179

Felipe J, Mehta A, Rhee C (2014) Manufacturing matters but it's the jobs that count. ADB economics working paper series no. 420

Gaston N, Trefler D (1997) The labour market consequences of the Canada-US Free Trade Agreement. Can J Econ 18–41

Ghose AK (2000) Trade liberalization, employment and global inequality. Int'l Lab Rev 139:281

Goldar B (2000) Employment growth in organised manufacturing in India. Econ Polit Wkly 1191–1195

Goldar B (2002) Trade liberalization and manufacturing employment: The case of India. ILO

Goldar BN (2011) Growth in organized manufacturing employment. Econ Political Wkly February

Goldar BN (2014) Globalisation, growth and employment in the organised sector of the Indian economy. IHD working paper no. WP 06/2014

Greenaway D, Haynes M, Milner C (2002) Adjustment, employment characteristics and intra-industry trade. Weltwirtschaftliches Archiv 138(2):254–276

Hasan R, Mitra D, Ramaswamy KV (2007) Trade reforms, labor regulations, and labor-demand elasticities: empirical evidence from India. Rev Econ Statis 89(3):466–481

Himanshu (2011) Employment trends in India: a re-examination. Econ Political Wkly 46(37), September

Hoekman B, Winters LA (2005) Trade and employment: stylized facts and research findings. The World Bank

IHD (2014) India labour and employment report 2014. Academic Foundation and Institute of Human Development

Jadhav K, Husain T (2016) Trade orientation of industries and employment performance in indian manufacturing: recent trends, patterns and implications. J Int Bus 3(1)

Janiak A (2006) Does trade liberalization lead to unemployment? Theory and some evidence. mimeo, Universite Libre de Bruxelles

Kakarlapudi KK (2010) The impact of trade liberalisation on employment: evidence from India's manufacturing sector. MPRA paper no. 35872

Kathuria V, Rajesh Raj SN, Sen K (2010) Organised versus unorganised manufacturing performance in the post-reform period. Econ Political Wkly XLV(24) (Special Article)

Kathuria V, Rajesh Raj SN, Sen K (2013) The effects of economic reforms on manufacturing dualism: evidence from India. J Comp Econ 41(2013):1240–1262

Krishna KL, Aggarwal S, Erumban AA, Das DK (2016) Structural changes in employment in India, 1980–2011 (no 262)

Kumar N (2007) Regional economic integration, foreign direct investment and efficiency-seeking industrial restructuring in Asia: the case of India. RIS discussion paper no. 123

Kumar N (2017) Reversing pre-mature deindustrialization for jobs creation: lessons for 'Make-in-India' from experiences of industrialized and East Asian countries. RIS discussion paper no. 208

Lall S (2000) The Technological structure and performance of developing country manufactured exports, 1985-98. Oxford Dev Stud 28(3):337–369

Lang K (1998) The effect of trade liberalization on wages and employment: the case of New Zealand. J Labor Econ 16(4):792–814

Mazumdar D, Sarkar S (2009) The employment problem in India and the phenomenon of the missing middle. Indian J Labour Econ 52(1)

Mehrotra et al (2012) Creating employment in the Twelfth Five-Year Plan. Econ Political Wkly XLVII(19)

McMillan M, Verduzco I (2011) New evidence on trade and employment: an overview. In Trade and Employment: From Myths to Facts, ed. Marion Jansen, Ralf Peters, José Manuel Salazar-Xirinachs, Geneva: ILO, pp 23–60

Milner C, Wright P (1998) Modelling labour market adjustment to trade liberalisation in an industrialising economy. Econ J 108(447):509–528

Mishra P, Kumar U (2005) Trade liberalization and wage inequality: evidence from India (No. 5–20). International Monetary Fund

Mohanty SK (2003a) Trade liberalisation in South Asia: an empirical assessment, paper presented at the ESCAP Expert Group Meeting on Regional Trading Agreements in Asia and Pacific, Bangkok, 30–31 Jan 2003

Mohanty SK (2003b) Regional trade liberalization under SAPTA and India's trade linkages with South Asia. Research and Information System for the Non-Aligned and Other Developing Countries, New Delhi-India

Mohanty SK (2012) Economic growth, exports and domestic demand in India: in search of a new paradigm of development. In: Zhang Y, Kimura F, Oum S (eds) Moving towards a new development model for East Asia—The Role of Domestic policy and Regional Cooperation, ERIA Research project 2011–10. Jakarta, ERIA, pp 191–222. http://www.eria.org/RPR_FY2011_No. 10_Chapter_6.pdf

Moreira MM, Najberg S (2000) Trade liberalisation in Brazil: creating or exporting jobs? J Dev Stud 36(3):78–99

Nagraj R (2017) Economic reforms and manufacturing sector growth need for reconfiguring the industrialisation model. Econ Political Wkly LII(2)

Nambiar RG, Mungekar BL, Tadas GA (1999) Is import liberalisation hurting domestic industry and employment? Econ Political Wkly 417–424

NCEUS (2009) The challenge of employment in India—an informal economy perspective. Report of the National Commission for Enterprises in the Unorganised Sector

Ohara M, Lin H (2011) Competition and management in the manufacturing sector in China and India: a statistical overview. In: Ohara M, Vijaybhaskar M, Hong L (eds) Industrial dynamics in China and India—firms, clusters, and different growth paths. Palgrave MacMillan and IDE-JETRO

Pavitt K (1981) Technology in British industry: a suitable case for improvement. Indus Policy Innov 88–115

Pavitt K (1984) Sectoral patterns of technical change: towards a taxonomy and a theory. Res Policy 13(6):343–373

Planning Commission, Government of India (2013) Twelfth Five Year Plan (2012–2017) social sectors volume III

Pradhan JP (2006) How do trade, foreign investment and technology affect employment patterns in organized Indian manufacturing? Indian J Labour Econ 49(2)

Raihan S (2008, April) Trade liberalization, growth employment and poverty in Bangladesh. In 11th Annual Conference on Global Economic Analysis, Helsinki

Raj SNR, Sen K (2012) Did international trade destroy or create jobs in Indian manufacturing?. Eur J Dev Res 24(3):359–381

Rajakumar JD (2011) Size and growth of private corporate sector in Indian manufacturing. Econ Political Wkly XLVI(18) (Special Article)

Rajakumar JD (2017) Measuring manufacturing comparing NAS and ASI. Econ Political Wkly LII(20) (Economic Notes)

Rani U, Unni J (2004) Unorganised and organised manufacturing in India: potential for employment generating growth. Econ Polit Weekly 4568–4580

Ramaswamy KV (2003) Liberalization, outsourcing and industrial labor markets in India: some preliminary results. Labour Market and Institution in India, 1990s and Beyond. New Delhi: Manohar

Rao KSC, Dhar B (2011) India's FDI inflows, trends and concepts. ISID working paper no. 2011/01

Ray AS, Bhaduri S (2001) R&D and technological learning in Indian industry: econometric estimation of research production function. Oxford Development Studies, vol 29, no 2, June

Revenga A (1997) Employment and wage effects of trade liberalization: the case of Mexican manufacturing. J Labor Econ 15(S3):S20–S43

RIS (2006) Towards an employment-oriented export strategy—some explorations (Report)

Rodrik D (2015) Premature deindustrialisation. NBER working paper no. 20935

Salvanes KG, Førre SE (2003) Effects on employment of trade and technical change: evidence from Norway. Econ 70(278):293–329

Sasidharan S (2015) Impact of foreign trade on employment and wages in Indian manufacturing. South Asia Econ J 16(2):209–232

Sen K (2008) International trade and manufacturing employment outcomes in India: a comparative study (No 2008.87). Research paper/UNU-WIDER

Sen K (2009) International trade and manufacturing employment: is India following the footsteps of Asia or Africa? Rev Dev Econ 13(4):765–777

Trefler D (2004) The long and short of the Canada-US free trade agreement. Am Econ Rev 94(4):870–895

UNCTAD (2013) How are the poor affected by international trade in India: an empirical approach

Veeramani C (2016) Inter-linkages between exports and employment in India, EXIM Bank of India Ocassional Paper, vol 179. https://www.eximbankindia.in/Assets/Dynamic/PDF/PublicationResources/ResearchPapers/Hindi/65file.pdf

Virmani A, Hashim DA (2011) J-curve of productivity and growth: Indian manufacturing post-liberalization. IMF working paper WP/11/163

Export-Employment Conundrum in India's Manufacturing Under Globalization: In Search of a Strategic Approach

K. J. Joseph and Kiran Kumar Kakarlapudi

1 Introduction

Ever since 1980s and especially after 1990s, there has been a change in the mindset of policymakers in the developing countries regarding the ways to bring about the much-needed growth and structural transformation of their economies. This was manifested in the swing in policy pendulum from the hitherto followed import substitution strategy to outward orientation with the state taking a back seat and the market playing the prime role. The process got momentum with the formation of World Trade Organization (WTO) and the drive towards globalization. With the opening up of the economies under globalization, the extent of market ceased to be a constraint to the division of labour (Commission on Growth and Development 2008). The outcomes have been profound with respect to growth and structural change in the countries concerned and even at the global level. The earlier episodes of higher output growth have been confined to relatively smaller economies like South Korea. In the era of globalization, even economies with continental size like China and India managed to sustain higher growth rates even for decades, which was unheard in their history and millions were lifted out of poverty. Thus, the developing countries were especially benefitted accompanied by an increase in their share in global merchandise and manufacturing value added increasing from 30 to 45% and 18 to 47%, respectively, during 1980–14, their share in global GDP increased by about 22% to reach 38% in 2014. This was almost entirely at the expense of industrialized countries whose share plunged from 78 to 57% (Nayyar 2016).

K. J. Joseph (✉)
Centre for Development Studies, Thiruvananthapuram, Kerala, India
e-mail: kjjoseph@cds.ac.in

K. K. Kakarlapudi
United Nations Economic and Social Commission for Asia and the Pacific: Subregional Office for South and South-West Asia (ESCAP-SSWA), New Delhi, India

© Springer Nature Singapore Pte Ltd. 2019
S. Chaturvedi and S. Saha (eds.), *Manufacturing and Jobs in South Asia*, South Asia Economic and Policy Studies,
https://doi.org/10.1007/978-981-10-8381-5_5

However, along with these impressive records at the aggregate level and at the level of a few countries, there is also evidence to suggest that there has been the exclusion of regions, of countries within regions, of regions within countries and of people within countries (Nayyar 2016).[1] There has also been a rapid increase in economic inequality among people almost everywhere in the world; while the share of the poorest 50% of the population in national income contracted almost everywhere (Palma 2011), the share of the richest 1% or even 0.1%, has risen rapidly almost everywhere (Atkinson et al. 2011). Hence, today, the focus of policies is increasingly shifting from growth to inclusive growth and no wonder one of the Sustainable Development Goals of the United Nations explicitly aims at reducing inequalities.

For most humanity, Sen (1983) reasons, the only commodity a person has to sell is his/her labour power. Hence, the person's entitlements depend principally on his or her capability to find a job, the wage rate for that job and the prices of commodities that he or she wishes to buy. Viewed thus, any exploration on the growing inequalities under globalization will lead to the doorsteps of employment conditions and labour markets. Scholars of eminence have been rather unanimous about the adverse effect of market-driven globalization on labour and employment. As Freeman (2011) argued, structural adjustment induced growth has been characterized by 'crises of structural adjustment' as there has also been growing unemployment, a main source of inequality and poverty. Stiglitz (2013) has been more emphatic when he observed that the dearth of jobs and the asymmetries in globalization have created competition for jobs in which workers lost and the owners of capital gained. Further as Rodrik (1997) pointed out, international trade under globalization makes domestic workers more susceptible and therefore, lowers their bargaining power (as cited in Ahsan and Mitra 2014). All else equal, both of these factors will lower the bargaining power of workers, as well as their share of income relative to other factors of production. Empirical evidence tends to support the above proposition. ILO (2011) reported that since the early 1990s, the labour share of national income has declined in three quarters of the 69 countries in they studied, with the decline being particularly pronounced in the developing countries. ILO (2012) further observed that around 670 million workers even in Asia, otherwise known for impressive performance, live on less than US$2 a day and that 322 million below US$1.25 per day pointing towards the poor quality of the employment generated.

Having joined the global bandwagon, India's experience has been hardly different. Trade, investment-driven growth rates in GDP have been higher during the post-reform period of globalization. At the same time, studies have found that the growth in employment lagged behind the trade-induced output growth and there has been widening wage differential, instrumental in -growing inequality (Chaudhuri and Ravallion 2006; Pal and Ghosh 2007). The trends in wage rates indicated

---

[1]To illustrate, between 1980 and 2014, while the share of Asia in world GDP more than doubled (11.5–26.7%) that of Latin America marginally improved (6.6–7.8%) and in case of Africa, its share declined from 3.6% in 1980 to 2.1% in 2000 and only marginally recovered to reach 3.1% in 2014 (see Nayyar (2016) for details).

rural–urban and casual–regular dualism. In urban areas, the wage gap between the secondary and tertiary sectors has been widening (Sarkar and Mehta 2010). It has also been argued that the link between trade and employment is rather complex. Trade liberalization and expansion are often accompanied by broader reforms and other macroeconomic changes, which makes it difficult to disentangle the effect of trade on employment empirically (UNCTAD 2013). In this context, it important to note the findings of a recent study (Veeramani 2016) that reinforced the findings of an earlier study on export and employment by RIS (2006). Using input–output analysis, Veeramani (2016) observed that the total number of jobs supported by merchandise and services increased from about 34 million in 1999–00 to 62.6 million in 2012–13, recording a growth rate of 3.4% per annum which is higher than the total employment growth in the country. As a result, the share of export-supported jobs in total employment increased from little over 9% in 1999–00 to 14.5% in 2012–13. The study also highlighted the important role of manufacturing exports in employment generation as its share in the total export-supported employment increased from 19.6% in 1999–00 to 24.5% in 2004–05 and 39.5% in 2012–13. This salutary evidence on the employment outcomes of exports notwithstanding, there are indications to be sceptical about its contribution to equity because of the quality of employment being generated—an issue of much concern today. If export competitiveness is built on comparative advantage based on low wage cost and informal/contract employment, welfare contributions of export are likely to be in suspect.

The observed outcomes, both in terms of the quantity and quality of employment and resultant deficit in inclusive development outcomes as manifested in increasing inequality cannot be delinked from the hitherto followed free trade policy. It has often been argued that the free trade policy under WTO was driven more by commercial interests than development concerns. To the extent that free trade has failed to deliver the desirable developmental outcomes and the sustainable development goals are being upheld, there arise the need for revising the process of globalization pursued so far. The core ingredient of such strategy is the reconfiguration of globalization from a large developing country perspective shall be towards 'globalizing on our own terms and at our own pace' to avert the plausible 'unmitigated disaster' arising out of unacceptable levels of inequality at different levels Stiglitz (2002). In this process, the role and relevance of the state cannot be overemphasized. Thus viewed, today, there is an increasing significance of the insights from the strategic trade policy (Brander and Spencer 1981, 1985), which called for state intervention to maximize national welfare. Such interventions, however, needs to be based on a precise understanding of the potential of different industries to contribute towards national welfare based on their ability to generate employment, both in terms of quantity and quality such that growth-led export contributes to shared prosperity. The firm-specific and interventions as articulated by the strategic trade policy could be more effectively implemented today by averting plausible rent-seeking by harnessing the potential offered by developments in Information and Communication Technologies (ICTs). From the perspective of long-term development, it is also important to locate the sectors of dynamic comparative advantage, which could be instrumental in higher export growth with high-quality employment. The present study is an attempt at locating such industries and evolving strategic approach towards enhancing their export performance.

The reminder of the paper is organized as follows; Sect. 2 informs about the database and its limits. Section 3 presents an overview of the emerging trends in exports and employment, both in terms of its quantity and quality, under globalization. Section 4 locates the industries with revealed employment advantage with high-quality employment and those with the dynamic comparative advantage in terms of maximizing exports and employment followed by the last section where in the concluding observations are presented.

2 Data, Scope and Limitations

The study draws data from three important sources. Given the focus of present paper on organized manufacturing, the data on value added, output, fixed capital, profits and data on other important characteristics are obtained at the 3-digit level of National Industry Classification 2004–04 from EPWRF. The EPWRF has concorded different NIC classifications in NIC 2004 at 2- and 3-digit level from 1973–74 to 2013–14. The data for the latest year (2014–15) is obtained from the Annual Survey of Industries (ASI) published by CSO. Similarly, we have taken the data on disaggregate employment; male, female, contract workers and wages from published records of ASI. The data from 1990–91 to 2014–15 is provided in NIC-1987, NIC-1997&2004 and NIC-2008. Using the concordance tables provided by CSO, we have concorded the data in 2004–05 NIC. We have taken data on exports and imports from Commodity Trade (COMTRADE) provided by United Nations Conference on Trade and Development (UNCTAD) and extracted the data through World Integrated Trade Systems (WITS). The data is extracted under International Standard Industrial Classification Rev. 3 (ISIC Rev. 3) which is consistent with NIC-2004. In this version, the data is available from 1988 to 2017. The latest year for the ASI data is 2014–15. Therefore, the period of analysis of the study is from 1990–91 to 2014–15. The data comprises of 55 3-digit manufacturing industries. We have constructed industry-wise Wholesale Price Index (WPI) in 2004–05 constant prices using the data provided by the economic advisor, industry to deflate the nominal values. Similarly, we have used the Consumer Price Index for Industrial Workers (CPI-IW) to deflate the wages and salaries. Trade data is obtained from UN-COMTRADE, which represents exports and imports of both organized and unorganized sectors, whereas output data from ASI represents only the organized sector. Hence, export intensity as measured in this paper could be an overestimation of the actual export and import intensity of the manufacturing. The comparison of organized sector's value addition to that of total manufacturing GDP suggests that organized sector contributes to nearly 70% of the total value added in 2014 and given higher trade orientation of organized sector as compared to the unorganized sector, it is reasonable to assume that export and import intensity follow the similar trend. The data on manufacturing value added is obtained from national account statistics as opposed to the annual survey of industries, which provides value addition in organized industries. In order to provide a comprehensive picture of the manufacturing sector accounting for both organized and unorganized sectors, we have used manufacturing GDP published by the CSO.

3   Export and Employment: Emerging Trends

The economic reforms in India were followed by the delicensing and import liberalization initiated in the 1980s. However, as Chaudhuri (2002) puts it, deepening of the reforms since the 1990s indicated a shift from the state-led domestic-oriented, capital goods focused, 'heavy' industrialisation strategy, towards a market-friendly regime, as advocated by development agencies, such as the World Bank. The rationale behind such approach was the anticipation that trade and investment liberalization increases competitiveness and efficiency particularly by reaping traditional comparative advantage, which could lead to the growth of labour-intensive industries and therefore addresses the problems of employment generation and poverty reduction. It is in this context, the literature on manufacturing sector performance, particularly after the economic reforms, focussed on three important aspects, viz. value added/output, export and employment. In what follows, we shall briefly discuss their trends.

3.1   Value Added

It was postulated that delicencing along with trade and investment reforms would foster the growth. Hence, a number of scholars have analysed the growth performance of manufacturing sector (Balakrishnan and Babu 2003; Chandrasekhar 1996; Chaudhuri 2002; Goldar 2011; Gupta et al. 2008; Gupta et al. 2008a, b; Gupta and Kumar 2010; Mani 1995; Nagaraj 2003, 2011, 2017; among others). Figure 1 shows the annual growth rates of manufacturing value added during the past 25 years after economic liberalization. The empirical evidence suggests the annual rate of growth of manufacturing has fluctuated considerably in the 1990s. In accord with the studies by Chaudhuri (2002) and Nagaraj (2017), the growth in value added increased consistently up to 1995–96 and decelerated thereafter (Fig. 1).[2] By comparing the growth of manufacturing in 1990s to that of 1980s, scholars (Nagaraj 2011) argue that there is no significant increase in the growth particularly after the reforms. The growth in the manufacturing sector's decadal average growth rates have remained less than 6% right from 1950s to 1990s (Nagaraj 2017). However, it is important to note that the growth picked from 2000–01 onwards and the sector experienced

---

[2]Chaudhuri (2002) points that fluctuations in growth of value added was observed from 1951 to 1952 onwards with high growth and low growth phase. Therefore, the post liberalization fluctuation in growth is an extension to what was observed in the previous decades.

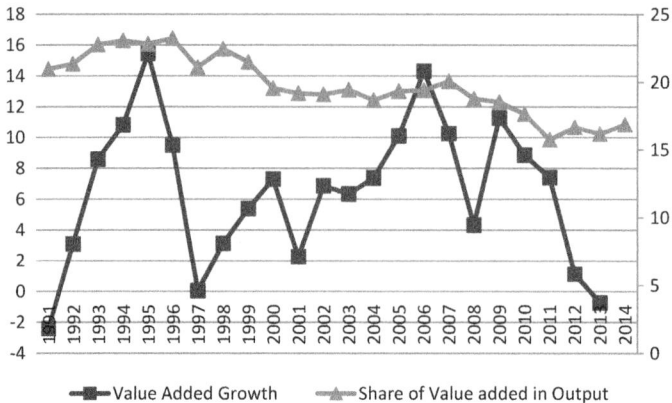

Fig. 1 Growth in value added and share of value added in output. *Source* Computed using ASI, various years and CSO

a slight rise in its average growth rate to 8% in the decade of 2000. More importantly, its performance since then has been worsening with growth rates declining since 2006 onwards (Fig. 1). The studies highlight that the growth in manufacturing is led by the fast growth of medium and high-tech industries such as electrical and electronics, chemicals, metal and non-mental and transport industries (Nagaraj 2011 for example). From Fig. 1, it appears that the value-added growth during the last 25 years presents a cyclical pattern instead of a sustained growth. It is also evident that in contrast to the shorter cycle length during the early years of reform, the cycle length expands as we move to the later period; an issue which needs further enquiry.

Figure 1 also presents the decline in value added over the years. It is evident from the figure that the Indian manufacturing sector has been experiencing a rising output but diminishing value added in total output with the trend becoming more pronounced since mid-1990s. The share of value added in output decreased from 23% in 1996 to 18% in 2004 with a marginal increase up to 20% in 2008 and declined thereafter. The declining manufacturing value added indicates an increase in the resource intensity of the manufacturing sector.

3.2 Trade Performance

The second important aspect that received substantial scholarly attention in the manufacturing is the trade performance after removal of tariff and non-tariff barriers as part of the economic reforms. Following the experience of East-Asian countries like South Korea, Taiwan, Singapore and China that exploited the domestic comparative advantages and embarked on export-oriented growth strategy, the trade reforms were expected to increase the exports of labour-intensive manufacturing products

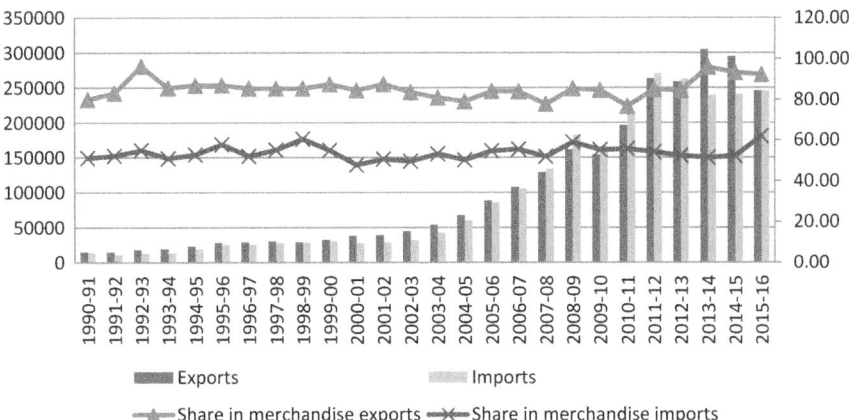

Fig. 2 Share of manufacturing in merchandise trade. *Source* Computed using RBI data and UN_COMTRADE

and foster employment. Figure 2 presents trends in exports (Rs million) and imports (Rs million) and the export share of manufacturing in total merchandise trade from 1990 to 2015. The simple annual growth indicates a steep decline in export growth for the first three years after the initiation of reforms followed by high fluctuations in the growth of export throughout the period under observation. However, it is important to note that the growth of exports is found to be higher than the growth of value added and employment for most of the years indicating increasing trade performance (Table 14). Similarly, the share of manufacturing in total merchandise exports increased from 79% in 1990 to 87% in 2002 and declined marginally thereafter. However, the manufacturing exports at present contribute over 93% of total merchandise exports, which indicates the increasing trade orientation of the manufacturing sector (Fig. 2). The share of manufacturing imports, on the other hand, in total merchandise imports shows a declining trend, which could be seen in the context of increasing oil, imports.

A number of scholars have provided a detailed analysis of trade performance of India's manufacturing sector and the aggregate findings are in conformity with the trends observed in Fig. 2 (Nambiar et al. 1999). Some scholars have argued that India's manufacturing export performance is, however, poor in comparison with other countries (Francis 2015). It was argued that the growth of Indian manufacturing sector is not an export-led growth but has been induced by domestic demand and imports (Banga and Das 2010). As opposed to the conventional trade theoretic view, which is based on static comparative advantage, the trends in export performance after liberalization indicate a structural shift towards capital-intensive and high-technology sectors (Veeramani 2012). The changing comparative advantage in favour of technology-intensive industries needs to be seen in the context of efforts towards reaping the dynamic comparative advantage. At the same time, scholars also highlight an increase in the dependence on imports particularly among high-tech industries and argue that liberalization has led to deindustrialisation in select sectors like electronics (Chaudhuri 2015).[3]

3.2.1 Employment

The third issue that has generated a long debate is employment generation within the manufacturing sector. A number of scholars have analysed the trends and patterns of employment growth in Indian manufacturing sector particularly after the liberalization (Goldar 2000; Nagaraj 2000, 2004; Kannan and Raveendran 2009; Goldar 2011; among others).[4] Figure 3 presents the employment scenario of total persons engaged during the last two and half decades. From the figure, three phases of employment growth are evident. In the first phase (1990–96), we observe an increase in the number of people employed. Goldar (2000) has shown that employment in the organized manufacturing sector (including electricity) registered an impressive annual growth rate of about 2.83% during 1990–96. This trend in the increase in absolute employment from 1990 to 1996 is evident from Fig. 3 wherein employment has grown from over 6 lakhs to over 8 lakhs. Goldar (2000) attributed the growth in overall employment to private and joint sector companies. The growth rate registered by the public sector was only 0.39% as against 3.72% by the other firms. However, Nagaraj (2000) contested the findings of Goldar (2000) and attributed the employment growth during the 1990s to the investment boom, witnessed in response to the industrial deregulation and trade policy reform. The second phase (1997–03) shows a decline in absolute employment. As Nagaraj (2004) pointed, 1.3 million employees lost their employment during 1995–96 to 2001–02 and these losses have been widespread across major states and industry groups. Further, he noted that jobless growth during the 1980s was followed by an employment boom for four years during 1992–96 and retrenchment thereafter. Similarly, Rani and Unni (2004) found that the initial economic reform policies have adversely affected employment in organized and unorganized manufacturing sectors, which got improved in the subsequent years. In another study, Kannan and Raveendran (2009) showed that employment growth has been negligible from 1980 to 2004 despite high levels of output growth. They found that some industries such as tobacco, textile, leather, paper, metals and non-metals, chemicals and electrical and non-electrical machinery have shown high output growth along with high employment growth. The scholars attributed the phenomena of jobless growth to increasing capital intensity and growth of real wages.[5]

---

[3]For details on premature deindustrialization in developing as a result of globalization, see Rodrik (2016).

[4]Bhalotra (2003) provides a comprehensive overview and summary of studies that dealt with employment and wages in manufacturing sector in India under the light of economic liberalization.

[5]For a detailed empirical analysis on the employment growth in Indian manufacturing sector, see Bhalotra (1998) and Fallon and Lucas (1993).

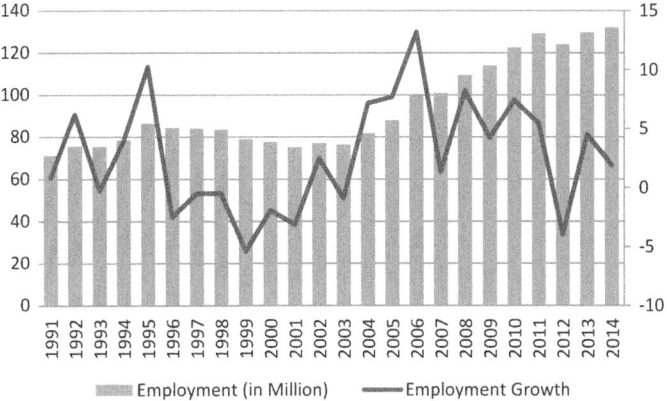

Fig. 3 Employment scenario in Indian manufacturing. *Source* Computed using ASI, various years

However, there is a significant increase in absolute level of employment from 2004 to 2011 with a marginal decline in employment afterwards. Goldar (2011) argued that employment has registered an annual growth rate of 7.5% during 2003–04 to 2008–09 after a negative employment growth in the second phase. While the marginal decline in employment after 2011 could be broadly attributed to general economic slowdown wherein industrial sector registered negative growth rates, the significant growth in employment (during 2003–11) is attributed to growth in a private sector where the labour intensity is higher than the other industry categories (Goldar 2011).

Figure 4 shows increasing labour productivity, which substantiates the argument in the literature that capital intensity has been increasing. Similarly, Fig. 4 also depicts declining employment intensity over the years. Given the employment generation potential of the Indian manufacturing, another strand of literature analysed the role of trade in observed patterns employment growth in Indian manufacturing (Kambhampati et al. 1997; Khambampati and Howell 1998; Goldar 2002; Hasan et al. 2003; Banga 2005; Sen 2008, 2009; Raj and Sen 2012; Rajesh raj and Sasidharan 2015; Goldar 2009; Uma et al. 2012).

While some studies argue that trade liberalization has led to employment generation through increase in employment elasticity (Kambhampati et al. 1997; Goldar 2002; Hasan et al. 2003; Deshpande et al. 2004; Banga 2005), few others argue that liberalization process has contributed to the downsizing of employment, switching towards capital-intensive production (Raj and Sen 2012; Rajesh raj and Sasidharan 2015; Goldar 2009; Uma et al. 2012). The existing studies on employment growth in the manufacturing sector have focused on aggregate employment while the quality of employment generated, as argued by other scholars, is important particularly in the light of increasing trade liberalization and to create inclusive employment opportunities which have ramifications on growing inequality.

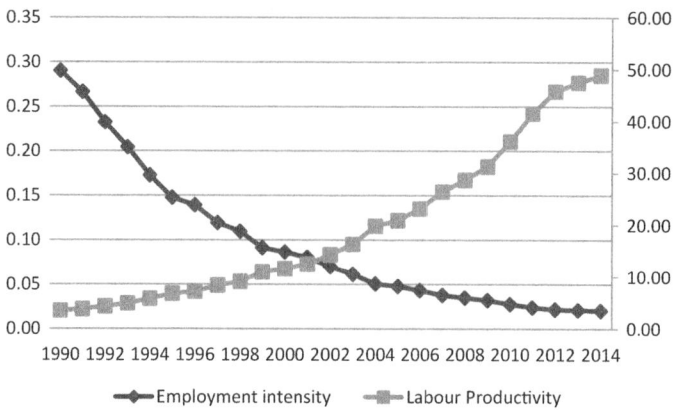

Fig. 4 Labour productivity in Indian manufacturing. *Source* Same as Fig. 3

3.2.2 Quality of Employment

While the recent evidence in terms of increasing share of manufacturing in merchandise along with increasing evidence for export-supported employment generation, the issue of much concern from equity and welfare perspective is quality of employment generated. It is generally understood that employment is key to the social and economic advancement of workers and provides them with a sense of identity, but it may also be associated with risks for health and well-being. Further the developments in the labour markets can be accompanied by challenges concerning the quality of employment. Hence, the quality of employment has been attracting the growing attention of the academia, policymakers and especially the multilateral organizations like the International Labour Organization (ILO). The focus of ILO, for example *today* goes beyond the quantity of employment to include worker rights; employment creation; social protection; and social dialogue between workers' organizations, employers' organizations and calls for *promoting opportunities for men and women to obtain decent and productive work.* In Europe, the Europe 2020 strategy identified employment and job quality as essential elements for smart, sustainable and inclusive growth. United Nations Economic Commission for Europe (2015) has suggested many indicators of the quality of employment, which include (1) safety and ethics of employment, (2) income and benefits from employment, (3) working time and work–life balance, (4) security of employment and social protection, (5) social dialogue (6) skills development and training and (7) employment-related relationships and work motivation. Since the focus in the Indian context is apparently on the quantity of employment, the quality considerations are yet to receive the attention of policymakers and we have very limited database on the above indicators. For the present purpose, we have gathered information on three aspects of quality, skilled and unskilled workers, contract and direct workers and male and female workers.

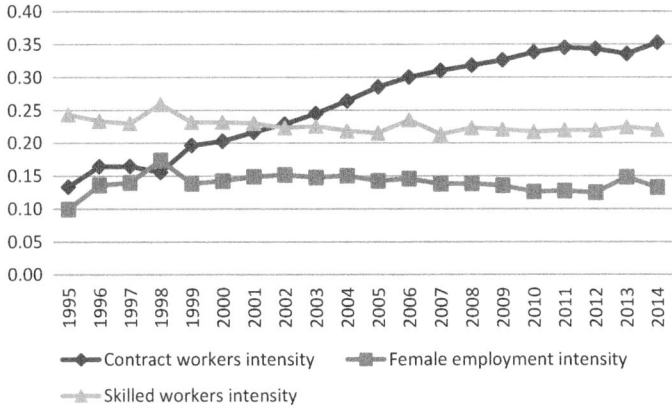

Fig. 5 Trends in quality of employment in manufacturing. *Source* Same as Fig. 4

Figure 5 presents the nature and quality of employment generated during 1995–2014. Due to data paucity on the employment of male and female prior to 1995, we restrict our analysis to 1995–2014 so that the numbers could be easily compared. We find that the share of workers (unskilled) in total employment has largely remained the same over years with minor variations. At the same time, the share of female in total employment has increased from 9.97% in 1995 to 15.15% in 2002. However, the share has gradually declined to 12.48% in 2012 with a minor improvement afterwards. What is of much relevance from the equity and welfare perspective is that in the share of contract workers there is an almost threefold increase from 13.34% in 1995 to 26.42% in 2004 and further to 35.39% in 2014.

As evident from the figure, thus today more than one-third of total workers are employed through contracts who do not come under the purview of any social security benefits. The observed trend clearly indicates the deterioration in the quality of employment that is being generated in the organized manufacturing sector. Along with the deterioration in the quality of employment, we also observe a sustained decline in the share of wages in the value added and a significant increase in the share of profit (see Fig. 6). The figure also, however, shows the recent increase in the share of wages and decline in profits. Such an increase in wage share has coincided with a decline in the real wage for workers. To the extent that wages of permanent workers are flexible downwards, the increase in the wage share could have been an outcome of increased employment mostly of contract workers at lower wage rate.

Drawing from three phases of employment generation, we divided the period of analysis into two sub-periods; period one (1996–04) and period two (2004–14). The first period represents the phenomenon of jobless growth where total employment growth was found to be negative (−0.56%) while the output growth was 8.39%. The second period corresponds to high output growth (10.05%) coupled with high employment growth (5.01%). As already discussed, the employment growth patterns at the aggregate level have been widely debated. Hence, given the focus of the

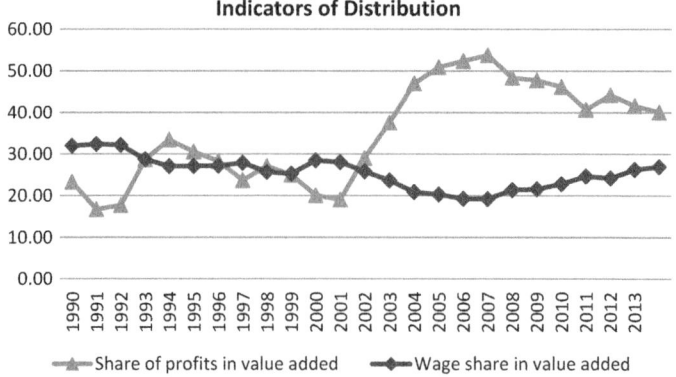

Fig. 6 Share of profit and wages in value added. *Source* Same as Fig. 4

present paper, we focus on the quality of employment growth. It is evident from Table 14 that the growth in employment in period one was mainly driven by the growth in contract labour (8.15%) and female employment (5.22%) while the growth of direct employment and male workers was found to be negative (−1.96% and −3.04%, respectively). In the second period, the growth of female employment declined (3.92%) as compared to the first period (5.22%) while the growth of male workers improved in the second period (3.59%).

Given the nature and quality of employment generation in India's manufacturing sector where we observed an increase in the share of contract workers, it is imperative to analyse its manifestations in terms of share of wages and profits in value added. From a distribution point of view, the roots of inequality could be identified through changes in relative shares of profits and wage share of workers. Figure 6 presents the share of wages and profits in value added. We find that the share of wages in total value added shows a declining trend from the beginning of reforms with a marginal increase from 2007 onwards. Similarly, the share of profits showed a declining trend from 1994 onwards till 1999 and increased significantly during 1999–07. The share has nearly doubled during the observed period followed by a declining trend from 2007 onwards. The observed trend in the share of wages and profits could be broadly attributed to: (1) changing production technique in favour of the capital-intensive mode of production and (2) the observed changes in the quality of labour. Though the observed trends in the share of wages and profits indicate severe implications on growing inequalities, Nayyar (2014) points out that profit-led growth and wage-led growth could be complementary to each other rather than substituting in nature.

3.2.3 Champions of Exports and Employment Generation

It is evident from our discussion in the previous section that manufacturing sector is not only having the potential for employment generation but also a major source of export earnings and that manufacturing exports has the potential towards contributing to employment generation. Veeramani (2016) observed that out the 13.3 million exports supported employment generated during 2010–11 to 2012–13, the bulk of it (75%) was brought about by the manufacturing sector. However, it was also observed that industries are not equally positioned with respect to addressing these two key policy objectives of employment and export generation. While exports and employment generation could be complementary in some of the industries, these policy objectives could be inimical in others. Therefore, the conventional approach of export promotion based mainly on the revealed comparative advantage need not necessarily contribute towards employment. In the current context of growing inequality, which cannot be delinked from the jobless growth, and much hope has been pegged on manufacturing export as a strategy towards employment generation, the relevance of an export strategy built on the twin pillars of exports and employment, therefore cannot be overemphasized.

Viewed thus, the aggregate measures of export orientation may conceal more than what it reveals about employment. When we analyse the trade-induced development from an employment generation perspective, it is important to identify industries that are capable of more exports and job generation potential. From the equity and distribution perspective, it is not just the employment generation that matters but the quality of employment created is equally important. This is because the strategy towards building competitiveness through cost reduction may entail, along with changes in production techniques, changes in the structure of employment leading to an increasing share of contract workers in the workforce with its implications on the quality of employment generated. Hence, a related issue pertains to the quality of employment generated through export promotion. However, with the plausible exception of Saha et al. (2013) and Banerjee and Veeramani (2017),[6] studies on trade and employment in Indian context have not paid adequate attention to the quality of employment generated through exports. Finally, in a large and diversified economy like India, while the relevance of harnessing static comparative advantage is important, equally important is the need to build up dynamic comparative advantage and locating such industries for evolving an employment oriented export strategy from a long-term perspective.

Towards identifying the export-driven employment-generating industries, we divide all the 3-digit manufacturing industries into four mutually exclusive categories based on their observed performance with respect to employment generation and export performance in comparison with the manufacturing sector as a whole. The first category, designated as export-employment champions, is those industries with employment intensity and export intensity higher than the industry average. Industries in this category, while being more labour intensive, are also highly export-oriented such that they hold the potential for employment generating not only because

---

[6]Studies have pointed out the increasing contract worker intensity in total employment particularly after the liberalization and changes brought in the labour laws (Ramaswamy 1999; Sharma 2006; Neethi 2008; among others). However, these studies do not provide any evidence on the role of trade orientation therein…

of their labour intensity but also due to scale effect as they have higher export competitiveness. The second category, export champions-employment laggards, is of industries with export intensity higher than the industry average but the observed employment intensity is lower than the industry average. The observed performance could be attributed to more capital-intensive production and that more employment generation could take place mostly through scale effect through increased exports. The third category, export laggards-employment champions, are those industries with export intensity lower than the industry average while the employment intensity higher than the industry average. In the case of these industries, high employment generation capacity notwithstanding is not having export competitiveness. Hence, building export competitiveness in these industries is important for more employment generation. Finally, we have the export-employment laggards, characterised by lower than industry average export intensity and employment intensity. These are the industries with higher capital/technology intensity and greater domestic market orientation. While export promotion could be helpful for employment generation in all the industries, the return to the export promotion in terms of employment generation is likely to be higher in case of export-employment champions and employment champions-export laggards. A definite conclusion, however, is not warranted especially because higher export intensity need not necessarily always translate into a higher level of exports and similarly higher labour intensity may not be leading to higher number of jobs. Further, as already indicated, larger number of jobs may not always be leading to favourable outcomes as regards equity and welfare on account of the quality of the employment generated. In what follows, we shall locate and map the industries at the 3-digit level based on above categorisation and examine their relative contribution towards export and employment on the one hand and quality of employment generated by them on the other. We shall begin our analysis at the aggregate level and proceed with a more disaggregate level.

3.2.4 Empirical Evidence: Aggregate Analysis

Table 1 presents the distribution of industries (3-digit level) in India's manufacturing sector in terms of four categories that we have identified. It is evident that in 1990, a little over 25% of the number of industries were employment-export champions and 36% of the industries were export champions but employment laggards. These two groups of industries that displayed higher employment intensity accounted for nearly 61% of the total number of industries in India's manufacturing sector in 1991. As we move to 2000, their share further increased by 69% and declined marginally thereafter to reach 67% in 2014. The recent decline in their share notwithstanding, it appears that high employment intensity appears to be the hallmark of an overwhelming majority of manufacturing industries in India. The table also highlights two other interesting features of industries in India's manufacturing sector. First, there has been a steady increase in the share of export champions-employment laggards, which is evident from more than fourfold increase in the share of industries in this category from 3.6% in 1990 to over 16% in 2014. This indicates the increasing capital intensity

Table 1 Distribution of number of manufacturing industries (3-digit) based on their performance with respect to export and employment

Year	Champions of export and employment	Employment laggards and export champions	Employment champions and export laggards	Laggards in employment were export
1990	14 (25.45)	2 (3.63)	20 (36.36)	19 (34.54)
1991	15 (27.27)	1 (1.81)	20 (36.36)	19 (34.54)
1992	12 (21.81)	2 (3.63)	22 (40)	19 (34.54)
1993	9 (16.36)	3 (5.45)	23 (41.81)	20 (36.36)
1994	10 (18.18)	2 (3.63)	22 (40)	21 (38.18)
1995	13 (23.63)	1 (1.81)	21 (38.18)	20 (36.36)
1996	13 (23.63)	2 (3.63)	21 (38.18)	19 (34.54)
1997	13 (23.63)	1 (1.81)	20 (36.36)	21 (38.18)
1998	10 (18.18)	4 (7.27)	22 (40)	19 (34.54)
1999	9 (16.36)	3 (5.45)	22 (40)	21 (38.18)
2000	13 (23.63)	1 (1.81)	25 (45.45)	16 (29.09)
2001	11 (20)	3 (5.45)	23 (41.81)	18 (32.72)
2002	12 (21.81)	2 (3.63)	23 (41.81)	18 (32.72)
2003	13 (23.63)	1 (1.81)	27 (49.09)	14 (25.45)
2004	17 (30.9)	2 (3.63)	25 (45.45)	11 (20)
2005	12 (21.81)	3 (5.45)	26 (47.27)	14 (25.45)
2006	13 (23.63)	6 (10.9)	25 (45.45)	11 (20)
2007	12 (21.81)	5 (9.09)	26 (47.27)	12 (21.81)
2008	13 (23.63)	6 (10.9)	23 (41.81)	13 (23.63)
2009	14 (25.45)	5 (9.09)	23 (41.81)	13 (23.63)
2010	13 (23.63)	5 (9.09)	24 (43.63)	13 (23.63)
2011	14 (25.45)	4 (7.27)	25 (45.45)	12 (21.81)
2012	14 (25.45)	5 (9.09)	26 (47.27)	10 (18.18)
2013	13 (23.63)	7 (12.72)	24 (43.63)	11 (20)
2014	12 (21.81)	9 (16.36)	25 (45.45)	9 (16.36)

Note Figures in the parenthesis indicate the share of the number of industries
Source Same as Fig. 4

in India's manufacturing sector. Whether the observed shift also involves a strategic shift towards dynamic comparative advantage is a related issue which we shall take up later in this section. Second, in 1990, a large proportion (34.5%) were export and employment laggards indicating their low labour intensity and greater domestic market orientation. It is encouraging to note that there has been a steady decline in the number of such industries and their share in 2014 is found to be only 16.4%. These points towards increasing export orientation of manufacturing industries in India.

3.2.5 Contribution to Export and Employment

Analysis in terms of export intensity and number of industries, while being indicative, need not necessarily convey the real contribution. Hence we shall now look at the contribution of the different groups of industries with respect to exports and employment generation. Table 2 presents the trends in the share of the four categories in terms of export and employment during 1991–2014. In 1990, the employment and export champions accounted for over 55% of the total manufacturing exports, which declined over the years to reach the present level of 20%. When it comes to employment, their share has shown fluctuations from year to year and yet their contribution is over 19% in 2014. Thus, we have a situation wherein 22% of the manufacturing industries that we have designated as export-employment champions, today account for 19% of the employment and 21% of the exports. In case of employment champions-export laggards, while their export share has increased to reach as high as 21% in 2007 there has been a decline thereafter to reach the present level of 18%. When it comes to their employment contribution, it continues to remain as high as 59%. Thus viewed, it appears that these two categories of industries put together accounts for nearly 78% of total employment, while they account for only 38% of the total exports. From the employment generation perspective, any attempt to enhance their international competitiveness is bound to give rich dividends in terms of employment. The table further reveals that export champions and employment laggards today drives the manufcaturing exports as their share in total exports increased from less that 7% to over 50%. These industries are known to be poor candidates for job generation as their share in employment is only 8% of the total manufacturing employment.

When it comes to employment-export laggards, their share both in exports and employment has steadily declined—employment from 21% 1990 to 11% in 2014 and export from 32 to 13.7% during the corresponding period. From the above discussion, it appears that any strategic approach towards increasing employment shall focus on the first two categories (export-employment champions and employment champions-export laggards). The third category could also be helpful in increasing employment through enabling their scale of exports.

As already indicated, higher employment need not necessarily contribute towards equity and welfare if increased job creation is not accompanied by a concomitant increase in the quality of employment. Hence, we explore the plausible qualitative dimensions of the employment generated by the four categories of industries.

3.2.6 Quality of Employment

Contract Labour Intensity
An important dimension of quality of employment, which has been often highlighted relates to the contract labour intensity (Ramaswamy 1999; Sharma 2006; Neethi 2008; Saha et al. 2013; among others). Contract labour employment by their very nature is perceived to be of low quality because unlike their permanent counterparts, their entitlements towards social protection are limited. Table 3 presents data on the

Table 2 Relative employment and export share of category to total manufacturing

Year	Employment-export champions		Employment laggards-export champions		Employment champions-export laggards		Employment laggards and export laggards	
	Exp	Emp	Emp	Exp	Emp	Exp	Emp	Exp
1990	7.38	55.47	2.17	6.91	58.16	16.23	32.29	21.38
1991	23.91	62.46	2.08	7.37	37.78	5.73	36.22	24.45
1992	6.63	33.69	2.63	27.06	59.03	17.41	31.71	21.84
1993	7.25	29.8	2.89	30.23	57.67	17.07	32.19	22.9
1994	23	40.7	2.84	28.41	39.59	6.03	34.58	24.85
1995	27.95	63.05	1.99	7.73	37.76	6.57	32.3	22.66
1996	24.28	56.16	5.29	12.23	38.35	7.19	32.08	24.43
1997	25.48	57.21	2.12	8.4	39.43	9.2	32.98	25.19
1998	23.89	39.95	7.01	32.61	41.6	8.77	27.49	18.67
1999	24.76	39.02	3.89	30.76	39.52	8.73	31.83	21.49
2000	28.09	59.69	1.86	6.4	45.77	11.86	24.28	22.06
2001	25.35	36.64	3.82	25.01	39.88	9.79	30.96	28.56
2002	25.89	34.09	2.33	22.03	45.5	13.41	26.28	30.47
2003	27.43	31.81	1.59	20.42	53.7	20.29	17.27	27.48
2004	33.03	51.88	4.57	11.84	50.41	15.76	11.99	20.52
2005	16.14	21.99	6.08	29.48	60.77	21.31	17.01	27.21
2006	19.74	20	7.78	46.68	57.61	20.28	14.87	13.04
2007	16.92	18.28	5.64	43.56	60.07	21.07	17.37	17.09
2008	17.32	16.89	5.88	43.57	59.76	21.16	17.03	18.38
2009	25.07	27.34	5.36	44.47	52.17	12.73	17.4	15.45
2010	14.17	16.01	5.57	46.42	62.2	21.49	18.07	16.09
2011	17.01	18.42	4.8	46.18	59.24	19.45	18.94	15.95
2012	24.12	23.48	6.64	48.11	54.47	15.62	14.77	12.79
2013	25.05	22.62	7.77	51.03	53.22	14.96	13.96	11.38
2014	19.21	20.1	8.22	50.51	58.81	18.05	13.76	11.33

Note Exp Exports, *Emp* Employment

intensity of contract labour (represented by the share of contract workers in total workers) in the manufacturing sector as a whole and for the four categories that we have identified. In sync with the findings of the earlier studies, Table 3 shows that for the manufacturing sector as a whole, the share of contract labour almost increased threefold from 13% in 1990 to 35% in 2014. This tends to suggest that more than one-third of total workers in India's manufacturing are contractual labour, not entitled to any social security benefits, indicating a drastic deterioration in the

Table 3 Contract labour intensity in different categories of industry and the manufacturing sector

Year	Export-employment champions	Employment laggards and export champions	Employment champions and export laggards	Laggards in employment export	Total industry
1992	4.20	24.67	12.56	9.03	11.35
1995	7.07	22.20	18.36	12.47	13.34
1998	9.13	33.33	15.77	16.88	15.55
2001	10.13	25.06	27.98	23.14	21.64
2004	15.26	40.24	32.83	26.43	26.42
2007	18.43	35.45	32.95	35.91	31.02
2010	18.36	38.00	34.21	44.29	33.81
2013	27.65	38.86	32.07	47.33	33.57
2014	21.03	38.82	37.66	43.76	35.29

Source Same as Fig. 4

quality of employment in the manufacturing sector as a whole. In contrast to the trend observed in the manufacturing sector as a whole, the level of contract labour intensity is only 21% in case of export-employment champions.

In case of export champions-employment laggards that account for 50% of the total exports the contract labour intensity, similar to other two categories, is above the manufacturing sector as a whole. Incidentally, it is interesting to note that the share of contract labour intensity is found to be the highest in export and employment laggards. The contract labour intensity in such industries increased from 9% in 1992–93 to 19% in 2000–01 and their share increased significantly to 44% by 2014–15, indicating that regardless of whether the industry is export oriented or domestic market oriented, making use of contract labour, presumably with a view save on labour cost, appears to have emerged as a major competence building strategy. Saha et al. (2013) also reported similar findings wherein it is shown that import-competing industries hire more contract workers. To the extent that wage, while being a cost for the producers, is income for workers and hence a source of demand for the industry, implications of such immersing competence building strategy prevalent in all the categories, except the export-employment champions calls for further scrutiny. Perhaps, it is high time to reflect on the relevance of sustainable competitiveness for which there is hardly and shortcut other than being innovative.

3.2.7 Female Labour Intensity

The second indicator of employment quality that we have considered is the female employment intensity. Table 4 indicates that for the manufacturing sector as a whole, there is no marked increase in female labour intensity, instead, the share of females in

Table 4 Female labour intensity in different categories of industry and the manufacturing sector

Year	Export-employment champions	Employment laggards and export champions	Employment champions and export laggards	Laggards in employment export	Total industry
1995	10.88	9.54	12.73	5.27	9.97
1998	17.09	13.40	22.86	9.94	17.41
2001	19.25	16.44	16.36	8.32	14.89
2004	19.86	5.89	15.48	1.91	15.04
2007	28.46	6.41	12.93	3.59	13.78
2010	30.94	5.67	11.03	4.67	12.61
2013	23.31	8.24	14.63	3.74	14.80
2014	26.95	09.16	11.48	3.29	13.34

Source Same as Fig. 4

total workers declined from 17% in 1998 to 13% at present. It appears that industries choose between contract workers and female labour since we find that industries with low contract intensity are found to have higher female employment intensity. However, we find significant inter-group variations with respect to female labour intensity. In 2014–15, the female employment intensity is found to be the highest in export-employment champions with females accounting for 27% of the workforce as compared to only 13% for the manufacturing sector as a whole. When it comes to the 'employment champions-export laggards' and the export champions-employment laggards, the female labour intensity (11 and 9%) is found to be only marginally lower than the manufacturing sector as a whole (13%). But the female labour intensity is found to be the lowest with a declining trend over time, in case of the export-employment laggards.

3.2.8 Skilled Labour Intensity

Table 5 presents data on skilled labour intensity measured in terms of the share of supervisory and management staff in total employment. An increase in the share of skilled labour may be taken as an indicator of skill-biased technological change on the one hand declining employment for the workers on the other. Data presented in the table, however, tends to suggest that, for the manufacturing sector as a whole there has not been any major shift towards skill-biased employment because the share of skilled manpower remained at 22–23% during the period under consideration. However, when it comes to export-employment laggards, the skilled labour intensity is higher than that industry average. But it is also evident that there has been a marked decline in the share of the skilled labour force over time (from 29% in 1990–91 to 23% in 2014–15) indicating an increase the share of workers, which as we have already noted coincided with increased intensity of contract workers. From Table 5, it is also

Table 5 Skilled labour intensity in different categories of industry and the manufacturing sector

Year	Export-employment champions	Employment laggards and export champions	Employment champions and export laggards	Laggards in employment export	Total industry
1990	22.71	27.43	19.14	29.39	22.89
1993	20.71	26.43	20.55	30.56	23.95
1996	17.09	24.42	22.03	29.42	23.33
1999	17.06	26.47	22.27	28.59	23.16
2002	17.10	22.94	21.17	29.26	22.28
2005	17.69	25.70	20.36	27.55	21.48
2008	18.38	25.58	22.01	25.85	22.24
2011	18.22	26.07	21.54	25.22	21.89
2014	19.71	25.16	22.07	23.02	22.00

Source Same as Fig. 4

evident that in case of export champions-employment laggards, the skilled labour intensity is the highest with only a marginal decline (from 27.5 to 25%) during the period under consideration indicating that their export competitiveness is driven, at least to some extent, by skill and technology. With the share of skilled labour intensity remaining more or less unchanged in the other two categories (export-employment champions and employment champion-export laggards) that accounts for nearly 8% of the manufacturing employment trends to suggest that low labour cost continue to be the major driver of competence building in India's manufacturing sector.

The analysis of the three aspects of quality of employment generation in India's manufacturing sector using the four categories of export and employment generation revealed several interesting patterns. First, export-employment champions provides higher jobs to unskilled workers as compared to skilled workers, employs a higher proportion of female labour and lower number of contract workers. This clearly indicates that export-driven employment industries not only create more employment but also the high quality of employment. Second, export champions-employment laggards industries also seem to be providing a better quality of employment as is evident from their skill intensity, contract intensity and female employment intensity as compared to their capital-intensive counterparts. Hence, promotion of export orientation in these employment-generating industries would further increase both quantity and quality of employment.

3.2.9 Implications on Equity

Our central concern in analysing export–employment relationship in the manufacturing sector is to explore the employment generation through exports towards addressing the observed deficits in inclusive development. To address this issue further we have examined distribution aspects of the different categories of industries that we have identified. Here, our focus is on the share of wages and profit in value added. Before taking up this issue of distribution, in the light of our finding in section one that the depth of manufacturing and that the share of value added has been declining over time, we shall begin with the share of value added in the output in four categories that we have identified.

The observed trend in value added across our industrial categories shows a certain encouraging trend in the sense that the export-employment champions showed a relatively higher value-added share as compared to the manufacturing sector (Table 6). The observed share is found to be the highest in export-employment champions followed by employment champions-export laggards (21.07%). Especially, notable is that these two groups of industries managed to maintain their share at 21% over time. When it comes to export champions-employment laggards, though their value-added intensity is lower than the manufacturing average at present, they have been able to record a marginal increase. Finally, we observe a drastic decline in case of export-employment laggards wherein the share of value added in output declined from about 22% during 1990s to 16%, thereafter and 13% at present (Table 6). On the whole, we are inclined to infer that though there has been a decline in value added and depth of manufacturing, inter-alia, on account of increasing integration, globalization and global production network, we could identify a few group of industries, which managed to generate more value addition in the domestic economy.

With respect to the distribution of value added in terms of profit and wages which is often being construed as indicators of equity, we find that the profit share has been showing a steady increase over the years to reach the highest level of 54% in 2007 and declined thereafter to reach the level of 40% in the terminal year. Correspondingly, the share of wages declined over the years to reach the lowest level of 19% in 2007 and increased thereafter to reach 27% in the terminal year (Table 7).

The recent increase in the share of wage bill, however, does not imply that the workers are better off. As is evident from Table 8, the share of workers in the wage bill has shown a steady decline not only for the manufacturing sector as a whole but also for the four categories we identified. Hence, the observed increase in the share of the wage bill in value added has to be attributed to an increase in the share of professional and managerial staff in the wage bill. To the extent that there has not been any increase in the share of professional/managerial staff in the workforce, the observed increase in their share in wage bill needs to be seen in the context of higher rate of increase in their salaries (Table 8). On the whole, the emerging trend appears to be one wherein the professionals (high skilled) and capitalists gained and the workers appears to have lost. The above discouraging trend notwithstanding, the distribution of profit and wage bill across the four categories that we have identified has certain encouraging highlights. To begin with, with respect to employment and export champions, the wage share is significantly higher than the other categories. Moreover, the share of wage almost doubled as move from the initial year to the terminal year (Table 7). Correspondingly, the profit share is the lowest, notwithstanding the recent upward trend therein. The next category with more favourable equity outcomes is the export

Table 6 Value-added share in different categories of industry and the manufacturing sector

Year	Export-employment champions	Employment laggards-export champions	Employment champions-export laggards	Laggards in employment export	Total industry
1990	22.32	8.91	23.49	20.99	21.37
1991	22.10	6.98	26.25	19.86	20.96
1992	22.03	8.59	21.63	22.37	21.34
1993	25.40	13.24	23.48	22.97	22.75
1994	23.99	11.24	25.67	22.85	23.05
1995	18.76	9.16	25.15	24.32	22.81
1996	22.31	10.11	26.00	24.23	23.22
1997	20.65	9.11	20.97	22.19	21.09
1998	21.33	9.69	24.71	24.44	22.44
1999	20.28	12.79	25.40	21.14	21.48
2000	19.87	7.29	22.04	18.84	19.55
2001	19.24	11.89	24.55	17.70	19.17
2002	19.79	18.94	21.32	17.87	19.09
2003	19.17	11.54	22.27	17.73	19.44
2004	19.17	15.39	21.30	17.37	18.66
2005	20.09	15.16	21.26	18.81	19.34
2006	20.34	15.63	22.46	19.46	19.40
2007	20.69	17.11	22.32	19.87	20.08
2008	21.09	15.96	22.64	15.87	18.77
2009	25.68	13.21	21.18	17.36	18.54
2010	21.40	14.03	22.37	13.74	17.65
2011	20.20	9.32	21.85	12.60	15.74
2012	24.95	11.53	20.87	13.32	16.67
2013	24.29	10.96	19.65	14.28	16.17
2014	21.84	13.52	21.07	13.07	16.87

Source Same as Fig. 4

laggards and employment champions, wherein wage share increased in the recent past presumably at the cost of profits. What is striking is the distribution of profit and wages in export champions and employment laggards, wherein the profit share is significantly higher than the industry average; the wage is not even 50% of the industry average (Table 7). What is more important is the share of wages in this category has shown a steady decline over the years. The observed trends in the share of wages cannot be delinked from the trends in employment and its quality that we have already discussed. The categories of industries that generate more jobs along

Table 7 Share of profits and wages in the value-added in different categories of industry and the manufacturing sector

Year	Export-employment champions		Employment laggards and export champions		Employment champions and export laggards		Laggards in employment export		Total industry	
	Profits	Wages	Profits	Wages	Profits	Wages	Profits	Wages	Profits	Wages
1993	49.31	22.22	51.65	16.43	18.93	35.02	31.64	21.96	28.63	28.71
1994	28.13	29.16	47.13	17.92	25.07	31.39	38.13	20.77	33.43	27.07
1995	11.58	37.17	34.05	18.08	25.39	36.56	37.71	20.66	30.55	27.12
1996	12.35	31.29	32.77	17.64	22.53	33.43	35.07	19.28	28.26	27.16
1997	7.19	35.19	37.05	18.27	13.34	37.54	32.06	19.47	23.70	27.89
1998	8.09	32.41	42.20	18.98	17.15	30.42	35.67	17.32	27.09	25.72
1999	−0.33	33.78	45.37	19.45	20.90	28.23	32.13	19.11	24.99	25.28
2000	9.90	33.99	28.99	19.67	20.18	30.03	23.61	22.07	20.08	28.47
2001	1.45	37.18	34.95	22.50	20.30	28.20	21.77	23.04	19.03	28.03
2002	10.95	35.56	41.30	21.50	22.37	30.34	36.79	18.51	29.02	25.84
2003	12.51	35.11	37.46	32.18	33.74	25.75	48.28	15.61	37.54	23.69
2004	25.74	33.18	45.71	14.37	39.33	24.04	63.61	11.27	46.99	20.89
2005	33.24	34.32	48.32	15.45	40.65	24.57	63.38	12.96	50.88	20.33
2006	31.52	32.30	67.69	8.58	44.09	22.53	56.87	16.84	52.40	19.30
2007	30.67	35.19	71.84	7.88	44.00	22.60	58.27	16.35	53.75	19.24
2008	26.97	34.81	67.71	9.81	44.05	21.62	45.66	21.75	48.35	21.38
2009	45.99	25.95	62.90	10.15	39.08	22.25	49.84	21.00	47.73	21.59
2010	26.62	37.71	63.14	10.80	44.61	22.29	40.81	24.68	46.18	22.83
2011	20.56	38.49	56.56	12.90	41.93	23.05	35.49	25.05	40.73	24.66
2012	46.84	27.55	66.93	9.78	37.47	25.81	32.38	26.51	44.22	24.20
2013	44.71	29.54	62.30	12.53	30.84	28.89	36.63	26.77	41.61	26.28
2014	24.80	43.22	65.00	11.48	33.92	30.68	29.60	24.43	40.08	26.95

Source Same as Fig. 4

with better quality of employment tends to have better distributional outcomes as compared to others.

This argument could be further substantiated with the analysis of profit share in gross value added. The analysis reveals that profit share is relatively low in export-driven employment industries and employment industries with export potential as compared to others. This reinforces our argument that export-driven industries create equitable growth as compared to export-oriented capital-intensive industries and domestic-oriented capital-intensive industries. Viewed from employment generation perspective and equity point of view, it is important to promote industries with export generation potential.

Table 8 Workers wage share in total wages in different categories of industry and the manufacturing sector

Year	Export-employment champions	Employment laggards and export champions	Employment champions and export laggards	Laggards in employment export	Total industry
1992	69.20	69.06	71.51	59.90	65.84
1993	66.72	62.51	68.05	57.79	63.33
1994	75.39	64.14	63.93	58.57	63.61
1995	74.48	58.85	63.25	57.29	62.95
1996	72.74	63.30	62.14	56.32	61.68
1997	70.64	59.61	62.64	56.01	61.48
1998	70.06	65.90	60.14	52.90	59.38
1999	70.09	55.89	58.23	53.63	58.48
2000	67.65	58.25	57.06	52.44	57.69
2001	68.06	53.78	58.15	50.91	56.71
2002	67.52	63.08	57.03	50.50	56.71
2003	66.37	64.46	51.86	51.97	55.04
2004	59.97	48.32	53.11	54.48	55.11
2005	60.77	50.91	54.87	49.58	53.73
2006	59.51	53.58	52.80	48.69	52.78
2007	57.58	54.05	51.86	46.03	51.21
2008	55.93	48.17	49.93	44.41	48.99
2009	47.57	48.53	54.65	45.35	49.81
2010	55.32	47.77	50.29	45.10	49.19
2011	56.04	46.08	48.68	47.49	49.07
2012	46.23	46.44	51.18	48.18	48.97
2013	45.98	47.61	51.38	46.95	48.73
2014	51.49	46.05	46.37	49.76	47.73

Source Same as Fig. 4

3.2.10 Analysis at the Disaggregate Level

From the perspective of a strategic approach towards locating industries for export and employment promotion, the analysis at the aggregate level is not adequately helpful. It is especially because, in each of the group identified, there is bound to be differences across industries therein. Therefore, in the present section, our focus shall be to locate specific industries in each group. Such identification is important for devising export-oriented employment promotion policies. In order to identify industries over the years and their movement from one category to another, we select three time points and compare the industries that remained in the same category over

Table 9 Distribution of industries

	Employment champions	Employment laggards
1990		
Export Champions	172, 173, 181, 191, 192, 223, 289, 319, 321, 332, 342, 343, 351, 369	151, 314
Export laggards	153, 154, 155, 160, 171, 201, 202, 221, 222, 261, 269, 273, 281, 292, 293, 315, 322, 331, 352, 361	152, 182, 210, 231, 232, 233, 242, 243, 251, 252, 271, 272, 291, 311, 312, 323, 341, 353, 359
2001		
Export champions	171, 172, 173, 181, 191, 192, 221, 289, 319, 332, 353	151, 331, 369, 370
Export laggards	154, 155, 160, 182, 201, 202, 210, 222, 223, 251, 252, 261, 269, 273, 281, 292, 293, 315, 321, 342, 343, 352, 361	152, 153, 231, 232, 233, 242, 243, 271, 272, 291, 311, 312, 314, 322, 323, 341, 351, 359
2014		
Export champions	172, 173, 181, 191, 192, 221, 289, 292, 319, 331, 351, 353	151, 232, 233, 243, 272, 293, 322, 332, 369
Export laggards	154, 155, 160, 171, 182, 201, 202, 210, 222, 223, 242, 251, 252, 261, 269, 273, 281, 291, 311, 315, 321, 342, 343, 352, 361	152, 153, 231, 271, 312, 314, 323, 341, 359

Note Due to space constraint, we report only NIC codes. The details of industry names corresponding to NIC is provided in the appendix to chapter

the years and industries that changed from one category to another. Identifying industries that changed from one category to another is also important as far as policy is concerned. Table 9 presents the mapping of industries based on their employment and export intensity. For our analysis, we shall begin with the first column that represents export and employment champions and employment champions and export laggards. The first category included industries known for India's comparative advantage like textiles products (171, 172, 173) and leather, fabricated metal products, electric and electronic components.

The export-employment champions industries are: Other textiles (172), Knitted and crocheted fabrics (173), Wearing apparel, except fur apparel (181), Tanning and dressing of leather (191), Footwear (192), Other fabricated metals (289), Special purpose machinery (292), Other electrical equipment (319), Medical appliances and instruments (331), Building and repair of ships and boats (351), Aircraft and spacecraft (353). Similarly, employment champions and export laggards are; other food products (154), Beverages (155), Tobacco (160), Spinning weaving textiles (171), Dressing and dying of fur (182), Sawmilling and planning (201), Wood products (202), Paper products (210), Printing (222), Recorded media, (223), Other chemicals (242), Rubber products (251), Plastic products (252), Glass products (261), Non-metallic products (269), Casting of metal (273), Structural metal products (281),

Electronic capital goods (291), Electric motors (311), Electric lamps (315), Electronic valves and components (321), Bodies for motor vehicles (342), Parts and accessories of motor vehicles (343), Railway locomotives (352) and Furniture (361). In what follows, we present the distribution of industries under each category and their corresponding trends in quality of employment generation, and their equity implications by looking at profit share, wage share and value addition.

3.3 Export-Employment Champions

We have presented the relative export and employment share of each industry in the category as well as total manufacturing industries (see Table 10). Though at the aggregate level, these industries indicate higher export and employment intensity than the total manufacturing sector, all the industries under each category may not contribute uniformly to employment and export generation. Given this plausible inter-industry variation, we identify champion industries based on their relative contribution to the category and presents the trends in quality of employment and other indicators, which assume importance from the perspective of distribution. For our analysis, champion industries considered are those with a contribution in either employment or export exceeding 10%. Given their higher performance within the group, their contribution towards overall manufacturing is also expected to be significant (Table 10). Using this approach, we identified six champion industries such as other textiles (172), Knitted and crocheted fabrics (173), Wearing apparel, except fur apparel (181), Other fabricated metals (289), Special purpose machinery (292), Aircraft and spacecraft (353), which contribute significantly in terms of exports and employment generation. All the above industries except the last three are considered as low-technology industries as per OECD classification. Hence, it could be inferred that for most of these industries in this group, export and employment is based on their static comparative advantage. Among the industries in this category, wearing apparel industry contributes to 24.41% of exports and 28.11% of employment. The trends in quality of employment of wearing apparel indicate that skilled worker intensity (15%) is lower than the group average (20%), indicating its ability to absorb a large amount of unskilled labour force. Similarly, the contract labour intensity is lower than the group average, which further indicates its potential to create quality jobs as opposed to many other industries where employment generation is primarily taking place through hiring contract workers. It is interesting to note that nearly 50% of the workers in wearing apparel industry are females (49%) which is double that of the group average. When it comes to distributional aspects of this industry, we find that its value addition and the share of wages in value addition is higher than the group average and the share of profits is much lower than the group average. Similar trends in quality of employment generation and distributional aspects could be found in manufacture of fabrics (173) and footwear (191) where we find the lowest contract intensity among all the industries in the category and female employment intensity is much higher than the group average. Not only the quality of employment is better, but its performance in terms of value addition and the share of wages in value addition and the share of profits in value addition is also better as compared to other champion industries in this category.

The other industries that tend to generate employment with export are fabricated metals (289), special purpose machinery (292), aircraft, and spacecraft (353). These industries, according to OECD classification, are considered as high-tech or medium-tech industries on account of their higher R&D intensity, the potential for knowledge generation and innovation. Thus viewed, they have the potential to get benefited from the dynamic comparative advantage. However, their performance with respect to quality of employment and equity aspect is found to be not highly desirable. At the same time, it is pertinent to note that in case of industries like aircraft and spacecraft with high-skilled labour intensity, the contract labour intensity is relatively low and the share of value added is higher. More or less similar is the case with special purpose machinery. However, their performance with respect to share of wages in value added and female labour intensity is much to be desired.

3.4 Export Champions-Employment Laggards

This category, as discussed in the previous section, represents industries with low employment generation capacity as well as poor quality of employment. We have identified five out of 9 industries having either employment or export share more than 10% (Table 11). However, these industries together account for over 50% of India's manufacturing exports. The unique characteristics of industries in this group are that they belong to either medium or high-tech industries as per the OECD classification, the only exception being food processing industry which is a low-tech industry. While being technology intensive, we could identify five out of nine industries as having either employment or export share more than 10%. This points towards the potential of these industries to reap the dynamic comparative advantage. However, we find that three out of these five industries show lower skilled labour intensity and only one out of these five industries show contract intensity lower than the group average as well as the total manufacturing average. Petroleum products industry which contributes to 41 of exports in the group and 20% of total manufacturing exports employs 64% of contract workers, which is nearly double that of manufacturing average. Correspondingly, female participation in this industry is almost negligible. Among all other industries, petroleum industry accounts for highest proportion of profit (84.56%), which gets reflected in their lowest wage share (1.84%). On the contrary, the contract labour intensity in other manufacturing industry (369), which accounts for 25% of relative exports and 22% of relative employment share, is only about 20% which is lower than the group average as well as total manufacturing average. Not only the contract intensity low, but female employment intensity in other manufacturing is higher than the group average and total manufacturing average. Now coming to employment contribution, we have basic chemicals (26%) followed by food processing, basic metals and other manufacturing.

Table 10 Distribution of disaggregate industries employment-export champions in 2014

NIC	Export share	Employment share	Skilled intensity	Contraction	FEI	Share of GVA	Wage share	Share of profits GVA
Group Average	20.1	19.21	19.71	21.03	26.95	21.84	43.22	24.8
Other textiles (172)	12.98 (2.6)	12.03 (2.31)	17.25	21.82	15.83	19.89	21.84	26.16
Knitted and crocheted fabrics (173)	5.71 (1.14)	10.79 (2.07)	12.69	7.84	37.96	19.51	35.84	16.75
Wearing apparel, except fur apparel (181)	24.41 (4.9)	28.11 (5.4)	15.25	11.85	48.83	26.14	32.75	16.66
Tanning and dressing of leather (191)	4.85 (0.97)	3.85 (0.73)	17.56	28.78	18.60	15.09	29.04	−34.28
Footwear (192)	5.04 (1.01)	9.03 (1.73)	13.69	17.84	37.67	19.43	30.21	19.96
Other fabricated metals (289)	11.68 (2.34)	15.79 (3.03)	21.83	34.55	4.54	22.40	17.02	36.90
Special purpose machinery (292)	11.87 (2.38)	12.34 (2.37)	33.90	30.23	2.01	22.60	11.94	35.40
Other electrical equipment (319)	1.89 (0.38)	2.41 (0.46)	27.36	39.31	7.35	18.95	15.79	29.30
Medical appliances and instruments (331)	0.64 (0.12)	4.1 (0.78)	33.70	28.64	16.71	34.17	8.57	44.81
Building and repair of ships and boats (351)	7.68 (1.54)	0.97 (0.18)	20.45	74.50	0.29	7.29	86.29	−681.78
Aircraft and spacecraft (353)	12.7 (2.55)	0.53 (0.1)	34.98	19.87	3.17	40.19	12.15	45.33

Source Same as Fig. 4
Note FEI - Female Employment Intensity

Table 11 Distribution of disaggregate industries employment laggard-export champions in 2014

NIC	Export share	Employment share	Skilled intensity	Contraction	Fei	Share of GVA	Wage share	Share of profits GVA
Group average	50.51	8.22	25.16	38.82	9.16	13.52	11.48	65
Food processing (151)	9.28 (4.68)	23.04 (1.89)	22.48	38.62	17.81	5.81	14.46	32.83
Petroleum products (232)	41.4 (20.91)	8.65 (0.71)	27.22	63.66	1.26	14.51	1.84	84.56
Basic chemicals (233)	11.26 (5.69)	26.16 (2.15)	30.22	46.92	1.76	13.94	9.40	35.00
Man-made fibres (243)	1.16 (0.58)	2.32 (0.19)	21.46	26.83	2.42	19.71	9.55	44.52
Basic metals (272)	6.03 (3.04)	9.92 (0.81)	24.40	42.84	2.06	18.86	5.83	58.79
Domestic appliances (293)	3.41 (1.72)	4.06 (0.33)	24.17	38.75	9.05	20.40	6.96	63.71
Electronic components (322)	0.92 (0.46)	2.81 (0.23)	32.10	52.34	7.37	18.72	10.71	31.80
Optical instruments (332)	1.35 (0.68)	0.3 (0.02)	47.41	12.53	20.44	29.46	10.95	40.51
Other manufacturing (369)	25.15 (12.7)	22.69 (1.86)	21.00	20.38	14.63	8.08	16.56	33.70

Source Same as Fig. 4

However, in all these industries, contract labour intensity is higher than the industry average yet the wage share in value added is higher than the group average. In general, the available evidence tends to suggest while these industries have the potential to be internationally competitive based on their science, technology and innovation potential through intensified product, process and other innovations, their current comparative advantage depends on low labour cost advantage. This strategy need not be sustainable in the long-run and hence, the need for a change in the strategy cannot be overemphasized. At the same time, evidence also suggests that there is the need for appropriate institutional interventions to ensure that the higher value addition arising out of their innovation capability is shared in such a way that labour is not deprived.

3.4.1 Employment Champions-Export Laggards

We find the maximum number of industries under this category indicating a huge employment potential sans export competitiveness. With respect to exports, we observed that there are three industries whose relative export share is more than 10% of group average. These industries include; spinning and weaving of textiles (171), other chemicals (242) and automobile components (343). With respect to employment share, we have other food products (154) and non-metallic products (269). To begin with, we note that there are two industries wherein export share and employment share are higher than 10%. These are spinning, weaving, and other chemicals (242). When it comes to quality of employment and distributional aspects of industries with high export and employment share, we find significant differences. Spinning and weaving with low skilled labour intensity is found having, low contract labour intensity, high female labour intensity, high wage share in value added and low profit share. These characteristics are highly desirable from the perspective of equity. This tends to suggest that spinning and weaving of textiles, while harnessing static comparative advantage is able to ensure higher export performance along with higher quantity and quality of employment. On the contrary, in case of other chemicals, its higher export performance is associated with high-skilled labour intensity along with high contract labour intensity, lower share of wages in value added and higher profits.

It is further evident that this group comprises of high-tech, medium tech and low-tech industries and hence the industries with potential for dynamic and static comparative advantage. Therefore, the strategic approach to this category of industries shall comprise of both export promotion and innovation promotion along with institutional interventions to ensure equitable distribution (Tables 12 and 13).

3.4.2 Employment-Export Laggards

As already discussed in the previous section, employment-export laggards not only create low employment but also generate poor quality of employment. Following

Table 12 Distribution of disaggregate industries employment champion-export laggard in 2014

NIC	Export share	Employment share	Skilled intensity	Contraction	Fei	Share of GVA	Wage share	Share of profits GVA
Group average	18.05	58.81	22.07	37.66	11.48	21.07	30.68	33.92
Other food products (154)	4.73 (0.85)	10.65 (6.26)	20.13	18.11	30.71	14.22	19.14	17.85
Beverages (155)	0.71 (0.12)	2.06 (1.21)	23.26	51.57	6.48	21.75	10.08	43.97
Tobacco (160)	0.5 (0.09)	5.64 (3.31)	4.39	72.83	16.94	38.18	11.37	74.08
Spinning weaving textiles (171)	18.14 (3.27)	15.86 (9.32)	15.25	12.69	17.11	14.70	24.92	1.69
Dressing and dying of fur (182)	0 (0)	0.01 (0)	12.79	44.50	15.93	28.25	36.75	31.84
Saw milling and planning (201)	0.06 (0.01)	0.09 (0.05)	29.69	8.05	10.51	10.98	24.44	32.06
Wood products (202)	0.56 (0.1)	1 (0.59)	23.68	25.60	6.08	18.55	16.16	28.89
Paper products (210)	1.92 (0.34)	3.1 (1.82)	21.83	27.67	8.24	15.95	16.86	15.65
Printing (222)	0.28 (0.05)	2.18 (1.28)	36.54	20.26	7.83	26.68	13.80	26.52
Recorded media (223)	0 (0)	0.02 (0.01)	37.23	29.33	10.12	33.90	17.93	40.14
Other chemicals (242)	36.98 (6.67)	13.04 (7.67)	33.91	42.43	13.03	28.11	7.29	56.03
Rubber products (251)	5.08 (0.91)	2.39 (1.4)	20.61	33.66	4.52	21.81	15.76	46.15

(continued)

Table 12 (continued)

NIC	Export share	Employment share	Skilled intensity	Contraction	Fei	Share of GVA	Wage share	Share of profits GVA
Plastic products (252)	5.08 (0.91)	5.28 (3.11)	23.79	33.09	7.58	17.66	12.22	35.94
Glass products (261)	1.3 (0.23)	0.87 (0.51)	19.05	42.12	2.63	21.49	17.20	−2.12
Non-metallic products (269)	4.79 (0.86)	11.94 (7.02)	17.94	61.68	4.27	25.76	12.82	31.77
Casting of metal (273)	0 (0)	2.94 (1.73)	21.92	44.25	1.24	14.66	20.52	7.07
Structural metal products (281)	2.63 (0.47)	2.88 (1.69)	25.48	49.29	0.78	18.49	19.58	24.27
Electronic capital goods (291)	0.75 (0.13)	5.36 (3.15)	32.16	34.92	1.73	24.70	11.84	34.81
Electric motors (311)	3.77 (0.68)	2.67 (1.57)	29.58	34.09	6.52	20.47	17.87	29.14
Electric lamps (315)	0.48 (0.08)	0.61 (0.36)	20.11	45.44	12.76	17.91	29.43	9.63
Electronic valves and components (321)	1.3 (0.23)	1.02 (0.6)	26.17	30.09	17.27	21.28	19.71	21.36
Bodies for motor vehicles (342)	0.13 (0.02)	0.75 (0.44)	24.64	50.99	0.83	20.04	22.54	0.88
Parts and accessories of motor vehicles (343)	9.14 (1.65)	8.32 (4.89)	20.96	48.54	3.73	19.49	19.32	21.16
Railway locomotives (352)	0.23 (0.04)	0.43 (0.25)	23.39	41.37	0.74	19.18	15.63	35.78
Furniture (361)	1.31 (0.23)	0.73 (0.43)	28.44	26.50	3.92	21.13	15.65	25.77

Source Same as Fig. 4

Table 13 Distribution of disaggregate industries employment-export laggards in 2014

NIC	Export share	Employment share	Skilled intensity	Contraction	Fei	Share of GVA	Wage share	Share of profits GVA
Group average	11.33	13.76	23.02	43.76	3.29	13.07	24.43	29.6
Dairy products (152)	1.22 (0.13)	7.91 (1.08)	25.45	43.93	4.22	7.16	16.54	31.30
Grain mil products (153)	25.43 (2.88)	21.52 (2.96)	26.62	37.99	7.79	7.36	13.00	21.00
Coke even products (231)	0.06 (0)	1.57 (0.21)	21.32	33.62	2.78	14.49	20.15	25.86
Basic iron and steel (271)	34.53 (3.91)	36.71 (5.05)	20.30	47.81	0.75	13.61	13.96	10.94
Electricity and control apparatus (312)	6.86 (0.77)	5.11 (0.7)	21.36	45.91	7.07	11.15	12.59	28.03
Accumulators, primary cells and batteries (314)	0.62 (0.07)	2.82 (0.38)	18.50	40.47	9.92	19.29	11.84	41.11
TV and radio receivers (323)	1.91 (0.21)	1.44 (0.19)	30.05	50.86	6.74	14.15	6.15	30.66
Motor vehicles (341)	22.34 (2.53)	10.3 (1.41)	27.80	34.49	0.80	17.43	7.76	52.49
Transport equipment (359)	6.99 (0.79)	12.57 (1.72)	20.47	48.22	1.64	18.72	11.80	56.10

Source Same as Fig. 4

the similar approach to identify the industries, we have identified four out of nine industries whose relative export and employment share is more than 10%. Among others, basic iron and steel industry accounts for 34.53% of exports and 36.71% of employment under this category. Not only the employment-generating capacity is low but the contract intensity is higher (47.81%) than the group average. Correspondingly, the share of wages in value added in basic iron and steel industry is lower than the group average. Another industry, Grain mill products, accounts for 25.43% of exports and 21.52% of employment shows lower contract intensity and female employment intensity as compared to the group average. However, value addition is one of the lowest in this industry as compared to other industries. The possible exceptions are transport and motor vehicle equipment which are high-tech industries and account for part of the export and employment share while having significant value addition capacity as compared to others in the group. Nonetheless, the quality of employment in this group is generally very low. Hence, there appears to be the need for strategic interventions help building their dynamic comparative advantage along with institutional to ensure fair distribution.

4 Summary and Conclusion

There is a growing consensus that while the strategy of growth under globalization has enabled many of the developing countries to enter the high growth road, the returns to such growth has not been manifested in shared prosperity on account of growing inequalities at different levels. One of the underlying factors, often cited, for this undesirable outcome, which necessitated 'addressing inequality' as one of the core concerns of sustainable development goals, is the observed decline in the share of labour in national income. In a context of trade and investment-driven growth under globalization, international competition makes domestic workers more susceptible and therefore lowers their bargaining power. Given the failure of market-led model (as proposed by Washington consensus) in delivering equitable developmental outcomes, there is a growing concern towards reconfiguring a growth and development strategy, which is, equitable and sustainable. In this context, facilitating inclusive employment opportunities have become a key strategy to increase economic growth that is inclusive and sustainable. Highlighting the relevance of such a strategy, the recent economic survey (2018–19), GoI (2018) called for building a manufacturing growth strategy with a focus on creating inclusive employment opportunities. Given the potential of manufacturing exports in generating employment opportunities, high hopes have been pegged on to exports as a means of generating employment driven inclusive growth. However, notwithstanding the potential of exports for job creation, the issue of much significance in the context of flexible-deregulated labour markets is the quality of employment generation, as it matters in inequality and workers welfare. Hence, it is important to locate sectors/industries that are competitive in the international market and contribute to employment generation in terms of both quality and quality.

As opposed to the existing literature on trade and employment, which focussed mainly on the quantity of employment at the aggregate level, the present study focuses on both the quantity and quality of employment generated. Further, we argue that while the aggregate analysis offers useful insights regarding the causal relationship between trade and employment, from a policy perspective, it fails to locate the specific industries that are crucial for export competitiveness and employment generation. Hence, 'one size fits all' policy based on the aggregate analysis is likely to be incompatible with inclusive employment opportunities and calls for appropriate policies specific to the industry's characteristics. Using industry's employment intensity and export intensity relative to total manufacturing, this study identifies four industrial categories; (1) Export-employment champions, (2) Export champions-employment laggards, (3) Export laggards-employment champions and (4) Export-employment laggards. From the policy point of view, such an identification strategy enables us to locate industries with employment potential with or without export potential, which is crucial for devising appropriate export and employment promotion policies. Having identified four categories, we have analysed the nature and quality of employment generated along with its implications on equity. Constrained by the data availability on various aspects of quality of labour as identified in United Nations Economic Commission for Europe (2015), we have focussed on three aspects: (1) indirect employment (contract labour), and (2) female employment and (3) skilled employment. We have focussed on the share of wages and profits in value added to shed light on equity implications of quality of labour in four identified industrial categories.

The empirical evidence based on our aggregate analysis with respect to four industrial categories reveal that export-employment champions and export laggards-employment champions contribute to more than 60% of total employment generated in the manufacturing sector with an increasing trend over the years. However, their contribution to exports has been declining over the years to reach 38% in the terminal year. When it comes to quality of employment generation, we found considerable variation across four categories of industries. There has been an increasing informalization of work, which is evident through threefold increase in contract labour intensity at the aggregate level as well as in all the four categories. However, the extent of informalization is much lower in export-employment champions as compared to all the other three categories and aggregate manufacturing. Similarly, the share of female employment, though increased until 2004, shows a declining trend in all four categories. The share of female employment is the highest in export-employment champions (where their share is double that of manufacturing average) and export champions-employment laggards as compared to the other two categories. While the share of skilled employment has mostly remained the same during the period under consideration, its share is relatively low in export-employment champions and export champions-employment laggards. From the aggregate analysis, it appears industries with higher female employment has lower contract intensity indicating a trade-off between contract labour and female labour. The analysis of trends and patterns of wage share and profit share in value added to reflect on equity implications indicate an increase in profit share and a decrease in wage share with a mild trend reversal in the recent past. The observed trend reversal, however, has been on account of the increase in the share of professional managerial staff in the wage bill implying that workers are not really the beneficiaries. Among the four categories, while profit share is the highest and wage share is the lowest in export champions-employment laggards, wage is highest in export-employment champions and profit share is lowest in export laggards and employment champions. Overall, our analysis reveals that employment-export champions, export laggards-employment champions create better quality of employment as compared to total manufacturing as well as other two categories. Further, our analysis of wages and profits in value added reinforces the fact that industries, which create a better quality of employment, are the ones with more equitable distribution and highlights the role of quality of employment in equitable distribution of income.

The disaggregate analysis enabled us to locate the specific industries with potential for export and employment both in terms of quantity and quality along with the nature of their comparative advantage. It is observed that bulk of the employment generated by the export-employment champions are accounted by those industries that are conventionally known for static comparative advantages like textiles, garments, footwear and others. We also find other industries like food products, which are known to be highly employment intensive, appear to be in the group employment champion-export laggards. To the extent that these industries also generate high equality employment, any policy intervention to enhance their international competitiveness is likely to contribute towards more inclusive/equitable developmental outcomes.

From a long-term development perspective, a large economy like India has to adopt a strategy of walking on two legs reaping both static and dynamic comparative advantage. It is rather salutary note that industries in the second category, (export champions-employment laggards) which accounted for over 50% of total manufacturing exports in 2014–15, are either medium or high-tech industries. We also find the presence of a few medium and high-tech industries in the other two categories—employment-export champions and employment champions-export laggards. However, the available evidence tends to suggest that most of these industries that are presumably reaping dynamic comparative advantage because of their high technological base are showing poor performance with respect to the quality of employment that they generate. Though these industries have the potential for building dynamic comparative advantage based on their deep science, technology and knowledge base, the current strategy appears to involve building competitiveness based on low labour cost advantage. Hence, we make the case for appropriate policy interventions to help building dynamic comparative advantage based on product, process and other innovations. It also appears that there is the need for appropriate institutional interventions to ensure that innovation induced value addition and depth of manufacturing contributes towards the generation of high-quality employment such that international competitiveness and growth leads to shared prosperity. The industry/firm oriented strategic interventions which we call for could be implemented without the risk of rent-seeking if we effectively harness our capabilities in information and communication technologies.

Appendix

See Table 14.

Table 14 Annual average growth rates of output, employment and trade

	1996–03	2004–14	1996–14
Output growth	8.39	10.05	9.26
NVA growth	5.78	8.99	7.47
Capital stock growth	4.93	11.12	8.19
Export growth	10.60	14.75	12.78
Import growth	10.76	14.04	12.48
Total employment growth	−0.56	5.01	2.37
Unskilled employment growth	−0.19	4.96	2.52
Direct workers	−1.96	3.60	0.97
Contract workers	8.15	8.14	8.14
Male workers	−3.04	3.59	0.45
Female workers	5.22	3.92	4.54

NIC	Description	NIC	Description
151	Production, processing and preservation of meat, fish, fruit vegetables, oils and fats	269	Manufacture of non-metallic mineral products NEC
152	Manufacture of dairy product [production of raw milk is classified in class 0121]	271	Manufacture of basic iron and steel
153	Manufacture of grain mill products, starches and starch products and prepared animal feeds	272	Manufacture of basic precious and non-ferrous metals
154	Manufacture of other food products	273	Casting of metals [this group includes casting finished or semi-finished products producing a variety of goods, all characteristic
155	Manufacture of beverages	281	Manufacture of structural metal products, tanks, reservoirs and steam generators
160	Manufacture of tobacco products [tobacco-related products are also included while preliminary processing of tobacco leaves is class	289	Manufacture of other fabricated metal products; metalworking service activities
171	Spinning, weaving and finishing of textiles	291	00—Manufacture of general purpose machinery + manufacture of office, accounting and computing machinery.
172	Manufacture of other textiles	292	Manufacture of special purpose machinery
173	Manufacture of knitted and crocheted fabrics and articles	293	Manufacture of domestic appliances, NEC
181	Manufacture of wearing apparel, except fur apparel [this class includes manufacture of wearing apparel made of material not made in]	311	Manufacture of electric motors, generators and transformers
182	Dressing and dyeing of fur; manufacture of articles of fur	312	Manufacture of electricity distribution and control apparatus [electrical apparatus for switching or protecting electrical circ]
191	Tanning and dressing of leather, manufacture of luggage handbags, saddlery and harness	314	Manufacture of accumulators, primary cells and primary batteries
192	Manufacture of footwear	315	Manufacture of electric lamps and lighting equipment
201	Sawmilling and planing of wood	319	Manufacture of NEC

(continued)

(continued)

NIC	Description	NIC	Description
202	Manufacture of products of wood, cork, straw and plaiting materials	321	Manufacture of electronic valves and tubes and other electronic components
210	Manufacture of paper and paper product	322	Manufacture of television and radio transmitters and apparatus for line telephony and line telegraphy
221	Publishing [this group includes publishing whether or not connected with printing]. Publishing involves financial, technical, artist	323	Manufacture of television and radio receivers, sound or video recording or reproducing apparatus, and associated goods
222	Printing and service activities related to printing	331	33—Manufacture of medical appliances and instruments and appliances for measuring, checking, testing, navigating and other purposes
223	Reproduction of recorded media [this class includes the reproduction of records, audio, video and computer tapes from master copies, re]	332	Manufacture of optical instruments and photographic equipment
231	Manufacture of coke oven products [this class includes the operation of coke ovens chiefly for the production of coke or semi –coke]	341	Manufacture of motor vehicles
232	Manufacture of refined petroleum products	342	Manufacture of bodies (coachwork) for motor vehicles; manufacture of trailers and semi-trailers
241	33—Manufacture of basic chemicals + processing of nuclear fuel	343	Manufacture of parts and accessories for motor vehicles and their engines [brakes, gearboxes, axles, road wheels, suspension shock]
242	Manufacture of other chemical products	351	Building and repair of ships and boats
243	Manufacture of man-made fibres [this class includes manufacture of artificial or synthetic filament and non-filament fibres].	352	Manufacture of railway and tramway locomotives and rolling stock
251	Manufacture of rubber products	353	Manufacture of aircraft and spacecraft
252	Manufacture of plastic products	359	Manufacture of transport equipment NEC
261	Manufacture of glass and glass products	361	Manufacture of furniture
		369	Manufacturing NEC

References

Ahsan RN, Mitra D (2014) Trade liberalization and labor's slice of the pie: evidence from Indian firms. J Dev Econ 108:1–16

Atkinson AB, Piketty T, Saez E (2011) Top incomes in the long run of history. J Econ Lit 49(1):3–71

Balakrishnan P, Babu MS (2003) Growth and distribution in Indian industry in the nineties. Econ Polit Wkly 38(38):3997–4005

Banerjee P, Veeramani C (2017) Trade liberalisation and women's employment intensity: analysis of India's manufacturing industries. Econ Polit Wkly 52(35):37–47

Banga R (2005) Impact of liberalisation on wages and employment in Indian manufacturing industries. *Indian Council for Research on International Economic Relations*

Banga R, Das A (2010) Role of trade policies in growth of Indian manufacturing sector. MPRA Paper No. 35198, Munich, Germany

Bhalotra SR (1998) The puzzle of jobless growth in Indian manufacturing. Oxford Bull Econ Stat 60(1):5–32

Bhalotra SR (2003) The impact of economic liberalization on employment and wages in India. Paper submitted to the International Policy Group, International Labour Office, Geneva

Brander JA, Spencer BJ (1981) Tariffs and the extraction of foreign monopoly rents under potential entry. Can J Econ: 371–389

Brander JA, Spencer BJ (1985) Export subsidies and international market share rivalry. J Int Econ 18(1–2):83–100

Chandrasekhar CP (1996) Explaining post-reform industrial growth. Econ Polit Wkly 31(35):2537–2545

Chaudhuri S (2002) Economic reforms and industrial structure in India. Econ Polit Wkly 37(2):155–162

Chaudhuri S (2015) Import liberalisation and premature deindustrialisation in India. Econ Polit Wkly 50(43):61

Chaudhuri S, Ravallion M (2006) Partially awakened giants: uneven growth in China and India, vol 4069. World Bank Publications

Deshpande Lalit K, Sharma Alakh N, Karan Anup K & Sarkar Sandip (2004) Liberalisation and labour: labour flexibility in manufacturing, Institute for Human Development, New Delhi

Fallon PR, Lucas RE (1993) Job security regulations and the dynamic demand for industrial labor in India and Zimbabwe. J Dev Econ 40(2):241–275

Francis S (2015) *India's manufacturing sector export performance: a focus on missing domestic inter-sectoral linkages*, vol 182. ISID working paper

Freeman C (2011) Technology, inequality and economic growth. Innovation Dev 1(1):11–24

International Labour Organization (ILO) (2011) World of work report 2011: making markets work for jobs. International Labour Office, Geneva, Switzerland

International Labour Organization (ILO) (2012) World of work report 2012: better Jobs for a Better Economy. International Labour Office, Geneva, Switzerland

Goldar B (2000) Employment growth in organised manufacturing in India. Econ Polit Wkly 35(14):1191–1195

Goldar B (2002) Trade liberalization and manufacturing employment: The case of India. International Labour Office (ILO)

Goldar B (2009) Impact of trade on employment generation in manufacturing in India. Institute of Economic Growth, New Delhi

Goldar B (2011) Growth in organised manufacturing employment in recent years. Econ Polit Wkly 46(7):20–23

Gupta P, Kumar U (2010) Performance of Indian manufacturing in the post reform period. MPRA Paper No. 24898, Munich, Germany

Gupta P, Hasan R, & Kumar U (2008) What constrains Indian manufacturing? ERD working paper series, 119, Asian Development Bank, Manila, Philippines

Gupta P, Hasan R, Kumar U (2008a) Big reforms but small payoffs: explaining the weak record of growth and employment in indian manufacturing, MPRA Paper No. 13496, Munich, Germany

Gupta P, Hasan R, Kumar U (2008b) What constrains Indian manufacturing? ERD Working Paper No. 119, Asian Development Bank, Manilla, Philippines

Hasan R, Mitra D, Ramaswamy KV (2003) Trade reforms, labor regulations and labor-demand elasticities: empirical evidence from India (No. w9879). National Bureau of Economic Research

Kambhampati U, Howell J (1998) Liberalization and labour: the effect on formal sector employment. J Int Dev 10(4):439–452

Kannan KP, Raveendran G (2009) Growth sans employment: a quarter century of jobless growth in India's organised manufacturing. Econ Polit Wkly 44(10):80–91

Karmbhampati U, Krishna P, Mitra D (1997) The effect of trade policy reforms on labour markets: evidence from India. J Int Trade Econ Dev 6(2):287–297

Mani S (1995) Economic liberalisation and the industrial sector. Econ Polit Wkly 30(21):M38–M50

Nagaraj R (2000) Organised manufacturing employment. Econ Polit Wkly 35(38):3445–3448

Nagaraj R (2003) Industrial policy and performance since 1980: which way now? Econ Polit Wkly 38(35):3707–3715

Nagaraj R (2004) Fall in organised manufacturing employment: a brief note. Econ Polit Wkly 39(30):3387–3390

Nagaraj R (2011) Industrial performance, 1991–2008. India Development Report 2011, Oxford University Press, New Delhi, p 69

Nagaraj R (2017) Economic reforms and manufacturing sector growth. Econ Polit Wkly 52(2):61

Nambiar RG, Mungekar BL, Tadas GA (1999) Is import liberalisation hurting domestic industry and employment? Econ Polit Wkly 34(7):417–424

Nayyar D (2014) Why employment matters: reviving growth and reducing inequality. Int Labour Rev 153(3):351–364

Nayyar D (2016) Structural transformation in the world economy: on the significance of developing countries (No. 2016/102). WIDER Working Paper

Neethi P (2008) 'Contract work in the organised manufacturing sector: a disaggregated analysis of trends and their patterns. Indian J Labour Econ 51(4):559–573

Pal P, Ghosh J (2007) Inequality in India: a survey of recent trends. DESA Working Paper No. 45, United Nations Department of Economic and Social Affairs, New York, US

Palma JG (2011) Homogeneous middles vs. heterogeneous tails, and the end of the 'inverted-U': it's all about the share of the rich. Development and Change, 42(1), 87–153

Raj SNR, Sen K (2012) Did international trade destroy or create jobs in indian manufacturing? Eur J Dev Res 24(3):359–381

Raj SNR, Sasidharan S (2015) Impact of Foreign Trade on Employment and Wages in Indian Manufacturing. South Asia Economic Journal, 16(2), 209–232

Ramaswamy KV (1999) The search for flexibility in Indian manufacturing: new evidence on out-sourcing activities. Econ Polit Wkly 34(6):363–368

Rani U, Unni J (2004) Unorganised and organised manufacturing in India: potential for employment generating growth. Econ Polit Wkly 39(41):4568–4580

Rodrik (1997) Has globalization gone too far? Institute for International Economics, Washington, DC

Rodrik D (2016) Premature deindustrialization. J Econ Growth 21(1):1–33

RIS (2006) Towards an employment-oriented exports strategy: some explorations, Report for the Ministry of Commerce and Industries, Government of India

Saha B, Sen K, Maiti D (2013) Trade openness, labour institutions and flexibilisation: theory and evidence from India. Labour Econ 24:180–195

Sarkar S, Mehta BS (2010) Income inequality in India: pre-and post-reform periods. Econ Polit Wkly 45(37):45–55

Sasidharan S (2015) Impact of foreign trade on employment and wages in Indian manufacturing. S Asia Econ J 16(2):209–232

Sen A (1983) Development: which way now? Econ J 93(372):745–762

Sen K (2008) International trade and manufacturing employment outcomes in India: a comparative study (No. 2008.87). Research paper/UNU-WIDER

Sen K (2009) International trade and manufacturing employment: is India following the footsteps of Asia or Africa? Rev Dev Econ 13(4):765–777

Sharma AN (2006) Flexibility, employment and labour market reforms in India. Econ Polit Wkly 41(21):2078–2085

Stiglitz JE (2002) Globalization and its discontents, vol 500, Norton: New York

Stiglitz J (2013) The global crisis, social protection and jobs. Int Labour Rev 152(s1):93–106

Uma S, Joseph KJ, Abraham V (2012) Impact of trade liberalization on employment: the experience of India's manufacturing industries. Indian J Labour Econ (4)

Veeramani C (2012) Anatomy of India's merchandise export growth, 1993–94 to 2010–11. Econ Polit Wkly 47(1):94–104

UNCTAD (2013) The impact of trade on employment and poverty reduction. Accessed from https://doi.org/unctad.org/meetings/en/SessionalDocuments/cid29_en.pdf

Veeramani C (2016) Inter-linkages between exports and employment in India. Occasional Paper (179), EXIM Bank of India

Manufacturing Sector and Job Creation in Pakistan

Sajid Amin Javed and Abid Qaiyum Suleri

1 Background

Along with productivity growth, job creation has always remained a central focus of economic policies the world over. In this regard, industrialization has emerged as a major policy to create employment opportunities and manufacturing sector, as an employer, has earned a greater attention, the world over. Continuous creation of jobs becomes even more crucial for developing countries wherein the population growth continues to add to the army of unemployed and economic recoveries are more often jobless. We argue that manufacturing sector in Pakistan has the potential to serve as the key driver of growth and employment generation. And that these gains are contingent on restoring the external competitiveness of overall tradable sector of the country.

First, the agriculture sector in developing countries has considerable disguised unemployment already. And, youth is not interested to join low productivity jobs in the agriculture sector (IFAD 2014). Second, productivity growth in manufacturing can generate well-paid jobs in a range of skills and professions (ILO 2010). Third, manufacturing sector can create jobs not only through the production of goods but also through the creation of services as many large manufacturing companies are also services companies such as sales and design among others (Lanz and Maurer 2015). Fourth, manufacturing drives services while it is not true in reverse. Fifth, manufacturing drives technological change and it is easy to trade than services.

---

[1] There are four fundamental concept of Kaldor analysis of development including (1) increasing return in manufacturing sector, (2) effective demand-constrained growth, (3) agriculture–industry relationship; and (4) internal–external market relations.

S. A. Javed (✉) · A. Q. Suleri
Sustainable Development Policy Institute (SDPI), Islamabad, Pakistan
e-mail: sajidamin@sdpi.org

© Springer Nature Singapore Pte Ltd. 2019
S. Chaturvedi and S. Saha (eds.), *Manufacturing and Jobs in South Asia*, South Asia Economic and Policy Studies,
https://doi.org/10.1007/978-981-10-8381-5_6

Specifically, the channels through which manufacturing sector stimulates economic growth and employment can be understood through four fundamental concepts of Kaldor (1967).[1] According to the hypothesis, manufacturing has not only the characteristic of increasing return to scale but also dynamic increasing returns (Thirlwall 1983). Dynamic increasing returns is a special characteristic of the manufacturing in which the rate of growth of output in manufacturing causes an increase in growth of manufacturing, as well as an increase in overall productivity of the economy. A productive economy produces more (in excess of own demand). Hence, a productive economy has the capacity to employ more labours in skill-based jobs, which in turn increase their efficiency and further increases output to accommodate more unemployed labour force of the economy. Kaldor hypothesis has been found holding for South Asia (Das 2004).

The evidence suggests that the core driver of growth and employment generation for India is manufacturing sector (Madheswaran et al. 2007; Nagaraj 1994). Same holds true for Pakistan (Khan 2005). The development and growth in other sectors like service sector depends on the growth in demand which is caused by increasing GDP and increasing GDP is caused by higher growth in the manufacturing sector (Zalk 2014). This mechanism does not seem fit in case of Pakistan (Haider 2010).

According to the World Bank and Commission on Growth and Development (2008), unprecedented growth (7% per annual) of some countries[2] for more than a quarter century, since the end of World War II, was due to manufacturing growth. Recent examples include India and Vietnam achieving high economic growth based on fast-growing industrial sectors (Zalk 2014). Evidence suggests that rapid industrialization of these countries emanates from efficient exchange rate and capital allocation policies, infrastructure and skills development along with improved corporate sector, which provided required diversification of manufacturing products (Amsden 2003; Reinert 2008; Studwell 2013).

Recently, South Asian countries have been accumulating capital rapidly which is highly associated with positive growth. The remarkable growth in value addition of south Asian countries which represent the transformation of society in terms of working, living and investing in them become the source of their growth miracle (Nabi et al. 2010). International evidence suggests that manufacturing still play a significant role in the process of economic development (Levinson 2013).

Against this backdrop, and considering the chronic unemployment facing South Asian countries, a framework is required through which growth and employment would accelerate via contributions of the manufacturing sector. In South Asia, the manufacturing sector has contributed to job creation less than what it should have. In this chapter, we argue that manufacturing sector has the potential to serve as the key driver of growth and employment generation in Pakistan.

We then showcase that textile sector is the backbone of the manufacturing sector of Pakistan and needs to be focused specifically. Finally, highlighting the issues, challenges and way forward, we argued that some opportunities are emerging for

---

[2]Brazil, China, Indonesia, Japan, the Republic of Korea, Malaysia, Singapore, Taiwan, China and Thailand.

Pakistan pointing towards a good future of the manufacturing sector. But we conclude that final outcomes, in terms of growth gains from the manufacturing sector and its job creation capacity is contingent on restoring the external competitiveness of tradable sector of the country.

2   The Evolution of Manufacturing Sector in Pakistan

The diverse economy of Pakistan is divided into three major sectors, namely agriculture, industry and services. Further, the industry is divided into mining and quarrying, manufacturing, electricity generation and gas distribution and construction. Within manufacturing, large scale manufacturing comprises of 15 groups[3] of which the most dominant is textile sector.

Based on its forward and backward linkages, the manufacturing sector is a major source of economic growth and job creation in Pakistan. For instance, it contributed 13.5% to GDP and 13.8% to total employed labour force in the fiscal year 2016–17. A look into further classification of manufacturing sector showcases that Large Scale Manufacturing (LSM) contributed 10.7% to GDP, followed by Small Scale Manufacturing (SCM) which contributed 1.8% to GDP. Slaughtering's share in GDP was 0.9% in the financial year 2016–17[4] while Mining and Quarrying contributed 3.1% to GDP.

The industrial growth in Pakistan has been far away from being consistent. The annual expansion of the manufacturing sector during 1950s was about 16%, which slowed down to 7% during 1958s. During the non-plan period (1970–1977) the average expansion in manufacturing output decreased further to only 2.3% a year, which rebounded to 9.9% annual average between 1977 and 1982.

The growth remains a bit lower than the previous regime and stood 7.7% on average during the Sixth five-year plan (1983–88) and dipped down to 5.4% during the period of 1989 and 1992. The share of manufacturing in GDP was recorded as 17.3% during 1993 in which the share of Large-Scale Manufacturing (LSM) was 61% while Small-Scale Manufacturing (SSM) accounted for only 39%. The share of manufactured goods in exports was 64% in which the major share comes from low-technology driven areas of cotton textiles and garments during the same period.

From 1990s to 2016, Pakistan witnessed major changes in the structure of the economy. Noticeably, agriculture's share in GDP declined substantially from 25 to 20% while that of mining and quarrying increases significantly from 0.7 to 2.9%. Manufacturing's share dropped from 17 to 13%. Wholesale and retail trade sector share in GDP increased from 16 to about 19% during the period. Similarly, the

---

[3]Textile, Food, Beverages and Tobacco, Coke and Petroleum Products, Pharmaceuticals, Chemicals, Automobiles, Iron and Steel Products, Fertilizers, Electronics, Leather Products, Paper and Board, Engineering Products, Rubber Products, Non-Metallic Mineral Products and Wood Products.

[4]Ending on June 30 2017.

Table 1 Gross domestic product by sector, selected fiscal years, 1982–2016

(In percentages at current factor cost)

Sector	1982	1987	1992	1993	2016
Agriculture, forestry and fishing	31.6	26.3	25.6	25.0	20.4
Mining and quarrying	0.4	0.7	0.7	0.7	2.9
Manufacturing	15.1	16.7	17.5	17.3	13.5
Utilities	2.2	2.3	3.3	3.7	1.8
Construction	4.5	4.4	4.2	4.2	2.7
Wholesale and retail trade	15.1	15.7	17.0	16.1	18.5
Transportation and communications	9.4	8.7	8.4	10.3	13.3
Banking and insurance	2.5	3.2	3.1	2.9	3.4
Ownership of dwellings	4.5	4.9	4.4	4.4	6.6
Public administration and defence	7.3	9.9	8.4	7.8	7.6
Other services	7.3	7.4	7.5	7.6	10.2
Total[a]	100.0	100.0	100.0	100.0	100

Source Based on information from *Pakistan* economic survey various issues

[a] Brazil, China, Indonesia, Japan, the Republic of Korea, Malaysia, Singapore, Taiwan, China and Thailand

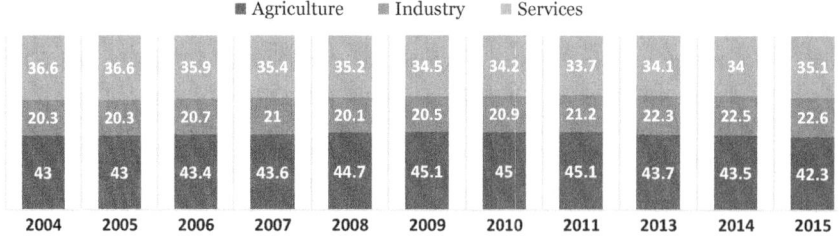

Fig. 1 Distribution of employment by economic sectors

increasing trend is recorded for transportation and communications and finance and insurance sector (Table 1).

Most importantly, however, no major shift has been documented for employment contributions of major sectors of the economy. Figure 1 shows the distribution of employment in different economic sectors comprising agriculture, industry and services. It could be observed that employment share in all the three sectors does not change significantly over the last 10 years and seem stagnant suggesting no structural transformation of the economy from the traditional agriculture sector to modern industry sector, when it comes to job creation.

A look into employment contributions of the sector does not present a pleasant picture. Being the third largest sector of the economy, this sector's contribution to employment was 13% in 2010 while the fixed investment as a share of GDP in this sector has declined sharply over the time (see Table 2). It is clearly evident that when the share of manufacturing to GDP has been growing, its contribution to the

Table 2 Share of manufacturing

Manufacturing % of	2000	2005	2010
GDP	14.7	18.3	18.5
Share in employment	11.5	13.6	13.0
Share fixed investment	23.0	22.0	16.2

Source Federal Bureau of statistics

Table 3 Manufacturing sector in regional countries (% GDP)

Country	1995	2007	2016
Pakistan	16.31	14.03	13.41
Bangladesh	15.29	16.73	17.61
India	17.3	18.3	16.58

Source Economic survey of Pakistan various issues and WDI data

employment of labour force actually declined from 13.6% in 2005 to 13% in 2010. Overall, manufacturing's share in GD grew double than its share in employment over the period 2000–2010. Moreover, Table 2 shows that manufacturing's share in fixed investment substantially declined from 23% in 2000 to 16.2% in 2010. This has implications for job creation and needs a careful examination and the factors responsible for this secular downward trend.

A comparison to Bangladesh and India seems worth looking into. Table 3 shows that in 2016 Pakistan has the lowest share of manufacturing as a percentage of GDP. Most importantly, manufacturing share in GDP in Pakistan witnessed a decline over the time falling from 16% in 1995 to 13% in 2016; Bangladesh documented an increase from 15 to 17.6% during this period. India though witnessed a decline but with much smaller magnitude in comparison to Pakistan.

LSM registered modest growth of 1.71% during the same period. The slight revival (a growth of 3.56%) of the manufacturing sector was recorded in the fiscal year 2011–12. LSM registered a growth of 4.26% in the fiscal year 2012–13 which increased to 4.5% in the fiscal year 2013–14—most probably because of improved energy supply as compared to previous years. Finally, the growth rate decreased to 2.5% in the fiscal year 2014–15, mainly because a reduction in exports of cotton yarn and gas shortage along with other sector-specific factors. Appreciation of Real Effective Exchange Rate of Pakistani Rupee (PKR) added to adversaries of already weak tradable sector through lost international competitiveness.

Despite the major constraint in the growth of the manufacturing sector, i.e. power shortage and the availability of the desired inputs, LSM grew at 5% rate in the fiscal year 2015–16. According to the latest economic survey (2016–17) of Pakistan, the Large-Scale Manufacturing registered an inspiring growth of 5.1%.

However, worrisome is the falling share of manufacturing in providing jobs. Figure 2 exhibits that the agriculture sector continues to absorb the major portion of the total labour force, though the share declined over the time. In contrast, the share of employment in services continuously increases while that of industry shows

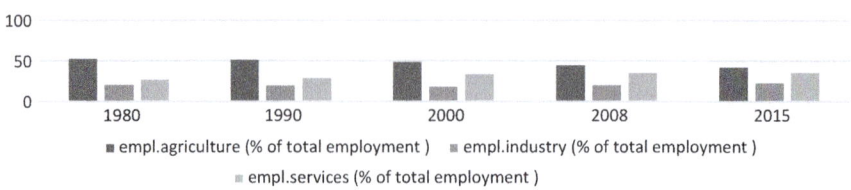

Fig. 2 Employment (% of total employment) by sector in Pakistan. *Source* Economic survey of Pakistan and WDI database

a constant trend. This highlights one of the structural weaknesses of transformation facing Pakistan.

The economy moved from agriculture to services sector without consolidating the industrial sector. This is very important to understand as this is one of the probable reasons behind the massive labour force remaining unemployed. As discussed in the opening section, the manufacturing sector has the capacity to provide jobs for a range of skills and has a larger room to absorb greater numbers as compared to the service sector. This is particularly true for unskilled and semi-skilled jobs. The bypassing of manufacturing left lesser room of job creation at one hand while weakened the growth foundations of the economy.

2.1   Intra Manufacturing Sector Value Additions

Preceding discussions takes us to the question—what is the share of value addition of different subsectors in the overall manufacturing sector? Figure 3 provides the answer. Textile and clothing outperform other sub-sectors in terms of value addition in manufacturing. The share of machinery and transport equipment in value addition of manufacturing remains at the bottom.

As is evident, the textile industry leads the contributions towards overall performance of the manufacturing sector. In this context, improving the performance of the manufacturing sector in Pakistan is heavily contingent on how well the textile

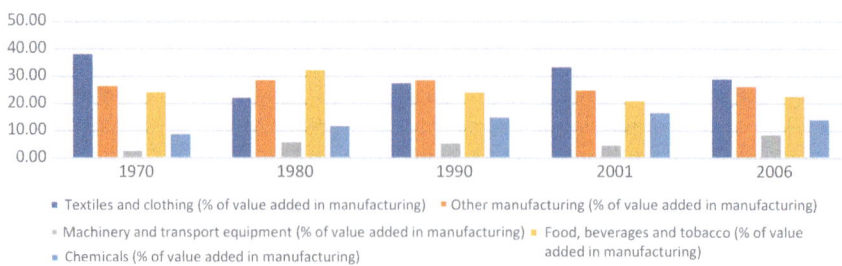

Fig. 3 Percent of value added in manufacturing. *Source* WDI database

sector performs. A recent dip in performance of the manufacturing sector also distills down to poorly performing textile industry. The impact of declining textile exports transforms to overall manufacturing sector in terms of growth rate, value addition and employment creation. Given its crucial role in the economy of Pakistan, the next section provides detail on the textile sector of the country.

3   The Textile Sector

The Textile industry of Pakistan contributes over 60% to total exports and accounts for 46% of the total manufacturing. Most importantly, 38% workers employed in manufacturing are in textile (Economic Survey, 2006–07).[5] In Asia, Pakistan is ranked eighth in the largest exporter of textile products. The contribution of the sector to GDP is 6% on average along with the provision of employment to around 15 million people which is 30% of the total workforce (49 million workforces) of the country.

After India and China, Pakistan is the fourth largest producer of cotton in Asia together with the third largest spinning capacity. The contribution of the spinning capacity to the world is 5%. The significance of this sector to the economy and society as a whole can be assessed by reviewing its contribution to the economy as shown in Fig. 4.s

Pakistan, soon after the independence, attached the highest priority to the development of the manufacturing sector by focusing more on textile and agro-based Industries based on cotton textile-led industrialization strategy. Pakistan also supported the man-made fibre industry through fiscal incentives and protection during 1960s and 1970s.

Due to successful textile-led industrialization strategies, Pakistan was counted as one of the fastest growing economies in the world in 1960s. Textile sector remained the top priority of industrialization strategies in Pakistan till 1990s. Although a short-term break in this textile-led industrialization were observed during 1970s when nationalization strategy was adopted.

The growth of textile industry during last one and a half decades is shown in Fig. 5. It is evident that the industry experienced an impressive growth during middle

Fig. 4 Contribution of the textile industry to the economy. *Source* State Bank of Pakistan, Ministry of Finance and All Pakistan Textile Mills Association

---

[5]It is the latest manufacturing census available.

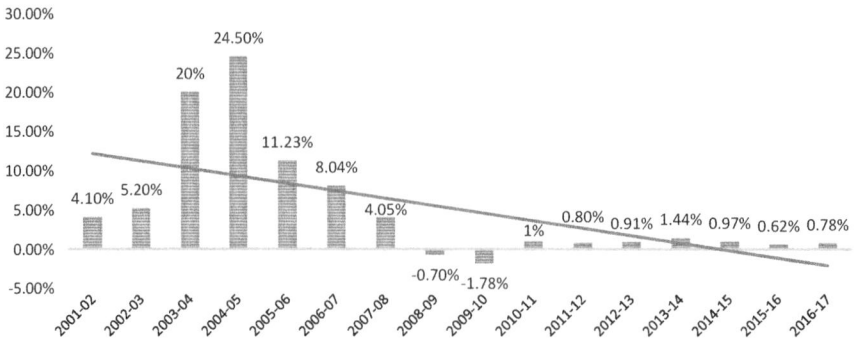

Fig. 5 Growth of textile industry during the last 16 years. *Source* Economic survey of Pakistan various issues

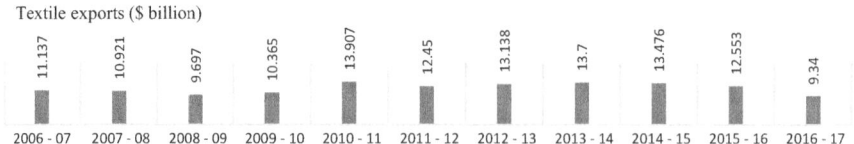

Fig. 6 Textile exports ($billion) (2016–17 value is for July–March). *Source* Economic survey of Pakistan various issues

of 2000s after a down during start of 2000s. The poor performance continued and the sector recorded a negative growth during end of 2000s. Thereafter, the industry registered a modest recovery but the average growth remain under 1% till recent. Overall, there is a sharp decline in industry growth in the period under consideration.

Along with other factors, secular decline in exports of Pakistan has contributed to the underperformance of textile sector. Textile, a major contributor of the tradable sector, has registered a huge decline in exports in recent years. Textile exports in billion dollars are shown in Fig. 6. As is evident, textile exports were recorded low in the fiscal year 2008–09 while record high during the fiscal year 2010–11 under considered period.

Major obstacles facing the textile sector of Pakistan include less than required development in the industry over the time, the high protection given to man-made fibre industry and the dominance of the spinning industry in textile policy making. Bangladesh garments exports were $20 billion in 2011 which were two thirds greater than Pakistan during that period. This impressive increase in Bangladesh garments exports is despite the fact that there were no cotton spinning mills in Bangladesh at the time of separation from Pakistan in 1971.

Textile and garments exports of Pakistan increased from $9.7 billion in 2005 to $11.9 billion in 2012, after the end of textile quota regime. In comparison with world exports of textile and garments, Pakistan share dropped from 2.46% in 2005 to 2.17% in 2012. One of the reasons behind it is that Pakistan did not get benefit from trade opening of textile and garments in 2005 due to unfriendly government

Table 4 Structure of Pakistan and world textile and garments exports

Product	HS code	Share of textile and garments Pakistan's exports (%)		Share of textile and garments world exports (%)	
		2005	2012	2005	2012
Low value-added cotton yarn	5204-07	12.6	18.9	2.4	2.7
Intermediate value-added cotton fabric	5208-12	21.5	21.9	6.8	5.4
MMF yarn and fabric	54	2.5	0.3	9.3	8.3
Knitted fabric	60	0.7	0.3	5.1	5.5
Textile madeups	63	31.8	27.6	8.5	9.9
High value-added knitted apparel	61	17.1	16.8	31.2	36
Woven apparel	62	13.8	14.2	36.7	32.3

Source Hamid et al. (2014)

Table 5 Main markets for Pakistan's textile and garments exports (%)

Product	2005			2012		
	EU	US	China	EU	US	China
Cotton yarn	6.19	9.52	16.77	3.99	1.02	63.75
Cotton fabric	13.16	14.67	2.74	17.72	4.43	12.30
Textile madeups	25.01	48.49	0.04	35.27	40.76	0.70
Knitted apparel	24.56	62.39	0.06	32.78	54.68	0.25
Woven apparel	42.22	39.83	0.02	57.40	28.35	0.40
Total	21.93	36.28	2.75	28.23	25.67	15.03

Source Adapted from Hamid et al. (2014)

policies and the resultant uncompetitive structure of Pakistan's textile and garments sector. It is evident from Table 4 that Pakistan textile and garments exports are low and intermediate value-added products.

Table 5 also shows that at the spinning stage, very little value is added in low and medium-count cotton yarn exports of Pakistan. In contrast, the share of yarn significantly increases between 2005 and 2012 in textile and garments exports. However, this increase was at the cost of intermediate value-added items including textile madeups (fall from 31.8 to 27.6) and man-made fibre (MMF) yarn and fabric (fall significantly from 2.5 to 0.3). A rapid increase in knitted apparel than in woven apparel could be seen for global exports while in Pakistan, the case is reverse where woven apparel exports increases more than an increase in knitted apparel exports.

The major chunk of Pakistan textile and garments goes to European Union (EU) and Unites States (US) market, the share of each in total textile and garments are 22 and 36%, respectively (see Table 5).

The major fall of textile and garments from US between 2005 (end of quota regime) and 2012 from $3.1 billion to $2.1 billion in the respective period were due to security environment in Pakistan. In contrast, during the same period exports to EU increased from $2.1 billion to $3.4 billion, which makes EU as a favourite market for Pakistani textile and garments. The third largest market for Pakistan textile and garments sector is China the share of which increased from 3 to 15% between 2005 and 2012. Interestingly, cotton yarn contributes to these increasing exports of textile and garments about 80% in 2012.

4 Employment in Textile Sector

Employment statistics related to textile sector of Pakistan are scarcely available in Pakistan for multiple reasons. First and foremost, the decline in textile sector capacity over the time, which has badly injured the employment prospects and restricted the entry of the new workforce. Second, no comprehensive surveys were conducted by the provincial government to update the stakeholders regarding current information on production, employment and other critical aspects of textile industry activity. One such study was conducted by Bureau of Statistics, Planning and development department, Government of Punjab in 2014. The data provided in the report is presented in Fig. 7. It reveals that total employment in sector remains also most stagnant over the time.

This can be most probably explained in hours worked on average as firms adjust number of work hours/a day (multiple shifts) to meet production targets rather than employing new labour. Number of hours worked per year per person is highest in India, followed by Pakistan while China has the lowest number (see Fig. 8).

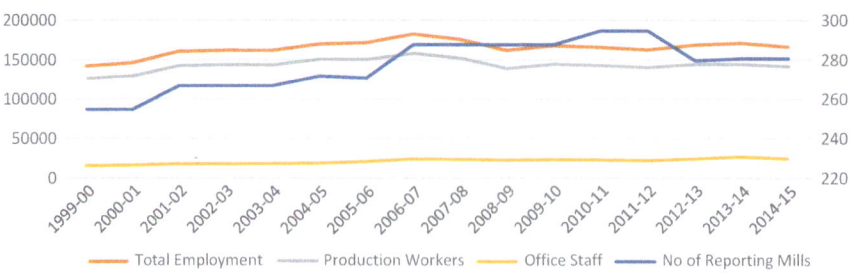

Fig. 7 Employment in textile sector (in numbers), no of reporting mills (right). *Source* Monthly survey of industrial production and employment in Punjab

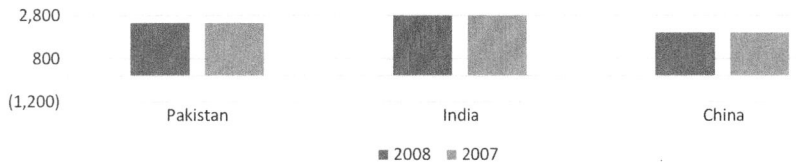

Fig. 8 Number of hours worked per year per person ('i.e. per full-time equivalents'). *Source* Pakistan Textile Statistics by All Pakistan Textile Mills Association (APTMA)

Furthermore, regarding capacity utilization, China and India are using active spindle per year the most while Pakistan using the least (see Fig. 9). It may reflect the underutilization of industrial capacity in textile sector.

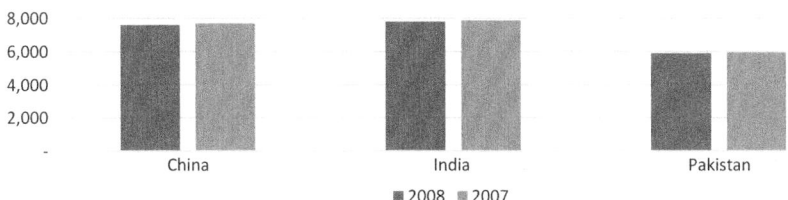

Fig. 9 Hours worked per active spindle/year. *Source* Pakistan Textile Statistics by All Pakistan Textile Mills Association (APTMA)

A similar position can be found in the case of using active looms per year (see Fig. 10).

A case study of textile industry in Sheikhupura, the textile sector hub in countryside of Lahore, however, reports that employers underreport employment to avoid outsourcing loophole, fines and compensation. In this context, manufacturing census which is ongoing can highlight some new trends and numbers.

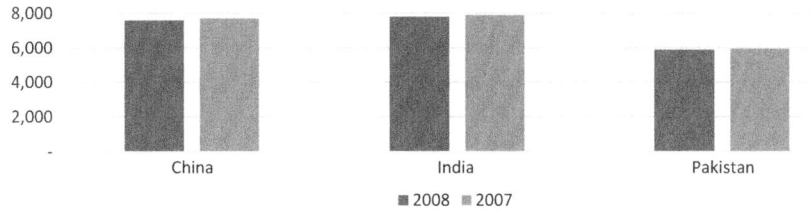

Fig. 10 Hours worked per active looms/year. *Source* Pakistan Textile Statistics by All Pakistan Textile Mills Association (APTMA)

5   Issues and Challenges to the Textile Sector—A Larger Perspective

Falling exports are associated with lower employment opportunities. Lower demand for exports creates excess supply (lower demand) for production; hence less labour is to be employed. Also, we believe that demand limited to indigenous sector has an upper limit and that it is tradable sector which serves as a major driver of investment and job creation. Unfortunate, tradable sector has not been doing well in Pakistan. This has resulted in poor job performance of the manufacturing sector of the country, including textile industry.

The continuous decline in exports sector (total exports fall by 3.06% during July—March 2016–17) and in the succeeding fiscal year of 2017–18 by 1.67% happen despite of several promotional measure announced in the Strategic Trade Policy Framework taken by the incumbent government like the establishment of the Exim Bank, the reduction of markup rate on Exports Refinancing Facility (ERF) from 9% in 2010 to 3% till date, the establishment of service trade development council by the ministry of commerce along with the reduction of Long-Term Financing Facility (LTFF) from 11.4 to 6%. All this shows the failure of the regulatory policies of the government. At the same time, however, one needs to bear in mind the partly overvalued rupee posing the most serious challenge to exports of the country.

Challenges of textiles manufacturing (some of which are common with manufacturing sector in general) include:

- Energy and other resource shortages.
- Integration into global value chains, i.e. climbing the sophistication ladder.
- Lack of product diversification.
- Stagnant growth options due to lack of sophistication.
- Lack of technological enhancement.
- Streamlined taxation system.

The above challenges show a massive problem inherent in this dominant sector—pure lack of competitiveness. The first and foremost issue is the lack of electricity to fulfil production needs. This has been an issue now for decades. However, in the near future, the issue seems to be resolved. The main issue, lower electricity generation in the country, seems to be resolved through intensive investment in the energy sector under China Pakistan Economic Corridor (CPEC). Presently, however, the energy crisis has had a significant negative impact on textiles sector. The lack of electricity has led to significantly lowered production, high wastage and overall stunted development. Energy has also not been distributed equally, leading to even more unequal economic development.

Higher cost of production is yet another issue which has contributed to lower international competitiveness. Constant supply of energy such as gas and electricity at viable prices to industrial unit is inevitable, but in Pakistan the prices is high. Comparing per unit electricity tariff with neighbouring countries (Bangladesh (7.3 US Cents), China (8.5 US Cents), India (US Cents 9), electricity tariffs in Pakistan (US

Cents 14) is the highest along with high gas prices per MMBTU relative to regionally competitive countries (Bangladesh (US $1.90), India (US $4.20), Sri Lanka (US $3.66), Vietnam (US $4.33) and Pakistan US $7.32) (The Nation).[6]

Similarly, the high cost of doing business (the factors being increase in minimum wages, Social Security 7% of wages, EOBI 6% of wages, stamp duty 0.2 on export, import documents, EDS 0.25% on exports, WWF duty on electricity 2%, line losses/Theft Rs 1.5 per unit) in Pakistan is also an obstacle in the way export competitiveness. Regarding freight cost including insurance in wake of war and terror, import and export, hike in Air freight charges due to no discount on freight bills had also added to the export decline in the country.

Riding the sophistication ladder is a steep climb and near impossible in the current climate. The reason for this is related to the lack of diversification and value addition. For decades[7] the product mix of textiles has remained stagnant and in the lower rungs of value added. Additionally, the lack of technological investment and sophistication efforts, either as a result of policy failure or poor implementation, has led to stale product design or barred access from upper tier markets. The sophistication efforts did not happen over time since the industry was not increasing its value-added chain length. As a result, for example, the clothing textiles area has remained and small and focused almost entirely on natural fibres and related materials. The world, however, had moved on to synthetic cloth and clothing, creating a whole higher tier of value.

The growth potential of textiles manufacturing has stagnated significantly for the last decade. To illustrate this, we examine the problem of value addition in the sector. The problem itself may be defined as the lack of breaking into higher tier markets. The GVCs have allowed other countries to increase their overall standards, quality and technological content in overall production. This resulted in an overall increase in the quality and standards of life.

In general, policy implementation has had a rather negative history in Pakistan[8] and therefore the main issue of technological enhancement policy is implementation. The problem can be surmised as follows: the technology frontiers in Pakistan have been more often than not prodded gently or poked, but not tested. This has been due to policy not being able to correctly estimate the requirements, sophistication, spread and type of technology needed to make a difference. Most importantly, initiatives like these lead to patchwork success, which was made even more disheartening by the subsequent issues and reversals. An example of a reversal would be the abuse of a technological subsidy etc.

Financial concerns run rampant in developing countries, and this remains the case in Pakistan. The taxation system is broken at worst, and at best severely ineffiecint. The taxation system exists to extract a portion of the income to be used for government

---

[6]Pakistan exports no more competitive.

[7]Cotton, Rice and Leather counted to almost 72% to total exports of country in first 9 months of 2016–17 showing a poor diversification (Pakistan Economic Survey 2016–17). Similar holds true poor diversification in terms of destinations of exports, wherein 60% of Pakistan's total exports are destined to OECD countries region having sluggish growth shrinking its capacity to import.

[8]ibid.

expenditure. However, the Pakistani taxation system is regressive and often too hard on the small businesses. This reduces the incentives to work and therefore to produce quality products. The taxation system is also complicated, causing problems for all businesses but more so for smaller businesses like SMEs. All in all, taxation system being stunted has an indirect but significant effect on the ease of doing business.

It must be admitted that the textile sector has not been very competitive lately. That needs to be fixed like the issues of labour productivity, poor entrepreneurship, energy crisis, poor innovation, etc. Pakistan made a policy choice by going after import substitution. Temporary setbacks should not make us renounce a good policy, which in the long term should be good for Pakistan. [Central Hypothesis] Surely, we need many more Joint Ventures; improved competitiveness; technology adoption; more market access; diversified investment in manufacturing; improve ease of doing manufacturing business; etc. If we summarize, following issues fall at the core of textiles manufacturing in Pakistan.

– **Lack of exports competitiveness**: textiles feature the bulk of exports, making them extremely important. The lack of competitiveness in exports, as mentioned earlier has led to dire issues of growth and development of the people. The exports competitiveness can only be achieved via sophistication and technological content increase. While machinery for this endeavour is obtainable.
– **Exchange rate overvaluation**: Appreciation in real exchange rates leads to lower price competitiveness as it makes the country's exports expensive for the rest of the world. This has been the case of Pakistan and therefore is a major problem. The problem of low-value exports already exists, but a real appreciation of PKR has damaged the international price competitiveness of Pakistan. Data from SBP show that PKR has appreciated approximately 25% in the last 5–7 years (REER 2010 = 100) in real terms. Historically, Pakistan has maintained PKR overvalued for political gains Javed et al. (2016) without paying any concern to its devastating effects on exports.[9] In addition to political gains, one plausible explanation for this attitude towards exchange rate can be inward-looking growth policy of the country. Now when Pakistan seems to move towards export-led growth, monetary policy needs to be tweaked in favour of exports, rather than be subverted b fiscal concerns. Already facing other forms of incompetitiveness including poor diversification, higher costs of production, lower labour productivity, efficient management of exchange rate becomes very crucial.
– **Skilled labour unavailability and low labour productivity**: one may import the machinery but their use by humans requires a lot of skill. These skill levels in terms of human resource are few and far between. Pakistan lacks the human resource in terms of number, quality and training facilities. Also, skill development in Pakistan, like other South Asian countries, has been focusing on employability rather than productivity. The focus must be shifted towards skill development for innovation. The capacity of vocational training institutions, however, may present a serious challenge.

---

[9]Refer to Javed and Vaqar (2016).

5.1 Way Forward for Generating Jobs in Textile Sector

Job creation in textile sector is dependent on its growth and increasing capacity which in turn depends on access to finance (on easy terms and condition), effective infrastructure network, efficient transport cost and pool of indigenous skills. Furthermore; state capability, commitment of the relevant authorities, availability of modern technology to make value additions possible and make the product competitive in international market would deliver stellar prospects for job creation, while the absence of all these factors would dampen the job opportunities.

Multi-prong comprehensive strategies are inevitable for the quick revival of textile sector which may include upgradation of the existing power looms which will switch the conventional textile to technical textile to increase the prices of the cloth. Moreover, the unorganized weaving sector needs dire attention of the government as this sector has insufficient resources like organized sector. This transition will reduce the cost of doing business and will subsequently increase the production capacity of the unorganized sector. In order to adopt new technologies, textile industries must synergize their efforts with the technical textile centre established in National Textile University Faisalabad.

The government policies that facilitate the textile sector for the possible financing of replacement of this old and obsolete machinery will enable the Small and Medium Enterprise (SME) to enhance the quality of the production along with quantity which will eventually lead to more employment opportunities in SME. The focus should be diverted to export and fashion garments from export of raw cotton yarn along with diversification in cotton chain. A wide range of products can be made possible by mixing polyester with cotton. The government must focus on this sector as it is the source of foreign earnings and provide jobs for the masses.

To increase the capacity of the yarn sector and to be competitive with India and China in the international market, Pakistan needs to overcome its power supply issues as Pakistan is facing the highest energy cost[10] in the region. Most of the textile industrial units are working only with 50% of the installed capacity. For full capacity, the government must ensure uninterrupted power supply to industrial unit working below full capacity. Furthermore, for smooth functioning and increased production of textile industry to generate more employment opportunities, it is high time that the government immediately pay the refund claims of the textile exporters and ensure continuity in their policies.

Pakistan needs to entitle certain percentage of rebate for Pakistani exporter to export their textile product to focus markets. This exercise has been made by the Indian government for their exporter to increase the export of their products to focus markets during GSP plus status granted for Pakistani exporter. The Pakistani markets are flooded by Indian yarn and fabrics because of the incidental inclusion of Pakistan in focus markets.

---

[10]Electricity and RLNG is, respectively, available at Rs. 11/kwh and Rs. 1000 MMBTU for the industry in Pakistan as compared to Rs. 7/kwh and Rs. 400 MMBTU in regional country of Bangladesh.

All ills (including low productivity, low local skills, energy crises, absence of research and development to improve productivity and profitability, uncertain and inconsistent polices, political instability among others) of textile sector are highly associated with state capability, political leadership, institutional reforms and commitment of the incumbent government to serve the interest of the nation. All the developed countries ensure dynamic and innovative institutional reforms to make and enforce laws for the betterment of their masses. However, the institutional structures in Pakistan are plagued by inefficiencies. Administrative and financial units have succumbed to the shambolic state of affairs. Clutches of exploitative elements have robbed the country of its precious gems. An exhaustive overhauling of the existing government apparatus is inevitable to ensure increased productivity and profitability in all sectors of the economy including textile sector.

Besides this; a true, inspirational and pragmatic leadership is need of the hour to devise alternative strategies to remedy ills afflicting all segments of the economy particularly the textile sector. A prudent policy, free of all political interest (depoliticization) can make the textile sector more productive and hence ensure more employment opportunities for the masses.

6 Future of Textile and Manufacturing Sector

A lot needs to be done for securing the future of the textile sector. It is not about uninterrupted energy supply, it is about supply at lower cost also. It is not only about developing the skills; it is about developing the skills for innovation. A comprehensive manufacturing sector policy is needed. Structural problems need to be resolved. If the past is any guide, the task is not easy. But, some indicators of hope are evident. CPEC provides us with one such opportunity. As we have a big comparative advantage in Textiles, we should prioritize Textiles to address the 'structural problems of manufacturing in Textiles' and enhance the CPEC-worthiness of Pakistan's Textiles sector. The supply–demand gap of energy is going to be matched soon which can be a new life for the industrial sector of Pakistan. However, from right now, authorities need to put policies in place to ensure energy supply at lower cost otherwise further increase in cost of production may offset the gains from the improved supply of energy.

Changing labour market, amid some major opportunities emerging from CPEC and Central Asia Regional Economic Corridor (CAREC) can provide opportunities for better human capital development for the industrial sector. This transition is pushing us to look into some questions of fundamental importance including skill gap, skill mismatch and institutional rearrangements. The success in the regard, however, depends on the efficient mapping of the set of skills increasing the productivity of labour and not only employability—as has been practice in past.

Most importantly however, the future of manufacturing (and textile) sector depends how efficiently Pakistan moves towards export promotion led growth and development. Exports potential of textiles must be explored to its best. A well-organized plan for product diversification can contribute substantially to future growth of overall industrial sector of economy. This requires a massive paradigm shift in policy making which include technological enhancement, global value chains and skill and labour productivity increase.

The problem here is that these are all long-term, long-act tools and so short-term answers will look far more attractive. The comparative advantage does exist for textiles, but it is often squandered in terms of lack of energy, low quality of products and lack of price competitiveness. Essentially, growth is linked to exports, which is linked to a revamped policy focused on sophistication and integration into global value chains. Immediately, Pakistan needs to focus on short-run sources of international competitiveness exchange rate management.[11]

Employment statistics related to the textile sector of Pakistan are seldom available in Pakistan mostly because of decline in textile sector capacity over the time which has badly injured the employment prospects and restricted the entry of the new workforce. Non-availability of textile sector employment data is also due to no comprehensive surveys conducted by the provincial government to update the stakeholders regarding current information on production, employment and other critical aspects of textile industry activity. The historical trend of total employment in textile sector shows a downward trend since 2006–07.

China reduced[12] the imports of Pakistani yarn since 2013–14 and therefore Pakistan needs to find new markets for its yarn so that its competitiveness position in international markets remain stable and yarn sector continuously provide employment to the masses. For smooth functioning and increased production of the textile industry to generate more employment opportunities, it is high time that the government immediately pay the refund claims of the textile exporter and ensure continuity in their policies.

Most of the textile industrial units are working only with 50% of the installed capacity. For full capacity, the government must show their commitment to overcome their power issues and provide uninterrupted power supply to the industrial unit working below full capacity. A move to the full capacity of the textile industries will create more employment opportunities. The future role of textiles is that it will continue to take centre stage in the manufacturing sector. The CPEC advent will allow greater diversification and revamp technological and sophistication levels, as well as bring more and high-skill labourers into the sector. This will help, as mentioned earlier, overcome the many traditional problems of the textiles industry. Furthermore, the transformative power of big change at a fast pace is on the horizon, as CPEC will allow investment levels not previously possible.

Technological change is part of the world's economy, and the sooner the policy implements tech-based reforms and incentives, the better the results will be. As discussed, the focus must be on SMEs, as they have the greatest potential for job

---

[11] Refer to Exchange Rate and External Competitiveness: A Case of Pakistan for details. https://sdpi.org/publications/files/ExchangeRateandExternalCompetitiveness.pdf.

[12] According to the most recent figures available, Pakistan has lost 10% percentage point to 18.5% of the market share of Chinese yarn in January 2016 as compared with the data from January 2015.

creation. Three prong policies ensuring price competiveness (competitive exchange rate), lower cost of production (ease of doing business) and improved human capital (skill development) needs to be out in place.

References

Amsden AH (2003) The rise of "the rest": challenges to the west from late-industrializing economies. Oxford University Press

Das DK (2004) The economic dimensions of globalization. Palgrave Macmillan, Houndmills, Hampshire, UK

Haider A (2010) Can sectoral re-allocation explain the jobless growth? Empirical evidence from Pakistan. Pak Dev Rev 49:705–718

International Fund for Agricultural Development (IFAD) (2014) Youth and agriculture: key challenges and concrete solutions

International Labour Organisation (ILO) (2010) A skilled workforce for strong, sustainable and balanced growth: a G20 training strategy

Javed SA, Vaqar A (2016) Political economy of exchange rate misalignment: a synthesis of lessons for Pakistan, monetary policy, brief#55. https://sdpi.org/publications/files/political-economy-of-exchange-rate-misalignment-a-synthesis-of-lessons-for-pakistan-pb-55.pdf

Javed SA, Vaqar A, Ali W (2016) Exchange rate and external competitiveness: a case of Pakistan, monetary policy series. http://sdpi.org/publications/files/exchangerateandexternalcompetitiveness.pdf

Kaldor N (1967) Strategic factors in economic development. New York State School of Industrial and Labor Relations, Cornell University, Ithaca

Khan JI (2005) Intra-model employment elasticities (a case study of Pakistan's small-scale manufacturing sector)

Lanz R, Maurer A (2015) Services and global value chains: some evidence on servicification of manufacturing and services networks. WTO staff working paper no. ERSD-2015-03

Levinson M (2013) Job creation in the manufacturing revival

Madheswaran S, Liao H, Rath BN (2007) Productivity growth of Indian manufacturing sector: panel estimation of stochastic production frontier and technical inefficiency. J Dev Areas 40:35–50

Nabi I, Malik A, Hattari R, Husain T, Shafqat A, Anwaar S, Rashid A (2010) Economic growth and structural change in south Asia: miracle or mirage?

Nagaraj R (1994) Employment and wages in manufacturing industries: trends, hypothesis and evidence. Econ Polit Wkly 29:177–186

Hamid N, Nabi I, Zafar R (2014) The textiles and garments sector: moving up the value chain. Lahore J Econ 283–306

Reinert ES (2008) How rich countries got rich and why poor countries stay poor

Studwell J (2013) How Asia works: success and failure in the world's most dynamic region

Thirlwall AP (1983) A plain man's guide to Kaldor's growth laws. J Post Keynes Econ 5:345–358

World Bank, Commission on Growth and Development (2008) The growth report: strategies for sustained growth and inclusive development

Zalk N (2014) What is the role of manufacturing in boosting economic growth and employment in South Africa? Econ3x3. www.econ3x3.org. Accessed 11 Feb 2014

Export-Oriented Manufacturing: A Viable Engine of Economic Growth and Labor Generation for Sri Lanka

Visvanathan Subramaniam

1   Introduction

A review of Sri Lanka's strategies to deliver substantial and equitable growth paints an arresting picture for those interested in understanding the dynamics of development endeavors in emerging Asia. When examined from a broader perspective, the island nation wields a track record antithetical to South Asia's postcolonial developmental woes. It has experienced marked success in raising human development indicators to a standard comparable with that of advanced nations while utilizing resources in a manner that belies its modest income levels.

However, in recent times, Sri Lanka's development story has been shadowed by sizeable growth magnitudes in the economies of regional partners. For instance, while South Asia is projected to experience a collective GDP growth rate of 6.9 and 7.3% per annum for 2017 and 2018, the Sri Lankan economy is expected to grow at a below average 4.5 and 4.8% per annum during a similar window (IMF 2017a, b). Such lackluster growth magnitudes are particularly worrisome given the current scenario; Sri Lanka has only recently emerged from a disastrous civil war that shackled development prospects.[1] Theoretically, the nation is supposed to be in the midst of a "peace dividend" wherein the economy experiences a sustained growth acceleration, much above the 5% threshold (Fonseka et al. 2012).

Contemporary shifts in the demographic composition of the labor force also place Sri Lanka in an unpropitious footing. Unlike most of its South Asian counterparts,

---

[1] As per a study conducted by Arunatilake et al. (2001), the Economic cost of the Sri Lankan war, as of 2000, was estimated at twice of Sri Lanka's 1996 GDP. This can be equated to roughly around US$26 billion. Given that the hostilities increased over the decade, the cost can only be expected to be much higher.

V. Subramaniam (✉)
Institute of Policy Studies, Colombo, Sri Lanka
e-mail: vishva.subramaniam@outlook.com

© Springer Nature Singapore Pte Ltd. 2019
S. Chaturvedi and S. Saha (eds.), *Manufacturing and Jobs in South Asia*, South Asia Economic and Policy Studies,
https://doi.org/10.1007/978-981-10-8381-5_7

Sri Lanka stands on the adverse end of a demographic dividend. In other words, the nation has already passed its peak inverse dependency ratio and now soon faces the challenge of mitigating the adverse economic effects of an aging population (World Bank 2011). Given this predicament, Sri Lanka cannot continue to compete on labor cost differentials since an aging working population will eventually precipitate a rise in wage rates. Sri Lanka's labor competitiveness can thus only be sustained (if not improved) by an emphasis on strategies that enhance productivity above and beyond any spikes in labor costs.

In such a scenario, it is essential that Sri Lanka implements a policy framework that propels growth while ensuring a sustained labor generation mechanism amenable to an aging, more expensive working population. Sri Lanka's locational advantages can be used as a leverage in this regard. The island's geographic proximity to fast-emerging economies (vis a vis India) and strategic maritime routes linking vital economic corridors makes it an ideal hub for producers wishing to target multiple high-value markets. However, a brief perusal of past history suggests that Sri Lanka has encountered mixed success in implementing liberalization reforms that aid in export orientation. The advancements made in clustered waves of liberalization have been offset by periods of economic uncertainty instigated by nationalist reforms.

This paper argues that it is in Sri Lanka's best interest to gradually and resolutely develop an export-oriented manufacturing sector which maintains an emphasis on inculcating a sophisticated, high-value export portfolio. This will spark a viable growth momentum by expanding export potential and increasing supply capacity. Simultaneously, such a policy will engender a larger shift to capital-intensive production processes that increase labor productivity.

The paper is structured as follows. It first provides an overview of Sri Lanka's experiments with liberalization before providing a review of the nation's manufacturing sector. Thereafter, it analyzes the labor market and provides brief synopses of distortions, especially relating to youth unemployment, skills mismatches, female unemployment, and public sector preferences. It then examines Sri Lanka's interactions with the South Asian region, with an emphasis on utilizing the burgeoning Indian middle class as a viable market for maximizing export potential.

2 Clustered Liberalization Reforms

Sri Lanka's development trajectory over the latter half of the twentieth century was heavily influenced by resolutions enacted by colonial administrators during the Colonial era. Tenets of laissez-faire liberalism were introduced to the island in 1832 through the Colebrooke–Cameroon Commission, which recommended the establishment of an open economy with nominal regulatory reach.[2] Consequently, a great impetus was placed on an export-oriented development strategy whereby—as per the-

---

[2]In "A History of Sri Lanka" (1981), K. M. De Silva argues that the recommendations made by the Colebrooke–Cameroon bear many similarities to Bentinck's reforms in India. However, according

ory—private sector participation and foreign investments fueled economic growth while state apparatuses ensured administration services (Waidyanatha 2001).

During the colonial period, the secondary sector—manufacturing included—was predominantly focused on home industries such as basket weaving, handlooms, and carpentry. The sector received scant attention as private (mostly British) entrepreneurs remained wary of channeling investments away from lucrative plantation crops to native sectors with scant global demand. Therefore, up until independence, Sri Lanka possessed a dual-sector open economy characterized by the coexistence, albeit in isolation, of an export-oriented plantation system controlled by minority interests, with a subsistence agricultural and traditional home industry sector that served much of the indigenous populace (Amjad et al. 2015).

The arrival of Independence in 1948 did not bring immediate respite to such discrepancies in capital and resource allocation. Strong commodity prices in international markets meant that significant revenue inflows shrouded imbalances in the economic structure. Sri Lanka (then Ceylon) posted substantial gains in per capita income and ensuing stability provided grounds for the establishment of well-accepted state welfare initiatives. Sri Lanka outperformed its regional partners during this period and was even dubbed by many as "the best bet in Asia" (Wriggins 1960). However, the island continued to function as an outward-oriented economy wielding a minimally diversified export basket composed of unsophisticated commodity products. Development was thus inexorably linked with the performance of its exported commodities, namely tea and rubber, in hitherto stable international markets.

Therein, the long-drawn decline in essential commodity prices experienced in the early 1960s had severe ramifications on the Sri Lankan economy. Falling export revenue resulted in a contraction of growth prospects and promulgated a balance of payment crisis. In response, the state increased import restrictions to address current account imbalances. As economic woes continued, the state responded by radically intensifying barriers to market entry. Such repeated interventions gradually induced a shift of economic emphasis away from export orientation toward import substitution.

The veer towards import substitution generated emphasis on the underdeveloped manufacturing sector as policy makers strived to stimulate native industries to produce consumer goods demanded by the domestic market.[3] Over a thousand medium- and small-scale industries commenced operations between 1960 and 1963 alone, compared to 500 operations started during the preceding 15 years (Dias 1987). Furthermore, real manufacturing output increased by 9.5% over the latter half of the decade, the highest increase recorded up to that time (Athukorala and Rajapathirana 2000).

Sadly, such gains were not sustained. Sri Lanka's limited resource base, coupled with the issue of slender investment capacity, meant that manufacturing enterprises

---

to De Silva, the former was "more far reaching in impact and more consistent in the application of liberalism."

[3] The manufacturing sector was briefly expanded during the Second World War due to the severance of trade routes by axis forces. However, development was quite miniscule as the initiative was state-driven with minimal private sector involvement.

did not have the financial strength to muster and sustain production processes. In addition, the nation possessed a relatively miniscule domestic market insufficient to sustain a large, capital-intensive production process. Crucially, import substitution mechanisms failed to mitigate Sri Lanka's crippling balance of payment deficit.

A perusal of existent literature suggests that restrictive trade policies were destined for failure as policy makers failed to take the input composition of contemporary and planned manufacturing enterprises into account. Industries producing light consumer goods for the domestic market were heavily dependent on imported raw materials (Athukorala and Rajapathirana 2000). Furthermore, domestic establishments lacked the technical know-how to establish and supply to capital-intensive production processes. Therein, manufacturing firms showed an overwhelming dependency on imported machinery and expertise for production (Dias 1987). Sri Lanka also continued to depend extensively on the three traditional plantation crops for export revenue in international markets. By 1977, nearly two decades into the protectionist era, the manufacturing sector accounted for a mere 15% of aggregate exports (Vidanapathirana 1993).

Concerns pertaining to stagnations in industrial development, retractions in consumption levels, and a persistent dependency on primary sector exports were bought to the forefront during the general elections of 1977. Resolute anti-incumbency brought into power a center-right government set on dismantling restrictions placed on trade policy. Ergo, the state introduced a series of fundamental liberalization policy reforms that marked a decisive break from decades of import substitutionary policies (Yiping et al. 2013).[4] The primary objective of reform initiatives was in achieving export-driven growth driven by a cheap yet skilled workforce and sustained by foreign investments.

Liberalization resulted in a plethora of positive developments. Economic growth surged from an average of 2.9% previously to over 6% during the immediate post-liberalization period (Yiping et al. 2013). The structure of the economy underwent a notable transformation as Sri Lanka gradually swayed from a land-intensive, plantation-dependent export portfolio to a more labor-intensive, manufacturing-oriented basket of goods. Instigated by such reforms, the share of manufacturing in total merchandise trade rose from 5% in the mid-1970s to over 70% by the year 2000 while the contribution of agricultural exports (primarily tea, rubber, and coconut products) recorded a fall from 78.7% in 1975 to 8% by 2016.

A surge of foreign investment into labor-intensive segments provided added impetus to Sri Lankan manufacturing. The textile and apparel sector soon emerged as the most significant manufacturing export, accounting for around 60% of aggregate manufacturing and over 45% of export earnings by 2016. The sector's rapid growth was fueled by the imposition of stringent quotas on apparel exports to developed nations as per the Multifiber Agreement (1977). Sri Lanka proved to be an ideal destination for apparel-led investments following liberalization as it held a comparative advan-

---

[4]Sri Lanka was the pioneer of policy liberalization initiatives in a South Asian context (at least on a postindependence perspective) with reforms implemented "a decade or more ahead of its neighbors" (Yiping et al. 2013)

tage in unskilled and semiskilled labor while possessing a virtually untouched quota pool (Athukorala and Ekanayake 2014).

Unfortunately, the growth surge proved to be ephemeral as the new government failed to sustain the momentum of liberalization. The new regime continued to divert funds for large-scale investment programs while inefficient state-owned enterprises remained in operation. Issues were further exacerbated by the escalation of conflicts between the armed forces and rebels in the North and East of the island.[5] Prevailing policy uncertainties and lingering socioeconomic issues hampered prospects of considerable progress in the manufacturing sector. Capacity utilization of manufacturing, which increased drastically from 60% in 1977 to 70% in 1980, stagnated over the subsequent years (Kelegama, Liberalization and Industrialization: The Sri Lankan Experience of the 1980s, 1992). In addition, lapses in planning and management resulted in the development of structural sector weaknesses. As Kelegama (1992) notes, the country was plagued by frailness exacerbated by an "erratic growth momentum, lop-sided growth and inadequate export orientation."[6]

Subsequently, to reinvigorate the economy, a renewal of liberalization endeavors was commenced in 1989. Often referred to as the "second wave of liberalization," the initiative involved extensive reforms to industrialization and economic policy. Yiping et al. (2013) provide a detailed perspective of such strategies: they state that "the wave of reforms involved ambitious privatization programmes, a drastic simplification of tariff structure, removal of exchange controls on current account transactions and a lax foreign investment regulations to reinvigorate outward orientation." Reforms also focused on implementing a more equitable development model. For instance, the Industrial Promotion Act, which was passed in 1990, focused extensively on promoting industrial diversification and enhancing the geographical spread of manufacturing industries.

Importantly, the second wave of liberalization had a significant impact on perceptions surrounding the impact of outward orientation on socioeconomic development. As Dunham and Kelegama (1997) state, "such reforms established a de facto consensus across the political spectrum that growth was viable on the basis of a pro-market open liberal economic policy regime." Initiatives that were implemented molded Sri Lanka's development trajectory for the next few decades.

Sri Lanka's manufacturing industry underwent further change following the arrival of a pro-nationalist coalition into political leadership in 2004. The new government's primary objective was to bring the curtains downs on the civil war by convincingly defeating armed rebels. A strong military campaign, reinforced by the international assistance, promulgated in a monumental and seemingly lasting victory for the armed forces. Therein, one of Sri Lanka's debilitating impediments to devel-

---

[5]The impact of the Sri Lankan civil war on industrial fortunes cannot be overstated. For a more ornate overview of the economic (and therein manufacturing) costs of conflicts, a perusal of Arunatilake et al. (2001) is encouraged.

[6]A contemporary overview of the manufacturing sector suggests that the noted weaknesses continue to persist. Sri Lanka experiences lopsided industrial growth due to a dependency on textile and garments manufacturing. Export orientation has been persistently inadequate with aggregate export revenue steadily declining over the recent past.

opment was resolved. Socioeconomic uncertainties that inhibited investor confidence (especially into the manufacturing sector) were now mitigated and a significant portion of the island's North and East were now open for development activities to commence.[7] Sri Lanka was expected to embark on an accelerated growth period in the backdrop of political stability.

However, in what appears to be a general trend in Sri Lanka's postindependence history, the enthusiasm pertaining to reform initiatives was not sustained. The cessation of conflicts paved the way for a reemergence of state interventions and import substitution schemes under the guise of populist and nationalist rhetoric. As such, large-scale infrastructural programs were implemented in rural areas and the role of state-owned enterprises (SOE) has shown signs of resurgence. Such organizations continue to be a large drain on state resources and have acted as an inhibitor to private sector development, especially in the manufacturing sector.

Moreover, the series of taxes and levies imposed since 2004 seriously hampered, if not reversed, the momentum of liberalization. An extensive study had been conducted by Pursell and Ahsan (2011) which concludes that Sri Lanka's total protection rate (customs duty + para-tariffs) increased marginally between 2002 and early 2004, but doubled between 2004 and 2009. Furthermore, the average protection rate for agriculture increased from 28.1 to 49.6% while the protection imposed for industrial products increased from 10.7 to 24.1%. In aggregate, import protections were increased from 13.4 to 27.9%. As a consequence of multiple stop-gap session of trade reforms, Sri Lanka's protectionist structure has accumulated intricacy to the extent that the island nation can be categorized as "the world record holder for the complexity of tariff system" (Pursell and Ahsan 2011). The authors attribute the spike to an increased use of para-tariffs by state officials to protect domestic industries while additionally gathering revenue for state coffers through non-direct mechanisms (Pursell and Ahsan 2011).

Thus, there was much expectation that new initiatives undertaken by the current government will place Sri Lanka back on the path of liberalization and assure industrial prowess inculcated through foreign investments. Sadly, clear discrepancies between performance and electoral promises have emerged—notable headway has not been made on many fronts.[8] Sri Lanka's economy remains in a precarious state with state activity (and inactivity)'compounding issues further. External borrowing has mushroomed, the trade deficit has deteriorated, foreign investments have trickled, and inflation threatens to make serious inroads into consumer welfare.

---

[7] Athukorala argues that the civil war was one of the primary reasons for Sri Lanka's virtual absence in Global Value Chains. Integrations into such networks require extensive domestic stability as corporations are wary of issues that disrupt the entire production process.

[8] Many observers consider the composition of the government as one of the primary inhibitors for policy reform. The presiding coalition comprises an uneasy alliance between a center-right party and a center-left party that have traditionally vied for power during much of Sri Lanka's postindependence history. The past two years have been marked by constant intra-governmental tussles and one-upmanships, precipitated by ideological differences.

3 Manufacturing Sector Performance

At the cusp of independence, Sri Lanka possessed an economy superior to that of most Asian states (World Bank 2004). However, seven decades later, the island nation finds itself lurching behind continental partners that now wield considerable economic prowess. Perhaps a primary reason for Sri Lanka's laggard performance is its failure to stimulate ample productivity gains in manufacturing. Staggered liberalization reforms and inconsistent policy advancements, as elucidated in the previous section, have impeded advancements in this sector. This section provides an overview of Sri Lanka's manufacturing sector with an added emphasis on labor generation capacity.

As evinced in Fig. 1, the manufacturing sector has been consistently plagued by instability and has failed to post consistent periods of uninterrupted growth above the national trajectory. Momentum garnered during periods of sustained growth has been counterweighed by bouts of languid performance (Aggregate performance). Since 2004, growth in the manufacturing sector has been eclipsed by economic growth. It was constrained by the civil war that raged until 2009 with cessation of hostilities resulting in a minor albeit staggered surge (1%) in growth over the subsequent period.

Table 1 provides an overview of variations in the sectoral composition of GDP over the past 40 years. As is evident, the share of agriculture in GDP has considerably deteriorated with substantial declines occurring particularly over the last 20 years. Akin to India's experience, Sri Lanka's industrial component—including manufacturing—has effectively leapfrogged as declines in the agricultural sector have been compensated by substantial gains in the service sector. As inferred above, stuttered growth in the manufacturing sector has resulted in minimal gains in GDP composition. Within the given 40-year window, manufacturing sector composition has increased by a mere 2.2%. In comparison, the services sector has expanded by 14.1% within a similar time period.

Fig. 1 Comparison of GDP and manufacturing sector growth rates (1960–2015). *Source* Central Bank of Sri Lanka, Annual Reports, various issues (Athukorala and Rajapathirana 2000)

Table 1 Composition of manufacturing in GDP (%)

Year	1975	1980	1985	1990	1995	2000	2004	2010	2015
Agriculture (%)	30.4	27.6	27.7	26.3	23	19.9	12.7	8	8.2
Industry (%)	26.4	29.6	26.2	26	26.5	27.3	30.2	26.6	27.3
Services (%)	43.2	42.8	46.1	47.7	50.5	52.8	57.3	54.6	57.3
Manufacturing[a] (%)	13.1	18.3	18.2	17.4	20.4	15.8	16.3	17.3	15.4

Source Central Bank, Annual Report, Various Issues
[a]Manufacturing is a component of Industry

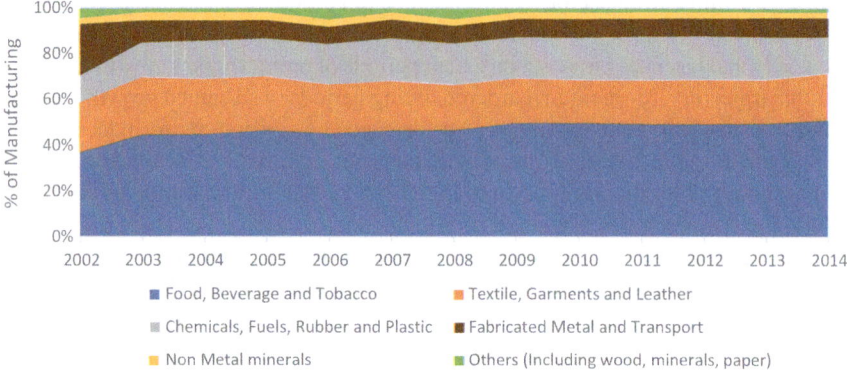

Fig.2 Value added by manufacturing subsectors (2002–2014). *Source* Central Bank of Sri Lanka, Annual Reports

Figure 2 depicts the share of manufacturing subsectors as a percent of aggregate manufacturing output. As is evident, the "Food, Beverages and Tobacco" subsector is the largest contributor to added value in manufacturing over the past decade and half, with the composition in value added increasing steadily from 37% of manufacturing in 2002 to 51% of manufacturing in 2014. Production in this segment is catered towards the domestic market. Meanwhile, export-oriented segments have experienced subdued growth in value addition. For instance, the share in value additions of textile and garments—the largest export-oriented sector—has stagnated between 20 and 25% mark over the last decade.

Table 2 depicts a sectoral breakdown of Sri Lanka's exports for select years over the past two and a half decades. As evinced, total exports have increased by approximately 407% over the given period. However, a closer examination reveals that growth has been staggered; momentum generated during periods of high acceleration has been dampened by durations of stagnation. For instance, aggregate exports doubled between 1991 and 1996 but increased by only 16% over the subsequent 5 year period. Similarly, while exports grew by 53% between 2006 and 2011, the decline in performance over subsequent years resulted in a 2% deterioration in value. Aggregate exports for 2016 stood at US$10.3 billion which, as denoted above, is a decline from previous performance.

Table 2 Sectoral breakdown of merchandise export value and composition for select years

	Export value (US$ Millions)						Composition (%)					
	1991	1996	2001	2006	2011	2016	1991	1996	2001	2006	2011	2016
Agriculture	808	1089	1107	1498	2568	2370	40	27	23	22	24	23
Industry	1226	3006	3710	5383	7991	7940	60	73	77	78	76	77
Total	2034	4095	4817	6881	10559	10310						

Source Central Bank of Sri Lanka, Annual Report, Various Years

Agricultural share of merchandise exports has decreased notably during this period. Declines can be attributed to volatile markets for produce and the gradual movement of capital away from the plantation triumvirate (tea, rubber, and coconut). Moreover, declines can also be ascribed to a step up the value chain. For instance, domestically grown natural rubber has been used to satiate the demands of local manufacturers of rubber products (EDBSL 2012).

Figure 3 illustrates the performance of Sri Lanka's key exports since the turn of the millennium. As evident, the island nation continues to wield a minimally diversified export basket with only two products—both from the apparel sector—wielding export revenue above the US$1 billion thresholds. As of 2016, approximately 59% of Sri Lanka's export revenue was derived from the apparel sector alone. [9] Therein, it can be surmised that heavy reliance on plantation crops has been replaced by a concerning dependence on apparel exports. On the bright side, processed rubber products—pneumatic tires and industrial gloves in particular—witnessed a surge in export revenue in the latter half of the previous decade. Subsequent drops in exports can be explained by steep declines in the price of natural rubber (HS 4001) which resulted in a contraction in the value of agricultural exports.

As evident in Fig. 4, Western regions—namely the United States and the European Union—are the primary markets for produce manufactured in Sri Lanka. This comes as no surprise. Sri Lanka's apparel sector is order-driven and caters to the tastes and preferences of affluent Western economies. Therein, given the sector's dominance in aggregate manufactured exports, export destinations are bound to be skewed towards the Occident. However, it can be inferred that Sri Lanka has increasingly moved toward Asian markets since the turn of the millennium. The principal export to these destinations includes pneumatic tires, electronics, and select articles of apparel.

Sri Lanka's failure to develop a comprehensive export basket can be elucidated when examining Table 3. The table provides a comparison of the aggregate "number of export products" (3 digit SITC) and export diversification as per the "Diversification Index," relative to select competitor states. In this regard, the "Diversification Index" calculates the "absolute deviation of a country's trade structure from contemporary world structure" with a higher index suggesting a greater divergence from

---

[9]This composition statistic denotes a decrease when compared with the export performance in 2001. In that year, apparel's composed approximately 59% of Sri Lanka's export revenue for the year 2016 was generated by the apparel sector alone

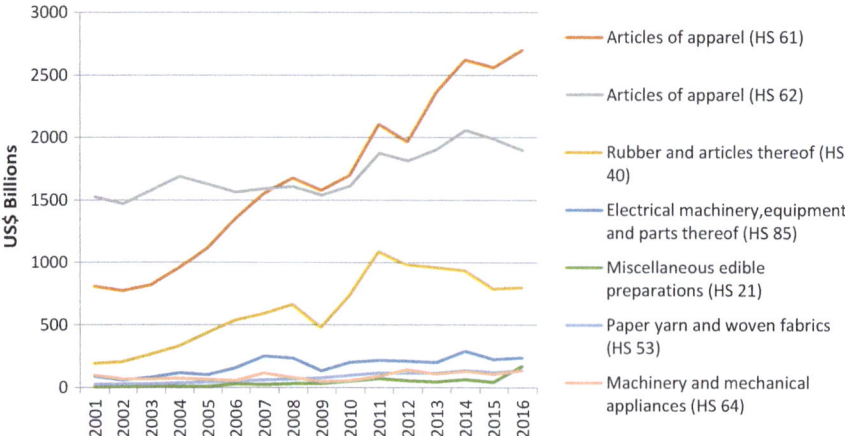

Fig. 3 Primary manufacturing exports as per 2 digit HS code (2001–2015). *Source* UN COM-TRADE statistics. https://comtrade.un.org/data/

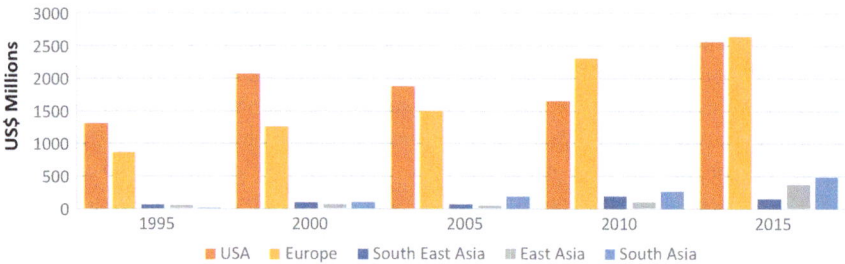

Fig. 4 Primary export destinations for manufactured products (select years). *Source* UNCTAD 2016, UNCTAD statistical database, merchandise trade matrix—product groups, exports in thousands of dollars, annual. http://unctadstat.unctad.org/wds/TableViewer/tableView.aspx

world patterns (UNCTAD 2012). Malaysia and Vietnam are utilized as comparator states given their past similarities with Sri Lanka's economic structure and their emphasis on manufacture-driven export-orientated strategy for development.

Over the given 20-year period, Sri Lanka has been able to expand its export portfolio by 13%. In comparison, Malaysia and Vietnam have enlarged export baskets by 2% and 26%, respectively. However, as evinced from the Table 3, the island nation has made miniscule headway in diversifying its export portfolio; in two decades, the index has improved by a mere 0.02 points. In comparison, Malaysia and Vietnam's export diversification initiatives have led to a drop amounting to 0.07 and 0.11 points, respectively.

Further due to a deficiency in product diversification, the Sri Lankan manufacturing sector also faces a dearth of high skilled labor and technology-intensive industries. Figure 5 provides a comparison between Sri Lanka's current and past labor, resource, and technology intensiveness. As indicated, the change in composition has been quite

Table 3 A comparison of diversification

	Number of export products		Diversification index	
	1995	2015	1995	2015
Malaysia	248	254	0.517	0.440
Sri Lanka	173	196	0.749	0.730
Viet Nam	199	251	0.670	0.551

Source UNCTAD 2016, UNCTAD statistical database, product concentration and diversification indices by economy
http://unctadstat.unctad.org/wds/TableViewer/tableView.aspx

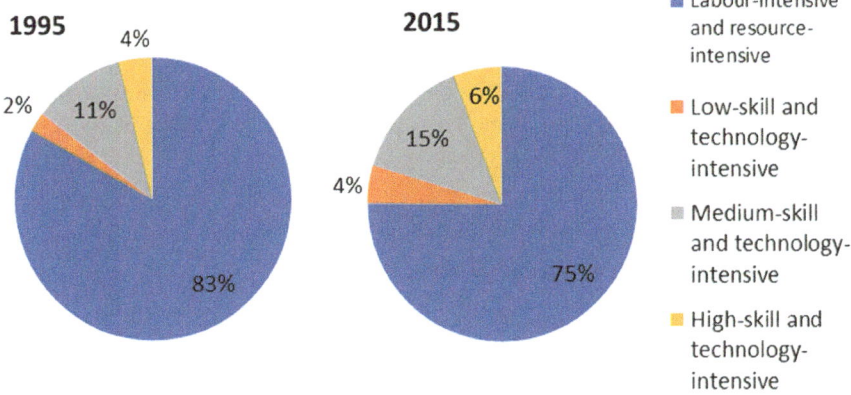

Fig. 5 Comparison of labor, resource and technology intensiveness of manufacturing exports (select years). *Source* UNCTAD 2016, UNCTAD Statistical Database, Merchandise trade matrix—product groups, imports in thousands of dollars, annual. http://unctadstat.unctad.org/wds/TableViewer/tableView.aspx

modest. "Medium-skilled and technology intensive" industries have expanded over the 20-year period, but the change is insufficient to swerve the dependency on labor- and resource-intensive industries.

The apparel domination of exports is a principal reason for the lack of progress in this regard. Indeed, Sri Lanka's major apparel manufacturers have made great strides in expanding into new lucrative and technology-intensive industries, but the industry, especially in the lower rungs, has not made enough progress to instigate sharp swings.

For the manufacturing sector to expand further, stakeholders from all industries should attempt to venture into higher value market segments.

4 Labor Market: Overview

An examination of Sri Lanka's labor market reveals paradoxes and conundrums dissimilar to those faced by other South Asian nations. While the nation has been able to rapidly develop socioeconomic conditions during the postindependence era, it has posted minimal success in eradicating certain labor market distortions and inadequacies that inhibit sector mobility. Particularly, the Sri Lankan labor force is plagued by issues arising from rigid labor laws, a skills mismatch, public sector dependency, and languid labor force participation rates for women.

As inferred to in the previous sector, there are signs that Sri Lanka is drifting toward sector-driven development akin to Singapore. However, policy makers should bear in mind that this model does not engender labor generation like the manufacturing sector. This is attested to by Chandrasiri (2011) who affirms that the manufacturing sector maintains the highest labor elasticity of demand and therein, considering Sri Lanka's relatively low manufacturing base, provides a larger chance of success in attracting high-value labor at the shortest possible interval.

4.1 Labor Market: General Overview

Table 4 provides contemporary statistics on the Sri Lankan labor force.

Table 4 Overview of Sri Lanka's labor market for 2016

Indicator	Total	Male	Female
Population (15 years and over)	15,468,203	7,168,508	8,299,695
Labor force in age group	8,354,841	5,369,143	2,985,698
Labor force participation rate (%)	54	75	36
Employed population	7,830,976	5,097,798	2,733,178
Employment rate (%)	94	95	92
Unemployed population	350,903.32	144,966.86	203,027.46
Unemployment rate (%)	4.20	2.70	6.80
Not in labor force	7,113,362	1,799,365	5,313,997
Average wage (US$)	190.4		

Source Department of Census and Statistics (2017)

As indicated in Table 4, Sri Lanka's participation rate hovers close to 54% of the working population which as per the World Development Indicators database places the nation slightly below the South Asian average of 55% (World Bank 2017). While aggregate unemployment hovers close to natural rates, the substantial gender disparity evident in participation rates is of particular concern, and will be expounded upon in a subsequent section.

Examining the sectoral breakdowns of Sri Lankan labour over a lengthened time horizon reveals trends paralleling fluctuations in economic priorities. For instance, agricultural activities were the primary employment provider over the decades following independence. However, the subsequent emphasis on domestic industry (including manufacturing) coupled with wavering fortunes of agriculture production led to increased labour flows from the latter to the former sector. Contrastingly, the labour composition in services deteriorated slightly over the initial liberalization period, only to increase substantially since the onset of the current century. The above shifts can be observed in Fig. 6 given below.

4.2 Youth Unemployment

Sri Lanka has been a poster child for educational advancement initiatives in Asia. Due to the success of focused policies spanning decades, the island nation possesses a highly literate populace without significant gender disparities. National surveys indicate an aggregate literacy rate of 93.2% with 94.1% of men and 92.4% of women estimated to wield basic language proficiency as of 2015 (Central Bank of Sri Lanka

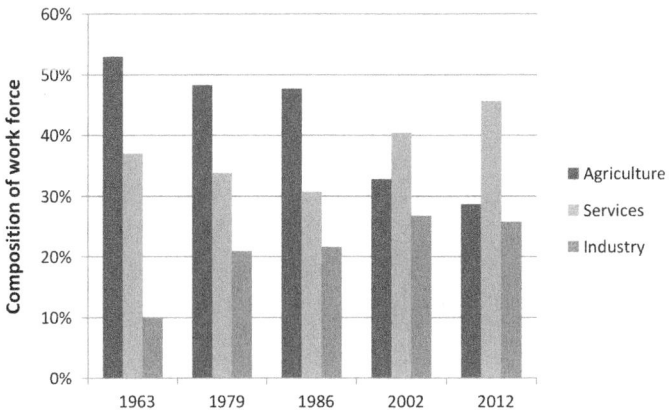

Fig. 6 Employment by economic sector (select years). *Source* Central Bank of Sri Lanka, Annual Report: 2016

Table 5 Employment and value added by subsector (2012)

Industry	Persons engaged	Value added (LKR. billions)
Apparel	266,750	177.9
Food product and beverages	115,890	208.4
Rubber and plastic products	52,413	62.9
Textiles	40,711	43.3
Furniture, manufacturing	20,330	22
Other	127,160	
Total	623,254	

Source Department of Census and Statistics (2015)

2017).[10] In addition, mean years of schooling in Sri Lanka were approximated at 10.8 years, a significantly higher value when compared to the South Asian average of 5.5 years (UNDP 2015). Such statistics place Sri Lanka on par with developed nations, with progress especially exemplary when examined on a regional perspective.

However, despite posting strong educational indices, Sri Lanka has failed to tackle the issue of persistent unemployment among younger segments of the working population. While many South Asian states face a similar challenge, Sri Lanka's problems appear more acute given the complexity and persistency of the issue. For instance

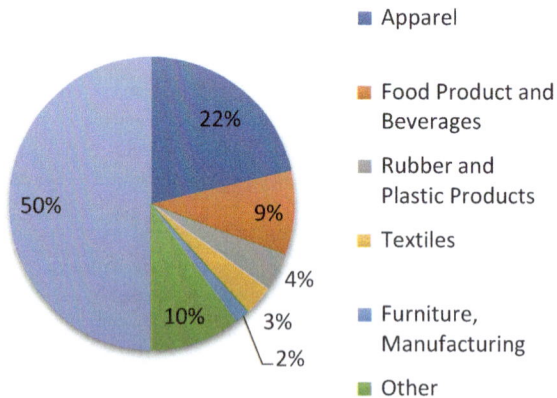

Fig. 7 Employment composition in manufacturing sector. *Source* Annual Survey of Industries, Department of Labor of Sri Lanka

---

[10]A UNESCO Institute of Statistics study estimates that the literacy rate for South Asia was 67% in 2013 with only 57% of women being able to read and write.

Table 6 Unemployment by select age groups

Age group	1990	1995	2000	2005	2010	2015
20–24	40.3%	38.2%	44.4%	24.6%	20.0%	19.8%
25–29	19.3%	20.1%	18.4%	9.5%	9.8%	9.7%

Source Department of Census and Statistics, Labor Force Survey, Various years

while aggregate unemployment rates for 2015 hovered at around 4.7% (Table 4 above), unemployment rates for citizens within the 25–29 age bracket stood at 9.7% during the same year. Furthermore, census data for that particular year reveals that 33% of the total population within this segment was categorized as economically inactive (Department of Census and Statistics 2016).[11]

To exacerbate issues further, statistics reveal that further education is not correlated to employment in Sri Lanka. As of 2015, the rate of unemployment for citizens who have completed the advanced level (Higher Secondary) examinations stands at 9.2%, while unemployment rates of those who have not completed the ordinary levels (Lower Secondary) examinations are measured at 2.7% (refer Table __ below). High rates of unemployment among the qualified workforce are affirmed by Vodopivec and Withanachchi (2010), who find that "in the first four years after university graduation, the proportion of unemployed graduates who found a job remained below 20% per annum." Therefore, in Sri Lanka's context, educational progress appears to be persistently correlated with medium-term unemployment.

This anomaly has been well studied, with contemporary literature attributing discrepancies to distortions in private sector and labor market expectations. Roughly surmised from a supply perspective, the low rates of labor absorption in Sri Lanka, particularly into the manufacturing sector, can be attributed to (i) a skills gap and (ii) a reduced enthusiasm among the younger segments of the populace to search for employment opportunities within the private sector. The paper examines these issues in closer detail.

4.3 Skills Mismatches

While Sri Lanka has registered success in attaining high primary and secondary enrollment, insufficient progress has been achieved in improving the quality of education. This issue has been noted in a World Bank study, which stresses that "although Sri Lankans spend more time in the education than neighbors in South Asia, questions regarding the system's quality and relevance seem to arise" (Dundar et al. 2014). The situation has been compounded by a lack of state funding into public education. As

---

[11] While this statistic does reveal discrepancies in participation rates, a closer examination suggests that an overwhelming majority—roughly approximated to around 65%—of this inactive population are women. Perhaps this is a symptom of a much larger issue elaborated in another section.

Central Bank reports, state expenditure into education averaged at 1.935% of GDP over the past 10 years which, per World Bank Development Indicators (WDI), falls below global and regional averages.

To exacerbate issues further, capital expenditure in education has been constricted to a miniscule 0.43% of GDP over the past 5 years. Such constrained allocations have forced authorities to continually forego development in certain avenues to balance budgets. Therein, persistent underinvestment has taken a toll on the public education system, with higher education and vocational training institutions bearing the brunt of the damage. Since the turn of the decade, capital expenditures into higher education and vocational training averaged approximately 8–10% of the aggregate budget allocated for educational activities.[12] It can thus be inferred that over the past six years, the state has spent a miniscule 0.18% of GDP on postsecondary education. Such paltry levels of investments are extremely unfortunate given the virtual absence of private universities in Sri Lanka. It has led to an abatement of capacity enhancement initiatives which in turn has aggravated a bottleneck constraining the transition from secondary to tertiary education. As a consequence, an increasing number of youth find themselves squeezed out of formal education after the completion of secondary level examinations. As of 2014, only 17% of students passing secondary level examinations gain entrance into universities while a further 30% proceed to technical and vocational training. Thus, in that year alone, approximately 140,000 youth—53% of new entrants—entered the labor market with no more than general secondary education and lacking job-specific skills (Dundar et al. 2014).[13]

Furthermore, an examination of the tertiary education, specifically focusing on Sri Lanka's halls of higher education, reveals discrepancies that inhibit skills development. Stagnation in standards and an imbalanced departmental emphasis have led to a system that produces graduates with skills not in sync with employee expectations. For instance, Sri Lanka's higher education system produces an abundance of students focused on the social sciences and humanities. As per the Department of Census and Statistics reports, 57% of the total graduates from the class of 2014 were from the "Arts" and the "Commerce" streams. These disciplines lack depth in the quantitative and technical skills required by manufacturing firms.

Technical and Vocational Education and Training (TVET) services are provided by a plethora of public and private institutions under the auspices of a central Tertiary and Vocational Education Commission (TVEC). As opposed to Sri Lanka's tertiary education sector, TVET initiatives place emphasis on delivering programs that match employer expectations. Thus, TVET programs and apprenticeships are well received by private sector institutions which utilize these initiatives to bolster workforce quality. As a result, over 20% of production workers in Sri Lanka receive training, compared with fewer than 10% of production workers in India and less than

---

[12]Figures have been derived from budget estimates provided by the Ministry of Finance. Capital expenditures into higher education and vocational training have been computed by referring to budgetary allocations to the Ministry of Higher Education and the Ministry of Skills Development and Vocational Training.

[13]Given the constraints to capacity, Dundar et al. (2014) estimated that approximately 10,000 students leave to study in halls of education outside the country.

5% in Pakistan and Bangladesh (Byiers et al. 2015). The wide acclaim of TVET, coupled with constricted university level admissions, has led to a higher cohort of youth enrolling in TVET programs when compared to other forms of the tertiary education sector.

However, such successes do not entail that TVET has been universally accepted as a substitute for higher education. For instance, despite orchestrating several promotion campaigns to raise the image of vocational training, the state has made minimal headway in increasing allure of TVET initiatives in the eyes of citizens. As Koralage and Hewapathirana (2012) state, "regardless of the employability aspects of vocational training, parents prefer that children pursue the highest education level possible, whether it leads to gainful employment or not" (quoted in Byiers et al. 2015).

Furthermore, several critics argue that TVET initiatives are designed to accommodate for labor-intensive sectors that require a large pool of low skilled labor. Such claims are not unfounded, a significant proportion of training programs focus upon the influential Textile and Garments (T&G) sector which has traditionally been labor intensive.[14] This emphasis is viewed with vexation in some corners as it is said to restrain focus on middle to higher level skills and therein promulgate a deficit in adept middle-management cadre. Shortages in higher level learning are affirmed by ILO reports, which indicate that only 2.2% of the workforce is trained in middle-level skills (cited in ADB 2016a, b).

4.4 Female Labor Force Participation

A perusal of existent literature and available data reveals that Sri Lanka, just like its regional partners, has failed to substantially increase decrepit female labor participation over the past three decades. The island nation's oversight is perplexing given the vast strides in educational parity achieved within this period. As per the most recently available census (2012), 13.6% of women completed advanced level examinations while 2.7% obtained a university degree. In comparison, 10.9% of men passed advanced level examinations while 2.6% obtained a degree. Despite women possessing a marginally better educational profile in the higher tier, their presence in the workforce is lacking—as of 2016, female labor force participation rates stood at 35.9%. While this compares well within the participation rates posted by fellow South Asian states, it falls below world (53§) and East Asian (65%) averages.[15] To compound issues, unemployment rates have traditionally been much higher for females than male counterparts. As per the most recent labor force survey (2016), the unemployment rate for females stood at 6.8% in comparison to 2.7% for males.

---

[14]Chandrasiri (2010) states that prominent TVET institutions construct programs designed for those with a lower secondary level of education. Thus, the depth of training tends to be quite low.

[15]Statistics given for World and East Asian states are derived from ILO databases where national statistics are adjusted to account for discrepancies.

In addition, census estimates indicate that approximately 74.7% of the economically inactive population in Sri Lanka is composed of by women. Family duties are the underlying cause for economic inactivity, with 61.4% of surveyed women indicating that engagements in housework render them unable to enter formal employment. However, this belies the actual impact that this segment of the population has on the economy. Approximately 24.2% of Sri Lankan households are headed by women with this proportion more pronounced in the war-torn regions of the North and East. Many remain statistically unemployed and depend on the informal sector for jobs to sustain households.

Literature pertaining to this issue has been shallow for much of the twentieth century owing to a larger emphasis on other contributors to unemployment in Sri Lanka. However, heightened enthusiasm since the turn of the millennium has precipitated into the denser contribution of research into this disparity. Such works suggest that much of the discrepancies in participation rates are funneled by a series of discriminatory tendencies akin to those experienced in much of Greater South Asia. For instance, rigid societal norms in the form of marital and household duties encumber women's participation in formal employment as the Sri Lankan work culture rarely accommodates to extraneous expectations. Past Governments have attempted to correct this imbalance by introducing new legislations that require establishments to provide paid maternity leave. However, these laws have proven to be counterproductive; as Maduruwala (2014) states, many employers believe that "providing maternity and child care benefits are an additional cost burden in a profit maximizing environment." Furthermore, the duties and responsibilities of those on maternity leave tend to be redistributed within the workforce thus resulting in an increased burden for fellow workers. This kindles animosity and propagates negative perceptions regarding female employment among middle and lower level cadre (Madurawala 2014). Such aversions precipitate to form a nascent discrimination against female recruitment as this labor cohort is often considered too expensive while wielding reduced productivity.

Female labor force participation is also hindered by sectoral bias wherein only select industries welcome enrollment. This is particularly true in manufacturing,

4.5 Public Sector Preference

As per contemporary norms, the appeal of public sector employment generally falls below that of the private sector due to the provision of a lower pay scale in the former. However, in the case of Sri Lanka, public sector pay "exceeds privates sector wages at the lower levels of employment" (Kelegama, Development Under Stress, 2006).[16] Given the additional benefits such as higher job security, pension eligibility,

---

[16]The existence of this preference is affirmed by a report prepared by (Arunatilake and Jayawardena, Explaining Labor Market Imbalance in Sri Lanka, 2014), which examines Jobsnet data to analyze labor market tendencies.

and mitigated work stress, new graduates are incentivized to solely apply for public sector vacancies. Kelegama (2006) states that this tendency—often referred to as the "Queuing Hypothesis"—has been pandered to by the Government, which in the past has initiated various schemes to enroll graduates into the public sector. Therefore, unemployed graduates prefer to wait for "good" job openings within the establishment as opposed to readily available "bad" jobs within the private sector (Rama 2003). Private establishments, particularly in the manufacturing sector, are severely affected by this distortion as they are plagued with further shortages in skilled labor, arising from reduced recruitment pools.

This phenomenon appears to be a relic of Sri Lanka's import substitution era. Yiping et al. (2013) believe that the constant interventions into the labor market during this period led to an increased dependency on the state as an "employer of last resort." In addition, the hostility towards foreign investments retarded labor returns in the private sector and further incentivized a switch in employee preference. The public sector soon outpaced the private sector in employment creation and by 1977 (dawn of liberalization initiatives), accounted for over 50% of employment in the manufacturing sector alone. Thereafter, subsequent stop-gap liberalization initiatives gradually eroded the importance of the public sector as a heightened inflow of investments elevated returns to labor in the private sector.

However, as explained earlier, the emergence of a populist–nationalist coalition to the helm of leadership in 2004 promulgated in a backtrack of liberalization reforms and increased state interventions. This facilitated a new wave of state enterprise expansion; the number of state-owned enterprises mushroomed from 107 to 245 while the number of employed in such institutions rose from 140,500 to a "staggering" 261,683 between 2009 and 2014 (Advocata Institute 2016). The fact that a large proportion of those employed were recent graduates is affirmed in an IPS report (2016) which asserts that 51,420 graduates were absorbed into the public sector under the "Graduate Employment Program" introduced by the previous government in 2014 alone (IPS 2016).[17]

Furthermore, the notion that public sector employment provides higher job satisfaction does not hold sway in recent times. Surveys conducted by the National Human Resource Development Council find that graduates employed (as of 2013) did not receive much satisfaction due to persistent political interventions and a misalignment between degree qualifications and job descriptions (NHRDC 2013).

5 Regional Integration—Expanding Indian Trade to Stimulate Manufacturing Capacity

The paucity of intra-regional trade within the South Asian region is a documented issue that has been well discussed in contemporary development parlance. As per

---

[17] Such recruitment drives tend to be staggered with employment provided in batches over a time period.

recent World Bank findings, intra-regional trade and investment among regional partners only constitute for approximately 5 and 4% of aggregate trade and investment conducted by regional partners (Kathuria and Shahid 2017). While attempts to foster integration and connectivity have been attempted frequently, their success has been largely mitigated by incessant political tensions, insufficient dissemination of regional opportunities, and a lack of infrastructural connectivity that impedes trade and investment mobility.

In further, discourses revolving around South Asian integration cannot discount the importance of India in fostering regional cooperation. India's sheer demographic and geographic scale, its strategic presence in the heart of South Asia, and its rapid growth acceleration over the last three decades places it in a position of influence within the subcontinent. Ideally, the nation's influence within the regional sphere can be leveraged to construct a symbiotic South Asian bloc wherein partners gain access to a large market base, share essential resources, and enhance technology transfers sans boundaries.[18] This has however not been the case. As eluded to above, various factors have permeated a cycle of mistrust among South Asian nations. Furthermore, while India's sheer comparative advantage, across several product lines, has enhanced its penetration into neighboring markets (on a bilateral level), its inability to curb age-old protectionist mechanics has caused distortions detrimental to the trade balance of its regional partners. Therein, given the difficulties in establishing a fluid and fruitful regional trade zone, the interests of many South Asian nations have gravitated towards distant international markets as a means to maximize export potential. Sri Lanka is no exception to this trend. Trade history shows an increased proliferation of imports from India, while aggregate exports to the region remain subdued.

An examination of Sri Lanka's postmillennial trade patterns suggests a preference to Western markets as a viable export destination. As of 2015, aggregate merchandize outflows to Europe and the United States accounted for approximately 58% of annual exports while exports to South Asia, despite locational proximity, encompassed a mere 9.7% of annual exports (Simoes and Hidalgo 2017). Conversely, South Asia has been a major import source, with the region accounting for 28% of aggregate imports for a similar period. However, imports from India alone accounted for 26% of aggregate imports for 2015, thereby indicating that a lion's share of Sri Lanka's intra-regional trade was accounted for by the Indo-Lankan bilateral partnership. This observation is elucidated in Figs. 8 and 9, which further elaborates on Sri Lanka's trade interactions with India and the rest of South Asia. As is evident, there appears to be a clear disparity in exports and import values between the two sectors over a 10-year period.

Such disparities will come as no surprise given India's geographic and cultural proximity to the island nation. Peninsular India is Sri Lanka's gateway to mainland South Asia, and both regions possess cultural similarities owing to shared religious beliefs, migration flows, and burgeoning trade ties stretching to the precolonial era. Furthermore, the two nations are inexorably linked due to a distinct topographic

---

[18]The region is home to approximately 1.76 billion citizens which surmounts to 24% of the world's population (World Bank 2017).

anomaly often referred to colloquially as the "Adams Bridge." The "bridge," a collective chain reef shoals and small islands, creates a quasi-isthmus in the Palk Bay that prevents large maritime vessels from traversing around the Indian peninsula. Therein, vessels traveling from the Eastern to the Western seaboards (and vice versa) of both nations are required to traverse around southern Sri Lanka to reach either coastline. Thereby, the establishment of sound, immutable bilateral ties is an essential task necessary to maintain the economic and military interests of both nations.

India and Sri Lanka are signatories to a bilateral "India-Sri Lanka Free Trade Agreement" (ISFTA) that came into effect in 2000 and recognized as the first treaty of its kind in the South Asian region (Kelegama and Karunaratne 2013). Furthermore, both nations are also signatories to the South Asian Free Trade Agreement (SAFTA), a Regional Trade Agreement signed in 2004 but whose performance has been shackled by circumspect trading lists and persistent conflicts among member states (De Mel 2007). As of 2016, India is Sri Lanka's the second largest import source, behind China, and the third largest export destination, behind the United States and the European Union (United Nations 2017).

However, such rankings and treaties belie the burgeoning trade imbalance inferred to earlier. As of 2016, aggregate merchandise imports from India were estimated at approximately US$3.8 billion while aggregate merchandise exports for the same year were valued at approximately US$750 million. The trade deficit for 2016 thus stood at a mammoth US$3.07 billion for 2016.

While a trade deficit should not necessarily be treated as an adverse phenomenon (since imports might consist of vital consumer goods and resources not available in the domestic market), the above imbalance in trade has received much attention given the somber growth in export penetration into India over the past decade. Such stagnations have been induced by a continued reliance on a low-value basket of exports that exhibits minimal diversification and sophistication (refer Fig. 10). For instance, as of 2015, primary products such as "Coffee, tea, mate and spices" (HS

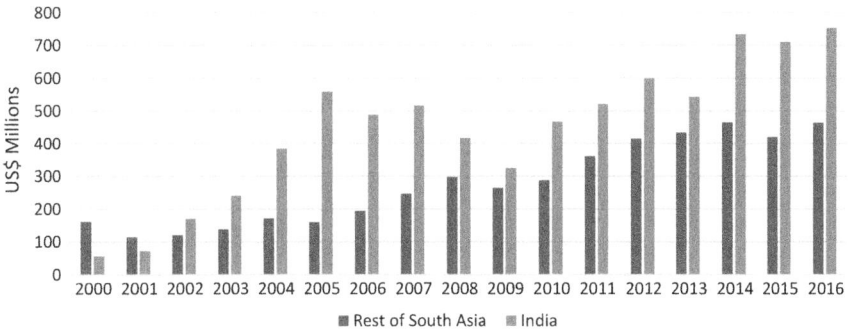

Fig. 8 Aggregate merchandize exports to India and Rest of South Asia (excluding India) for the period 2000–2016. *Source* UNCTAD 2016, UNCTAD statistical database, merchandise trade matrix—product groups, exports in thousands of dollars, annual. http://unctadstat.unctad.org/wds/TableViewer/tableView.aspx

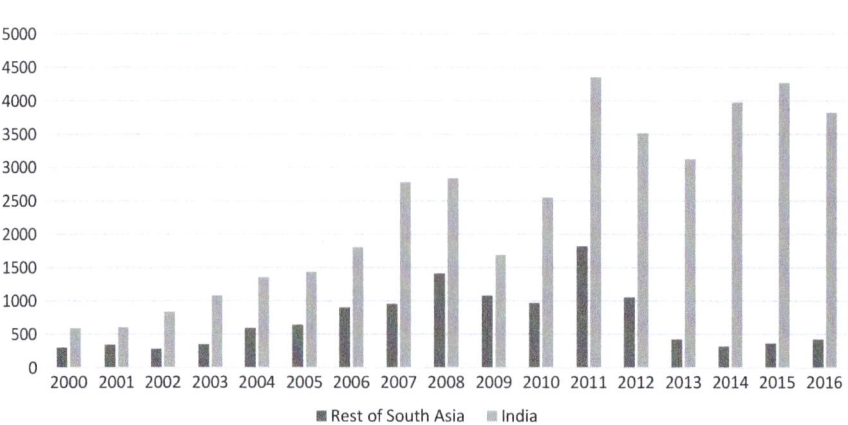

Fig. 9 Aggregate merchandize imports from India and rest of South Asia (excluding India) for the period 2000–2016

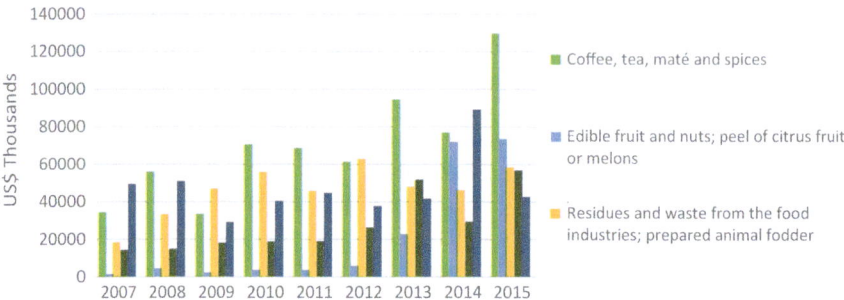

Fig. 10 Significant exports to India (2007–2015)

09), "Edible fruits and nuts" (HS 08), and "Animal fodder" (HS 23) are Sri Lanka's top exports to India. This is a concerning predicament given the limited scope of such products when attempting to expand export penetration at a hastened pace. With this being the case, Sri Lanka's best bet in maximizing trade potential, while simultaneously enhancing labor generation prospects, is to expand its bilateral export portfolio to include a wider plethora of manufactured goods catered to an Indian demographic.

This strategy serves a twin benefit to the Sri Lankan economy. For starters, domestic producers will now be able to tap into the consumer base of a nation often dubbed as one of the fastest growing major economies in the world (IMF 2017a, b). This is particularly advantageous given India's mushrooming middle class in its post-liberalization era. As per a recent study, India's middle class doubled in size between 2004–05 and 2011–12 and now amounts to nearly half of the entire population (Krishnan and Hatekar 2017). Targeting such a large cohort of consumers, in a rapidly emerging market close to home, will not only help producers garner additional revenue, but will help to mitigate risks induced by a lackluster economic performance in several Western nations. Heightened revenue yields will, in turn, incentivize producers to enhance supply capacity which consequently will stimulate labor generation and enhance economic growth prospects.

In addition, a concerted drive to penetrate the Indian market will help to lure inward Foreign Direct Investments (FDI) necessary to induce the scaling up of domestic industries and promote technology transfers. Sri Lanka's strategic location (nestled in the precipice of India, straddled by pivotal maritime routes), coupled with its efficient and educated workforce (when compared to other South Asian states), makes it an ideal destination for Indian investments looking to set up production centers catering to both the Indian and international markets. Evidence of such positioning already exists. Ceat, an Indian tire manufacturer, initially entered into Sri Lanka through a joint venture before acquiring a prominent Sri Lankan tire manufacturer. It has now significantly broadened its consumer base and now supplies pneumatic and non-pneumatic tires to 15 countries around the world, including India (Athukorola 2014).

However, potential forays into the Indian market has to be met. As mentioned earlier, the Indian market continues to be protected by archaic protectionist law of tariff and nontariff nature. Private sector stakeholders need to work in close tandem with the government to identify precise means in which markets can be opened.

6 Future Prospects

The creation of one million jobs by 2020 was a defining promise given by the current government during its successful election campaign. An examination of recent history suggests that this objective is wildly optimistic. From 2011 to 2014, the total number of employed increased by 237,689 which amounts to an increase of 78,230 per annum (IPS 2016). Thus, for the government to attain set targets, job growth rates have to be tripled within the shortest possible time period. Therein, given the heightened labor elasticity of the manufacturing sector, increased emphasis on the same will help increase labor generation rates and facilitate fulfilling the target.

References

ADB (2016a) Summary sector analysis: technical and vocational education and training. Asian Development Bank, Manila

ADB (2016b) Country assesment programme evaluation—Sri Lanka. Asian Development Bank, Manila

Amjad R, Chandrasiri S, Nathan D, Reihan S, Verick S, Yusuf A (2015). What holds back manufacturing in South Asia. Econ Political Wkly 36–45

Arunatilake N, Jayawardena P (2014) Explaining labor market imbalance in Sri Lanka. In: Gunatilaka R, Mayer M, Vodopivec M (eds) The challenge of youth employment in Sri Lanka. UNDP, New York, pp 69–90

Arunatilake N, Jayasuriya S, Kelegama S (2001) The economic cost of the war in Sri Lanka. World Dev 1483–1500

Athukorala P-C (2014) Intra-regional FDI and economic integration in South Asia: trends, patterns and prospects. South Asian Econ J 1–35

Athukorala P-C, Ekanayake R (2014) Repositioning in the global apparel value chain in the post-MFA era: strategic issues and evidence from Sri Lanka. Institute of Policy Studies, Colombo

Athukorala P-C, Rajapathirana S (2000) Liberalization and industrial transformation: Sri Lanka in international perspective. Oxford University Press, New Delhi

Byiers B, Kratke F, Jayawardena P, Takeuchi LR, Wijesinha A (2015) Manufacturing progress? Employment creation in Sri Lanka. Overseas Development Institute, London

Central Bank of Sri Lanka (2017) Annual Report: 2016. Central Bank of Sri Lanka, Colombo

Central Bank of Sri Lanka (Various Years) Annual Report. Colombo: Central Bank of Sri Lanka

Chandrasiri S (2010) Effect of training and labor market outcomes. In R. Gunatilake, M. Mayer, & M. Vodovipec, The challenge of youth employment in Sri Lanka (pp 91–114). Washington DC: The World Bank

Chandrasiri S (2011) Promoting employment intensive growth in Sri Lanka: ILO working paper series: no. 139 (pp. 1–58). Geneva: ILO

De Mel D (2007) South Asia: towards a viable free trade area. South Asia Watch on Trade, Economics and Environment

Department of Census and Statistics (2015) Annual survey of industries. Department of Census and Statistics, Colombo

Department of Census and Statistics (2016) Annual Report: 2015. Department of Census and Statistics, Colombo

Department of Census and Statistics (2017) Quaterly labor force survey. Department of Census and Statistics, Colombo

Dias S (1987) Industrialization strategy in Sri Lanka—Changes in policy and promotional measures. Sri Lanka J Soc Stud 51–82

Dundar H, Millot B, Savchenko Y, Aturupane H, Piyasiri T (2014) Building the skills for economic growth and competitiveness in Sri Lanka. The World Bank, Washington DC

Dunham D, Kelegama S (1997) Does leadership matter in the economic reform process?: liberalization and governance in Sri Lanka, 1989–93. World Dev 179–190

EDBSL (2012) Industry capability report: rubber products sector. Export Development Board of Sri Lanka, Colombo

Fonseka D, Pinto B, Prasad M, Rowe F (2012) Sri Lanka: from peace dividend to sustained growth acceleration. The World Bank, Washington DC

IMF (2017a) South Asia regional update. IMF, Washington DC

IMF (2017b) World economic outlook. IMF, Washington DC

Institute Advocata (2016) The state of state enterprises in Sri Lanka. Advocata Institute, Colombo

IPS (2016) State of the economy 2016: sustainable financing for development. The Institute of Policy Studies, Colombo

Kathuria S, Shahid S (2017) Boosting trade and prosperity in South Asia. In: De P, Rahman M (eds) Regional integration in South Asia: essays in Honor of Dr. M. Rahmatullah. KW Publishers, New Delhi, pp 7–35

Kelegama S (1992) Liberalization and Industrialization: The Sri Lankan experience of the 1980s. The Institute of Policy Studies, Colombo

Kelegama S (2006) Development under stress. SAGE Publications, New Delhi

Kelegama S, Karunaratne C (2013) Experiences of Sri Lanka in the Sri Lanka–India FTA and the Sri Lanka–Pakistan FTA. UNCTAD, Bangkok

Koralage KJ, Hewapathirane D (2012) Overcoming barriers to apprenticeship training in Sri Lanka. The Canadian Apprenticeship Journal, 27–37

Krishnan S, Hatekar N (2017) Rise of the new middle class in India and its changing structure. Econ Political Wkly

Madurawala S (2014) Female employment for inclusive growth: trends, issues and concerns of female labor force participation in Sri Lanka. The Institute of Policy Studies, Colombo

NHRDC (2013) Recruitment of graduates into the public service and their contribution to productivity vis-a-vis their job satisfaction. National Human Resources Development Council of Sri Lanka, Colombo

Pursell G, Ahsan F (2011) Sri Lanka's trade policies: back to protectionism. ASARC working paper

Rama M (2003) The Sri Lankan unemployment problem revisited. Dev Econ 510–525

Simoes A, Hidalgo C (2017) The economic complexity observatory: an analytical tool for understanding the dynamics of economic development. In: Twenty fifth AAAI conference on artificial intelligence

UNCTAD (2012, March 22). UNCTAD indicators to analyze countries' trade performance. https://vi.unctad.org/news-mainmenu-2/500-unctadstat12. Accessed 06 June 2017

UNDP (2015) Human development report. UN, New York

United Nations (2017) UN COMTRADE analytics. Trade Data: https://comtrade.un.org/. Accessed 25 August 2017

Vidanapathirana U (1993) A review of industrial policy and potential in Sri Lanka. Sri Lanka Economic Association, Colombo

Vodopivec M, Withanachchi N (2010) School-to-work transition of Sri Lankan. The World Bank, Washington DC

Waidyanatha W (2001) Rationale for liberalization of Sri Lankan economy. Econ Rev

World Bank (2004) Sri Lanka: development policy review. World Bank, Washington DC

World Bank (2011) More and better jobs in South Asia. The World Bank, Washington DC

World Bank (2017) World development indicators. World Bank, Washington DC. Retrieved from World Bank

Wriggins WH (1960) Ceylon: dilemmas of a new nation. Princeton: Princeton University Press

Yiping H, Athukorola P-C, Jayasuriya S (2013) Economic policy shifts in Sri Lanka: the post-conflict development challenge. Asian Economic Papers, 1–28

Economic Growth and Employment in South Asia

Ajit K. Ghose

1 Introduction

The South Asian countries, it is often said, have been achieving fairly rapid economic growth but this growth has been largely jobless so that they now face a daunting employment challenge. The story is not in fact quite so simple. Not all the countries of South Asia have been achieving rapid economic growth and economic growth has not been jobless in any of the countries. What can justifiably be said is that economic growth in these countries should have improved employment conditions much more than it actually did.

But what does this mean? Employment growth, as we shall see below, actually equalled labour force growth in all the countries. But this does not imply anything about improvement or deterioration in employment conditions. To understand why, we need to recognise that the economies of South Asia are dual economies à la Lewis with a formal or organised sector and an informal or unorganised sector.[1] The formal sector offers good jobs but employs only a small proportion of the workforce. The bulk of the workforce is in the informal sector, which holds large stocks of surplus labour in the form of underemployment and very low-productivity employment of many workers. Labour force participation also tends to be low as many people do not even look for work because they see this as a futile exercise. In this setting, economic growth improves employment conditions only when it reduces the stock of surplus labour (including the potentially available labour of many who are currently out of the labour force) through a process of transfer of those in underemployment and low-productivity employment in the informal sector to more productive jobs either in the

---

[1] Lewis (1954).

A. K. Ghose (✉)
Institute for Human Development, New Delhi, India
e-mail: ghose.ajit@gmail.com

© Springer Nature Singapore Pte Ltd. 2019
S. Chaturvedi and S. Saha (eds.), *Manufacturing and Jobs in South Asia*, South Asia Economic and Policy Studies,
https://doi.org/10.1007/978-981-10-8381-5_8

formal sector or within the informal sector itself. It is generating such a process of labour transfer that economic growth in South Asian countries has performed rather poorly.

But why has even rapid economic growth failed to rapidly improve employment conditions? The answer is to be found in the inappropriateness of the pattern of growth. Services have always been extraordinarily important (accounting for an unusually high share in GDP) in South Asian economies, which are still at early stages of development. Quite extraordinarily, moreover, economic growth in most of these countries (the only exception being Bangladesh) have also been services led. To add to the extraordinariness, the employment intensity of services has been and remains very low, a fact that stands in sharp contrast with what is observed in other countries of the world.

The growth process in South Asian economies, therefore, has brought too little structural change in employment. The movement of workers from agriculture to non-agriculture has been much too small and even this small movement has often been into low-productivity informal employment in non-agriculture.

Undoubtedly, the employment challenge that confronts the South Asian countries is formidable. The argument of this paper is that 'business-as-usual' growth, even if this can be sustained (there are reasons to think that services-led growth will be difficult to sustain), will do little to enable these countries to meet the employment challenge. The countries' own past experience makes this clear. A reorientation of the growth strategy is needed. Meeting the employment challenge will require rapid manufacturing-led growth.

The paper is organised as follows. In the section that follows, the growth experience of South Asian economies during the past decade and a half is scrutinised to see how growth affected employment conditions. In the third section, the employment challenge that these countries face is outlined. In the final section, the argument that rapid manufacturing-led growth is what is required to meet the employment challenge is sketched.

The statistical data used in the paper have been assembled from a variety of sources: SARNET database (built by collecting data from national sources) maintained at the Institute for Human Development (New Delhi), the World Bank (WDI database), the International Labour Organisation (KILM database) and the Asian Development Bank (Key Indicators database). Simple interpolations have sometimes been used to construct a dataset for five South Asian countries (Bangladesh, India, Nepal, Pakistan and Sri Lanka) covering the same period. Some data for a set of comparator countries—China, Indonesia, Korea, Taiwan and Thailand—have also been extracted from the same sources: The World Bank, the ILO and the ADB.

2 Economic Growth and Employment in Five South Asian Economies, 2000–2015

2.1 Characteristics of Employment

While economic growth during the past decade and a half cannot be said to have been poor in any of the five South Asian countries under consideration, it was reasonably rapid only in three of these—Bangladesh, India and Sri Lanka (Table 1). In Nepal and Pakistan, GDP growth was slow, just 4% per annum. The other more interesting fact is that no particular relation between GDP growth and employment growth is observed across the countries; India's GDP growth of 7% was associated with employment growth of only 1.5% while Pakistan's GDP growth of 4% was associated with employment growth of 3.3%. On the other hand, employment growth closely followed, indeed virtually equalled, the labour force growth in each of the countries.

These are the features that tell us that South Asian economies are labour-surplus dual economies. GDP growth is independent of employment growth in such economies; labour is in excess supply so that no 'labour constraint' on growth exists. On the other hand, most people do not have access to any kind of institutionalised social security and must work to survive. This means that most of those who are in the labour force are also employed. But many engage in work sharing (in self-employment and in casual wage employment) and many others engage in very low-productivity work. Very few remain unemployed and these few are educated (hence looking for good jobs in the formal sector) and generally belong to relatively well-off households (so that they can afford to remain unemployed). The employment problem manifests itself in poverty (which results from underemployment and low-productivity employment) and not in unemployment (which does not imply poverty). Employment growth reflects labour force growth and tells us little about growth in the demand for labour associated with economic growth.

Some of these characteristics of employment and unemployment are empirically discernible (Table 2a). Except in Sri Lanka, the formal sector employs a very small proportion of the workforce; a large majority (between 80 and 90%) of the workers work in the informal sector, either as self-employed or as casual wage employees. Even in Sri Lanka, where the formal sector employs 37% of all workers, the majority is still in the informal sector.

It is in self-employment and casual wage employment that there is much scope for work sharing; a given amount of work can be performed by a flexible number of workers. In the case of self-employment, the working members of a family share both the work and the income. In the absence of investment and technological change, an increase in the number of working members in families results in increased work sharing (i.e. increased underemployment). In the case of casual wage employment, not all the workers find employment on any given day but no worker fails to find employment on all days. In short, an increase in the number of persons seeking work in the informal sector results in increased employment (and not in increased unemployment) but also in increased underemployment. Given that the bulk of the labour force is in the informal sector, the same hold for the economy as a whole: labour force growth means employment growth but employment growth is often associated with rising underemployment.

On a snapshot view, therefore, underemployment, not unemployment, shows up to be the major problem (Table 2b). It should be said that the estimates of underemployment are not robust. In Nepal, for example, underemployment has almost certainly been seriously underestimated; in a situation, where 83% of the workers are in self-employment, underemployment has to be much higher than 6%. In Sri Lanka, too, underemployment appears to have been underestimated. Moreover, the estimates, even where they are reliable, are not comparable across countries as the definition is not uniform. They are presented here only to illustrate the point that underemployment of the employed is more significant than unemployment in South Asian economies. And unemployment, as noted above, is essentially confined to educated youth from relatively well-off households waiting in the queue for good jobs.[2]

Change in employment conditions, therefore, cannot be discerned from employment growth or change in unemployment. Employment growth in the formal sector and change in underemployment in the informal sector can tell us much about the change in employment conditions, but time-series data on these indicators are in general unavailable. Only the generally available information on change in the structures (sector shares) of output and employment associated with economic growth can be analysed to see if and to what extent the employment conditions have been improving.

Of the sectors, agriculture is almost wholly informal (except perhaps in Sri Lanka, which has a large plantation sector) while the non-agricultural sectors are themselves dualistic with formal and informal segments. Movement from agricultural employment to non-agricultural employment, therefore, is not equivalent to movement from informal employment to formal employment. However, even informal employment in non-agriculture is, as a rule, more productive and remunerative than agricultural employment. Thus, movement of workers from agricultural employment to non-agricultural employment usually does mean improvement in employment conditions. Such movement, when large, leads to a decline in employment in agriculture and thus to a rise in labour productivity in agriculture, which also means improvement in the conditions of agricultural employment (since it implies a decline in underemployment and in very low-productivity employment).

---

[2]A detailed analysis of these features of employment and unemployment in India is available in Ghose (2016).

2.2 Economic Growth, Structural Change and Employment

Historically, economic growth has been associated with persistent decline of agriculture together with rise of manufacturing at an early phase (when the income level is low) and with rise of services at a later phase (when the income level is high). In today's developed countries, the share of manufacturing in GDP increased for a long period before beginning to decline, which was also when the share of services began to increase rapidly.[3] The share in total employment in the economy followed the same trajectory as the share in GDP for both manufacturing and services. However, because technological change was important in manufacturing but not in services, growth of labour productivity was generally significant in manufacturing but quite insignificant in services. So, the share of manufacturing in total employment was always lower than its share in output while the share of services in employment tended to equal its share in output. In more recent periods, the same pattern of structural change has also been observed in the rapidly growing economies of East Asia (Table 3). Indeed, no country has yet attained even middle-income status without industrialisation.[4]

The growth experience of South Asian economies, which still are in early stages of development, defies the historically observed pattern. Economic growth in these economies during the last decade and a half has been services led (Table 4). And labour productivity growth has been much higher in services than in manufacturing, which is to say that the employment intensity of growth has been much lower in services than in manufacturing. Bangladesh stands out as the sole exception; here growth was manufacturing led and the employment intensity of growth was higher in services than in manufacturing.

The dominance of services in the economy is a feature that the South Asian countries inherited from their colonial past. In British India in 1946, services accounted for 38% of GDP while manufacturing accounted for 17%.[5] High share of services in GDP was thus a part of the initial conditions in the South Asian economies. The kind of growth that they experienced only increased the dominance of services. In 2000, the share of services in GDP ranged from 44% in India to 62% in Sri Lanka (Table 5a). It continued to grow in all countries except Bangladesh throughout the period 2000–2015. The manufacturing-led growth in Bangladesh did lead to a reduction of the share of GDP in services, but the share still remained high as it was already very high in 2000.

A comparison of the structural characteristics of South Asian economies with those of East Asian economies is illuminating. In 2015, the share of services in GDP ranged from 55% in Nepal to 66% in Sri Lanka (Table 5b). On the other hand, the share of manufacturing in GDP ranged from just 6% in Nepal to 19% in Bangladesh. In East Asian economies (some of which already counted as developed), around 2012, the share of services in GDP ranged from 40% in China to 66% in Taiwan

---

[3]Cf. Kuznets (1957, 1966) and Maddison (2006).

[4]See Szirmai (2012), ADB (2013) and Haraguchi et al. (2017).

[5]Cf. Sivasubramonian (2000).

(Table 6). The share of manufacturing in GDP, on the other hand, ranged from 25% in Indonesia to 36% in China and Thailand. Around the time, the lowest income East Asian country was Vietnam, the per capita GDP (in current international Dollars) of which was the same as that of India (the second richest country in South Asia) and the highest income country in South Asia was Sri Lanka, the per capita GDP of which was just above that of Indonesia (the second poorest country in East Asia).

The other contrasts between South Asia and East Asia relate to employment intensity of manufacturing and of services. In South Asian economies, the share of manufacturing in employment tends to be close to its share in GDP while the share of 'services' in employment is much lower than its share in GDP.[6] In East Asian economies, the opposite is true; the share of manufacturing in employment is much lower than its share in GDP, while the share of 'services' in employment is close to its share in GDP. Thus, labour productivity in manufacturing is much lower than that in services in South Asia while the reverse is the case in East Asia. The data in Tables 5b and 6 suggest that labour productivity in manufacturing was 2–2.5 times that in services in East Asia but 0.2–0.9 times that in services in South Asia.

The pattern of growth in East Asia was far more effective in improving employment conditions than the pattern of growth in South Asia (Tables 3 and 4). This can be seen most clearly from a comparison of India's experience during 2000–2015 with Korea's during 1963–1990 (the period during which Korea's economy underwent transformation from a low-income economy to a high-income economy). The growth rates of GDP in the two countries were not radically different: 7.2% in India and 7.5% in Korea and the rate of growth of agriculture was virtually the same: 3% in India and 2.9% in Korea. The rate of growth of non-agriculture was exactly the same: 8.2% in both countries. The big difference was in the composition of non-agricultural growth. This was driven by the growth of manufacturing (14.8% per annum) in Korea and by the growth of services (8.9% per annum) in India. Manufacturing recorded a growth of 7.5% in India and services recorded a growth of 6.6% in Korea.

The differences in the pace and pattern of employment growth were dramatic. The growth of employment was much slower in India (1.5% per annum) than in Korea (3.3% per annum). The growth of employment in non-agriculture (6.3% per annum) was very rapid in Korea so that employment in agriculture was declining fairly rapidly (at 1.5% per annum). In India, the growth of non-agricultural employment (3.2% per annum) was not rapid enough to turn the growth of agricultural employment negative. The far more rapid growth of non-agricultural employment in Korea is explained by two factors: the far higher growth of manufacturing and the far higher employment intensity of growth in services. In Korea, output growth of 14.8% per annum was associated with employment growth of 8% per annum in manufacturing; in India, output growth of 7.5% per annum in manufacturing was associated with employment growth of 2.3% per annum. So, even in manufacturing, the employment elasticity (i.e.

---

[6]These too are features that had been inherited from the colonial past and have not been altered by the growth process. In British India in 1946, the share of services in GDP was 38% while the share in employment was 16%. The share of manufacturing in GDP was 17% while the share in employment was 10%. Cf. Sivasubramonian (2000).

the ratio of employment growth to output growth) was actually higher in Korea (0.54) than in India (0.31). In services, output growth of 6.6% in Korea was associated with employment growth of 5.6% (implying an employment elasticity of 0.85), while in India, output growth of 8.9% was associated with employment growth of only 2.4% (implying an employment elasticity of 0.27).

We can draw two conclusions. First, the employment effect of growth depends on both the pace and the pattern of growth. In South Asian countries, growth did not significantly improve employment conditions both because it was not rapid enough and because its pattern was wrong. Only India had rapid economic growth but the particular pattern of this growth blunted its effectiveness in improving the employment conditions. Growth was slower in Nepal, Pakistan and Sri Lanka and the pattern of growth was similar to India's; the improvement in employment conditions was naturally less significant in these countries than in India. Bangladesh did have manufacturing-led growth with better effects on employment but the growth was not rapid enough.

A second conclusion is that services growth is much more employment intensive when manufacturing leads the growth process than when services lead it. In East Asian economies, where manufacturing led the growth process, services growth was far more employment intensive than in South Asian economies (except Bangladesh), where services led the growth process. Even in Bangladesh (a South Asian economy), where manufacturing led the growth process during 2000–15, services growth was more employment intensive than in other South Asian economies. The possible reasons are as follows. Services that lead the growth process are high skill and hence have low employment intensity; services that grow as complementary to growth of manufacturing are relatively low skill and have high employment intensity. These very features also imply that services-led growth engenders higher income inequality than does manufacturing-led growth. Higher income inequality, in turn, generates demand for skill-intensive services.[7]

3   The Employment Challenge in South Asia

The employment challenge that each of the South Asian economies faces is truly formidable. This can be seen from the results of an illustrative exercise reported in Table 7. Before discussing these results, however, we need to say something about the method used to derive the estimates of disguised unemployment, which relate exclusively to females. We have assumed that the currently low-female labour force participation rate in South Asian countries is explained by the fact that there are many 'discouraged workers' among women; many remain out of the labour force because they judge the prospects of finding work to be extremely poor. As employment

---

[7]Some of these features of India's services-led growth are brought out in Ghose (2015, 2016).

conditions improve, therefore, the female labour force participation rate in South Asian countries will rise and eventually be around 50% (this roughly is the observed global average). Except in Nepal, the participation rate currently is significantly below 50% and the difference between the number implied by a participation rate of 50% and the number implied by the current participation rate gives the number in disguised unemployment (i.e. the number that can be expected to enter the labour force as employment conditions improve).

In Nepal, the number in disguised unemployment turns out to be negative. The reason is that the current female participation rate is 80%, which is much too high and reflects widespread poverty and distress participation (such high female participation rates are also observed in the countries of sub-Saharan Africa). Here, the female participation rate is expected to decline as employment conditions improve and poverty declines. We should also recall that underemployment is most likely to have been seriously underestimated in both Nepal and Sri Lanka. For these reasons, we have chosen to leave these two countries out in carrying out the illustrative exercise.

The employment challenge is equally daunting in the three countries considered— Bangladesh, India and Pakistan—and we can focus on the group of three, i.e. SA-3, in outlining it. Between now and 2025, in SA-3, 10.4 million persons are expected to enter the labour force every year. If 10.4 million full-time jobs can be created every year, the number unemployed (25.2 million) and the number underemployed (82.5 million) will remain unchanged but the number in disguised unemployment will increase (by around 2 million per year). If underemployment and disguised unemployment are to be eliminated (so that the Lewis Turning Point is reached) by 2030, 23.6 million full-time jobs will need to be created every year (note that the number unemployed will still remain unchanged). The enormity of the task can be appreciated when we note that, between 2000 and 2015, employment increased by 8.8 million per year and only a part of the incremental employment was full time.

The point of the exercise is to underline the fact that growth-as-usual will not lead to a resolution of South Asia's huge employment problem in the foreseeable future. Both the pace and the pattern of economic growth will need to change; growth will need to be significantly faster and the growth of non-agriculture will need to be much more employment intensive. To meet these requirements, the South Asian countries will need to achieve rapid manufacturing-led growth as the East Asian countries have done. That manufacturing-led growth will be much more employment intensive than services-led growth has been is clear from the analysis in the preceding section. There are very good reasons to think that manufacturing-led growth will also be faster than services-led growth and we discuss these in the concluding section that follows.

4   The Need for Manufacturing-Led Growth: Some Concluding Observations

The empirical finding that, in historical experience, growth has always been manufacturing led at early stages of development and services led at later stages inspired the formulation of Kaldor's well-known 'growth laws'.[8] These can be summarised in the form of the following propositions. First, increasing returns to scale are highly significant in manufacturing so that output growth itself causes productivity growth.[9] Second, growth of manufacturing has important spill over effects on other production sectors and causes economy-wide productivity growth through reallocation of labour and other resources from agriculture and traditional services to the dynamic manufacturing sector.[10] Third, growth of manufacturing induces growth of modern services as complementary and ancillary to manufacturing. The upshot is that the greater is the excess of manufacturing growth over GDP growth, the faster is GDP growth. Manufacturing-led growth is also the fastest achievable growth.

There are demand-side factors that also lend strong support to manufacturing-led growth at early stages of development. At low levels of per capita income, the income elasticity of demand for manufactures tends to be higher than that for services so that domestic demand for manufactures grows faster than that for services. Moreover, manufactures are tradable goods *par excellence* and external demand can play an important role in supporting rapid growth of manufacturing.

Recently, in light of India's recent experience of rapid services-led growth, some economists have argued that certain services have now acquired the characteristics of manufacturing (as noted above), and hence can lead the growth process even in a low-income economy.[11] The prime example of such services is information technology (IT) and related services. India's rapid services-led growth in the 2000s, therefore, is not perhaps so surprising. Indeed, it is perfectly possible that other low-income countries will also achieve rapid services-led growth in the twenty-first century.

As it happens, India still remains the sole exception to the rule; it is the only country to have achieved rapid services-led growth (at least for a period) at an early stage of development.[12] More importantly, even a cursory look into India's growth process during 2005–12, the period of fastest growth, reveals that growth was not in fact led by the 'dynamic' services, the services that arguably have acquired the characteristics of manufacturing (Table 8). IT and communication services did grow very rapidly but these accounted for rather small shares of services and of GDP. On the other hand, financial services, which accounted for larger shares of services and of GDP, also recorded very rapid growth. We also know that the high-end segments of transport (e.g. air travel), trade (e.g. malls and supermarkets) and 'hotels and

---

[8]Cf. Kaldor (1967).

[9]This is referred to as Verdoorn's Law originally formulated by Verdoorn (1949).

[10]This is referred to as 'macroeconomic economies of scale' originally identified by Young (1928).

[11]See, in particular, Dasgupta and Singh (2005) and Amirapu and Subramaniam (2015).

[12]As observed earlier, other South Asian countries—Nepal, Pakistan and Sri Lanka—also had services-led growth, but their growth was significantly less rapid than India's.

restaurants' recorded rapid growth. What explains the rapid growth of these 'non-dynamic' services? These services are not exported. The rapid growth of IT services, which are exported, could not possibly have induced such rapid growth of the 'non-dynamic' services. Here is a possible explanation: the rapid growth of services, and hence the rapid services-led growth was actually sustained by large inflows of foreign finance (inflows of foreign capital and remittances amounted to 6–7% of GDP on average during the period) rather than by 'dynamic' services. India's rapid services-led growth has in reality been foreign-finance-led growth. This, of course, is a hypothesis and must remain so here. The point is that it is wrong to interpret India's services-led growth to have been driven by the services that have now acquired the characteristics of manufacturing.

There also are reasons to think that services-led growth cannot be sustained for long, not just in India but also in other South Asian countries. This kind of growth brings about a serious imbalance between the structure of domestic absorption (consumption plus investment) and that of domestic production. In India today, goods account for around 65% of domestic absorption but just over 40% of domestic production.[13] This means a high trade deficit. Continued services-led growth can only mean growing imbalance, and hence rising trade deficit, which can only be sustained if large inflows of foreign finance are sustained. Services-led growth is fragile.

South Asian countries need rapid employment-intensive growth to meet the employment challenge. And this means that they need manufacturing-led growth, which will be both rapid and employment intensive.

Appendix

Statistical Tables
See Tables 1, 2, 3, 4, 5, 6, 7 and 8.

Table 1 Growth rates (percent per annum), 2000–2015

	GDP	Employment	Labour force
Bangladesh	5.8	1.2	1.3
India	7.2	1.5	1.4
Nepal	4.0	1.8	1.9
Pakistan	4.1	3.3	3.2
Sri Lanka	5.5	0.5	0.3

---

[13] See Ghose (2015).

Table 2 (a) Structure of employment, 2015. (b) Underemployment and unemployment, 2015

(a)

(Percentage distribution)

	Self-employment	Wage employment	
		Formal sector	Informal sector
Bangladesh	61.9	12.6	25.6
India	56.0	19.1	24.9
Nepal	83.2	7.7	9.0
Pakistan	64.0	14.4	21.5
Sri Lanka	44.9	37.2	17.9

(b)

	Incidence (%) of underemployment	Rate (%) of unemployment
Bangladesh	20.4	4.1
India	11.7	3.5
Nepal	6.5	3.0
Pakistan	15.1	5.9
Sri Lanka	2.6	4.7

Table 3 Growth of GDP and employment in selected East Asian economies

(Per cent per annum)

	Agriculture	Manufacturing	Other industries	Services	Total	Non-agriculture
GDP						
China (1990–2010)	4.0	13.7	12.1	11.1	10.6	11.8
Japan (1955–1985)	0.4	9.1	6.6	6.7	6.6	7.2
Korea (1963–1990)	2.9	14.8	12.0	6.6	7.5	8.2
Taiwan (1963–1987)	3.0	13.8	7.6	9.2	9.3	10.3
Employment						
China (1990–2010)	−1.6	2.1	2.8	4.0	0.8	3.2
Japan (1955–1985)	−3.1	2.3	2.4	2.9	1.3	2.7
Korea (1963–1990)	−1.5	8.0	6.7	5.6	3.3	6.3
Taiwan (1963–1987)	−1.7	7.4	4.8	4.7	3.3	5.6

Table 4 Growth of GDP and employment in South Asian economies, 2000–2015

(Per cent per annum)

	Agriculture	Manufacturing	Other industries	Services	Total	Non-agriculture
GDP						
Bangladesh	4.0	8.3	7.5	5.4	5.8	6.2
India	3.0	7.5	6.6	8.9	7.2	8.2
Nepal	3.2	1.7	3.9	4.9	4.0	4.4
Pakistan	2.6	5.9	3.2	4.5	4.1	4.6
Sri Lanka	3.4	3.7	8.5	5.9	5.5	5.7
Employment						
Bangladesh	0.4	3.4	10.0	5.8	1.2	2.0
India	0.1	2.3	7.3	2.4	1.5	3.2
Nepal	1.5	2.4	2.3	3.1	1.8	2.7
Pakistan	2.6	4.6	6.8	3.1	3.3	3.8
Sri Lanka	0.0	0.0	4.0	0.4	0.5	0.8

Table 5 (a) Sector shares in GDP and in employment, 2000. (b) Sector shares in GDP and in employment, 2015

(a)

(Percentage distribution) 2000

	Agriculture	Manufacturing	Other industries	Services
GDP				
Bangladesh	19.4	13.4	7.5	59.7
India	26.1	15.9	13.6	44.4
Nepal	35.4	8.0	8.2	48.4
Pakistan	27.2	10.1	7.1	55.6
Sri Lanka	10.5	20.1	6.9	62.5
Employment				
Bangladesh	50.8	9.4	2.3	37.5
India	60.0	11.4	4.9	23.7
Nepal	78.0	5.9	4.2	11.8
Pakistan	48.3	11.4	4.7	35.6
Sri Lanka	31.9	18.1	6.9	43.1

(continued)

Table 5 (continued)

(b)

(Percentage distribution)

	Agriculture	Manufacturing	Other industries	Services
GDP				
Bangladesh	14.9	19.0	9.5	56.6
India	14.3	16.6	12.6	56.5
Nepal	31.9	5.8	8.1	54.6
Pakistan	21.8	12.9	6.2	59.1
Sri Lanka	7.9	15.7	10.5	65.9
Employment				
Bangladesh	45.1	12.9	8.0	34.0
India	48.8	12.9	11.3	26.9
Nepal	74.5	6.5	4.6	14.4
Pakistan	43.8	14.0	7.7	34.5
Sri Lanka	30.5	15.9	9.8	43.8

Table 6 Sector shares in GDP and in employment, some East Asian economies

(Percentage distribution)

	Agriculture	Manufacturing	Other industries	Services
GDP				
China 2010	9.1	36.5	14.7	39.7
Indonesia 2012	11.6	25.4	19.2	43.8
Korea 2010	3.5	35.2	10.4	50.9
Taiwan 2012	1.7	28.3	4.0	66.0
Thailand 2011	10.3	36.3	9.3	44.1
Employment				
China 2010	36.7	19.2	9.5	34.6
Indonesia 2012	34.4	12.8	7.5	45.3
Korea 2010	6.9	18.2	8.3	66.6
Taiwan 2012	5.0	27.4	8.3	59.3
Thailand 2011	38.7	13.9	6.7	40.7

Table 7 The employment challenge

(Number in millions)		Bangladesh	India	Pakistan	SA-3
Population (15+)	2015	113.6	933.9	125.3	1172.8
	2017	115.5	948.8	127.5	1191.8
	2025	133.1	1083.5	149.7	1366.3
Labour force (15+)	2015	70.7	501.5	67.5	639.7
	2017	72.9	517.5	70.1	660.5
	2025	82.2	581.8	80.7	744.7
Fresh entrants per annum (15+)	2017–25	1.1	8.0	1.3	10.4
Unemployed (15+)	2015	2.9	17.5	3.9	24.3
	2017	3.0	18.1	4.1	25.2
Underemployed (15+)	2015	13.8	56.6	9.4	79.8
	2017	14.3	58.4	9.8	82.5
Disguised unemployed (15+)	2015	3.9	105.2	16.1	125.2
	2017	4.0	108.7	16.7	129.4
Full-time jobs required per annum to eliminate underemployment and disguised unemployment by 2030	2017–30	0.9	10.6	1.7	13.2
Required increase in full-time jobs per annum	2017–25	2.0	18.6	3.0	23.6
Actual increase in number of employed per annum	2000–15	0.8	6.4	1.6	8.8

Note The projections of population for 2025 are from the United Nations Population Division. The projections of labour force are based on the assumption that the labour force participation rates will remain unchanged. In estimating the number of full-time jobs that are required to be created per annum, it has been assumed that (a) the number of unemployed will remain unchanged and (b) half of the underemployed will need to be moved to full-time jobs elsewhere

Table 8 India's services-led growth

	As % of services		As % of GDP		Growth (per cent per annum)
	2004/05	2011/12	2004/05	2011/12	2004/05–2011/12
IT services	4.1	5.7	2.2	3.3	14.9
Communication	3.1	6.9	1.7	4.0	23.0
Financial services	10.9	15.2	5.8	8.7	15.1
Research and dev + legal and accounting	1.9	2.6	1.0	1.6	17.8
Real estate and dwelling + transport and storage	23.8	19.7	12.6	11.3	6.7

(continued)

Table 8 (continued)

	As % of services		As % of GDP		Growth (per cent per annum)
	2004/05	2011/12	2004/05	2011/12	2004/05–2011/12
Trade + hotels and restaurants	31.1	28.9	16.5	16.6	8.5
Community, social and personal	25.0	21.2	13.3	12.2	7.2
All services			53.0	57.4	9.7
GDP					8.5

Source Central Statistical Organisation (Government of India), *National Accounts Statistics*

References

ADB—Asian Development Bank (2013) Asia's economic transformation: where to, how far and how fast (special chapter). In: Key indicators for Asia and the Pacific 2013. Asian Development Bank, Manila

Amirapu A, Subramanian A (2015) Manufacturing or services? An Indian illustration of a development dilemma. Working paper no. 409, Center for Global Development, Washington, D.C.

Dasgupta S, Singh A (2005) Will services be the new engine of Indian economic growth? Dev Change 36(6):1035–1057

Ghose AK (2016) India employment report 2016. Oxford University Press, New Delhi

Ghose AK (2015) Services-led growth and employment in India. In: Ramaswamy K (ed) Labour, employment and economic growth in India. Cambridge University Press, New Delhi

Haraguchi N, Cheng CFC, Smeets E (2017) The importance of manufacturing in economic development: has this changed? World Dev 93:293–315

Kaldor N (1967) Strategic factors in economic development. Cornell University Press, Ithaca

Kuznets S (1957) Quantitative aspects of economic growth of nations. Econ Dev Cult Change 5(4):2–80

Kuznets S (1966) Modern economic growth: rate, structure and spread. Yale University Press, New Haven

Lewis WA (1954) Economic development with unlimited supplies of labour. Manch Sch 22(2):139–191

Maddison A (2006) The world economy. OECD Development Center, Paris

Sivasubramonian S (2000) The national income of India in the twentieth century. Oxford University Press, New Delhi

Szirmai S (2012) Industrialization as an engine of growth in developing countries. Struct Change Econ Dyn 23(4):406–420

Verdoorn PJ (1949) Fattori che regolano lo sviluppo della produttività del lavoro. *L'industria* 1:45–53 [Translated into English as "On the factors determining the growth of labour productivity" and republished in Pasinetti L (ed) (1993), Italian Economic Papers 2. Oxford University Press, Oxford]

Young AA (1928) Increasing returns and economic progress. Econ J 38(152):527–532

Competitiveness, Skill Formation and Industrialization: The South Asian Experience

Lakhwinder Singh

1 Introduction

Global economy is steadily moving towards the fourth industrial revolution (4IR).[1] The 4IR is changing the nature of economic activities, organizations, businesses, institutions and the lives of the people across the globe (Schwab 2017). Historical experience of the industrially advanced countries and more recently the newly industrializing countries of East Asia show that the industrialization has remained the engine of economic growth and development. The industrialization has transformed the sources of livelihood of the people and sustained institutional changes. The spread effects of industrialization have also impacted on the structural and institutional changes across the countries. The central dynamic force behind the industrial revolution has been epochal innovation (Kuznets 1966), and each industrial revolution has its own distinctive innovation. The newly industrializing countries of East Asia also have unique innovations to catch-up with the advanced countries (Lee 2013). The technological innovations not only change economic activities but also undergo dramatic skill requirements. The technological innovations to succeed require suitable institutional changes and human capital formation. Where these conditions are not fulfilled, the industrial revolution either has not happened or distorted economic development. However, the industrial revolution in some parts of the world does affect the rest of the world in several dimensions. Even with the low level of development, the most of the developing countries are witnessing a trend towards

---

[1] The fourth industrial revolution is based on unique new technological innovations such as robotics, artificial intelligence, nanotechnology, quantum computing, biotechnology, the Internet of things, 3D printing and autonomous vehicles.

L. Singh (✉)
Department of Economics, Punjabi University, Patiala 147002, India
e-mail: lakhwindergill@pbi.ac.in

© Springer Nature Singapore Pte Ltd. 2019
S. Chaturvedi and S. Saha (eds.), *Manufacturing and Jobs in South Asia*, South Asia Economic and Policy Studies,
https://doi.org/10.1007/978-981-10-8381-5_9

high-tech industrial development and that also reflected in terms of increasing share of trade in high-tech manufacturing commodities (UNIDO 2015).

South Asian countries are also undergoing steady structural transformation of its economies in general and within industrial sector changes in particular that are determined by the pace of globalization. These countries host the world's largest poor due to lack of innovations and stagnation of their industrial sector (UNIDO 2015). The innovation system of South Asian countries is highly dependent on imported technologies. These technologies are neither suitable to the factor endowment of South Asian countries nor generates interlinkages across sectors. Therefore, the spread of technology transfer benefits remains very limited. Lack of inter-sectoral linkages between sectors and economic actors push the system towards low-productivity trap. The consequence of such deficiencies results in promoting rampant exclusion. Domestic base of human capital and technological capabilities are relatively weak. Resources devoted towards innovation are substantially low as per the requirement of the innovation system. The current model of science and technology policy adopted by the South Asian countries is highly centralized and need refurbishment on urgent basis while adopting decentralized approach. To overcome low-productivity and poverty trap, the South Asian countries should devote adequate resources towards investing in human capital, institutions, improving innovation system.

In South Asian countries, the workforce either disguisedly employed or employed in low-productive economic activities and do not match with the skill requirements for the competitiveness of their industrial sector and thus results in mass poverty. To overcome the industrial stagnation and skill formation gaps, the South Asian countries need to revamp their national innovation system for harnessing the ongoing industrial revolution and move onto the path of self-sustained economic development. This chapter is an attempt to explore the possibilities of industrial development and skill formation for making South Asian countries more competitive in the era of fast-changing global economy. It is divided into six sections. The second section examines economic theory and empirical literature emphasizes the need for skill formation for industrial development and competitiveness. The third section analyses the nature of economic transformation of the Asian Countries. Skill mismatches of South Asian countries are identified in the fourth section. The suitable strategy for overcoming the skill formation gaps and industrial development for South Asian countries is developed in the fifth section. Concluding remarks are presented in the last section.

2 Theory and Empirics on Skills and Development

The endogenous theory of economic growth has argued that the skill formation plays an important role in raising the productivity of economic activities. Lucas (1988) has developed the model of economic growth with human capital accumulation and argued that long-term economic growth is determined by the level of capital accumulation by the number years of school and also learning by doing. The level of skill has a direct effect on raising the level of productivity of the workforce. However, the indirect effect of schooling of the workforce is the spillovers or externalities that generate increasing returns to scale. The direct impact of skills on individual productivity results in higher returns to the workforce but indirect effects generate increasing returns to scale and raise the general level of productivity and are beneficial to the society at large. Both the effects combined together result in higher level of productivity and increasing returns to scale. Therefore, it is suggested that a simple rise in the level of skills imparted through schooling has long-term effects on economic growth of an economy. Thus, public policy of increasing expenditure on schooling can be the major instrument of enhancing the productivity of human capital and long-term economic growth.

The another variant of endogenous growth theory presented by Romer (1986) has put forward the idea of the higher the level of expenditure on ideas generation (research and development expenditure), the higher will be the long-run growth. Romer has outlined his model while dividing the workforce of an economy into two parts. One part of the workforce is engaged in usual economic activities and the other part is employed in producing new ideas. The accumulation of new ideas helps in generating new technologies/innovations that improve the arts of production and prevent diminishing returns to scale on capital. But susceptible to diminishing returns on the generation of new ideas. The overall impact of investment on generation of new ideas, while employing the scientific manpower, is reflected through generation of externalities that results in developing suitable environment of increasing returns to scale. This process generates boundless economic growth for the countries that have employed a larger workforce in generating new ideas. Thus, an important public policy implication that results from this model of economic growth is that the higher the level of investment in the scientific workforce and research and development, the higher will be the level of economic development.

UNIDO (2015) has shown that the engine of long-run growth and catch-up is industrialization because industrialization generates the economic dynamism of structural change that sustains growth by increasing its episodes and reducing its volatility. The industrial development is driven by technological progress, which is imitated or adapted from the industrially advanced countries. This process requires domestic technological capabilities that are further based on the capabilities developed by the national innovation system. The capabilities development is fundamentally based on education of the workforce and the allocation of human capital and investment in research and development (R&D). To bridge the gap of technological knowledge and move on the process of catch-up, the developing countries are required to develop absorptive capacities. It is significant to note that the determinants of absorptive capacities are continuous investment in human capital, as the industrial development of the developing economies is in transition and becoming increasingly more technology intensive. Thus, it is important for a developing country to reap the benefits of this manufacturing transition while investing in generating skilled technicians, scientists and engineers. The absorptive capacities and capabilities are fundamentally determined by the well-functioning national innovation system.

Jagannathan and Geronimo (2013) have examined the relationship between skills development and industrial competitiveness across Asia-Pacific economies. The authors have identified the phase of transition across developing countries and their changing skill requirements for enhancing the competitiveness of industries across the developing countries. It is recognized that skill credentials developed and endorsed by industry are crucial for preparing the workforce to be shifted from school to work. Skill imparting institutions should take care of the range of industries and their skill requirements. As the technology improves, it opens up a window of opportunity for high value-added industries and thus requires knowledge workers that enable industries to achieve high productivity on sustainable basis. It is asserted by the authors that skill improvements are also required for increasing intensity of services in the Asian countries. This also requires a massive investment in the education of the workforce for attaining competitiveness in knowledge-intensive services and support to the industry for in house training of the workforce to avoid redundancy of the employed workforce.

Fourth industrial revolution (4IR) driven by new technologies and fast pace of globalization is dramatically changing the existing model of business across all sectors. The emerging models of economic activities increase the speed of job destruction and job creation. WEF (2016) estimates show that the half the number of jobs are at risk because of automation. Furthermore, it is estimated that the automation will destroy 9% of jobs even in the low value-added occupations. The risk of the non-automatable workforce employed in economic activities is also very high and one-third of these jobs may be destroyed by 2020. On the contrary, the educational institutions have been imparting training to the population that is soon expected to be redundant or there will be no new employment demand. It is estimated that 65% of the school going age children are receiving education for jobs that do not exist today or are receiving education and skills that will not allow them to join jobs due to skill gaps. It is thus suggested by the report of WEF (2017) that as the 4IR is unfolding, there is a strong need for increased investment in human capital formation so that benefits of emerging technologies can be widely reaped. To achieve inclusive and sustainable industrial development, there is a need to fill the double gap, that is, the mismatch between the emerging economic activities and human capital and within human capital male–female skill gaps. Beyond this, it is suggested that mindset change is required both at institutional level and at individual level to move towards adoption of lifelong learning culture that provides lifelong employability and career security.

The foregoing brief review of studies allows us to conclude that the changing economic environment of productive economic activities generates skill mismatch. It is true for both developed and developing countries but skill mismatch is relatively more severe in the case of developing countries as compared to the developed countries. Moreover, the capability to tackle the skill mismatch is quite weak in the developing countries compared with the developed countries. South Asian countries are at higher risk in this context and therefore require urgent actions to address the skill mismatch in the foreseeable future to remain competitive and enable the population for sustainable livelihood.

3 Economic Transformation of South Asian Countries

Changes in the economic structure of an economy are the indicators of the direction in which the country's economy is moving. The process of modern economic development can be reflected from the structural transformation of the economy. The changing structure of an economy also affects the institutional arrangements and ideology. These changes are driven by the unique innovations and economic activities shift towards a higher level of productivity and wages (Kuznets 1966). The growth experiences of South Asian countries and also of the region are presented in Table 1. The average annual growth rates of GDP and three sectors, that is, agriculture, industry and services, based on 2010 constant prices for the period 2000–2016, show variations across South Asian countries. On the whole, the South Asian countries during the period 2000–2016 had remained fastest growing region of the global economy with 7% per annum growth rate. Agriculture sector has recorded 3.3% of annual growth rate which was the lowest across sectors. The services sector growth rate was 8.7%, which was highest among the sectors and also of the overall growth rate. Among the South Asian countries, Afghanistan, Bhutan and India recorded 8%, 7.7% and 7.5%, respectively, growth rates which were higher than the overall South Asian regions growth rate. Nepal and Pakistan were the slow-growing countries in the region. Industrial sector growth rate was higher in Bangladesh, Bhutan, Maldives and Pakistan during the period under study. It can be inferred that the industrial sector has remained an engine of growth in these countries, although industrial growth rates had remained higher than the agriculture sector growth rates except Nepal. The analysis of Table 1 clearly brings out the fact that service sector growth rates had remained usually very high but Afghanistan, India, Nepal and Sri Lanka where the services sector dominated. The region as a whole has also recorded the highest growth rate in the services sector. Thus, it can be safely observed that service sector-led growth has remained predominant feature in the South Asian region.

Table 1 Sectoral growth rates across Asian Countries (2000–2016 at 2010 prices)

Countries	GDP	Agriculture	Industry	Man.	Services
Afghanistan	8	2.9	7.5	3.2	10.4
Bangladesh	6	4.3	8.2	8.5	5.8
Bhutan	7.7	2	9.2	8.9	8.5
India	7.5	3.3	7.6	8.3	9.6
Maldives	6.3	0.5	6.7	1.7	6.3
Nepal	4.1	3.2	2.7	1.6	4.8
Pakistan	4.2	2.9	4.9	5.6	4.8
Sri Lanka	6	3.8	6.2	4.3	6.5
South Korea	7	3.3	7.4	7.9	8.7

Source World Bank (2016)

Table 2 Sectoral shares of GDP across Asian Countries

Countries	Agriculture % of GDP		Industry change		Services	
	2000	2016	2000	2016	2000	2016
Afghanistan	32	22.10	27	23.4	41	55
Bangladesh	20	15	25	29	56	56
Bhutan	23	16	37	42	40	41
India	20	17	34	29	47	54
Maldives	8	3	15	24	77	73
Nepal	36	33	18	15	46	52
Pakistan	21	25	27	19	51	56
Sri Lanka	12	8	30	30	58	62
South Korea	20	18	32	34	47	58

Source World Bank (2016)

The differential growth experience across countries and sectors may have affected differently the structure of productive sectors of the countries and is presented in Table 2. The distribution of gross domestic product (GDP) across three sectors, that is, agriculture, industry and services, between the period 2000 and 2016 shows that substantial changes in the structure of the South Asian countries have occurred over time. There is a general trend of decline of the relative share of agriculture in GDP and has declined between 4 and 10% point except in the case of Pakistan where it has increased 4% point. It is significant to note that four countries, that is, Afghanistan, India, Nepal and Pakistan, have shown falling relative share of industrial sector in the GDP, whereas the relative share of the industrial sector in the case of Bangladesh, Bhutan and Maldives has increased during the period 2000 to 2016. However, Sri Lanka maintained its share of industrial sector in the GDP. Except Maldives, the relative share of the service sector has increased in all the countries. On the whole, the relative share of agriculture sector has declined marginally in the region, the industrial sector gained marginally (2% points) and the services sector gained substantially during the period of 2000–2016. The analysis of Table 2 clearly brings out the fact that the service sector has remained the dominant sector in the process of transformation of the South Asian region.

As has been outlined by Kuznets (1966), that the changes in the production structure are followed by the changes in the workforce structure as well but with a time lag. The analysis of the changes in the workforce structure across countries and sectors shows that the workforce is still highly dependent on the agriculture sector for deriving their livelihood (Table 3). This is contrary to the relative share of production sector precisely because of the low capacity to absorb labour in both the industrial and service sectors. Among the South Asian countries, Afghanistan and Nepal are having 61.6 and 72.7%, respectively, of the workforce that is engaged in the agriculture sector. However, other countries such as Bhutan, India, Pakistan and Bangladesh are also employed by more than 40% of their workforce in the agriculture sector.

Table 3 Workforce structure across South Asian countries

Countries	Agriculture		Industry		Services	
	2000	2016	2000	2016	2000	2016
Afghanistan	69.4	61.6	11	10.0	19.6	28.5
Bangladesh	59.5	41.7	9.9	18.9	38.0	39.4
Bhutan	54.2	57.4	16.2	4.7	29.6	32.8
India	59.9	45.1	16.0	24.3	24.1	30.6
Maldives	14.4	7.9	20.0	22.9	65.6	69.2
Nepal	73.0	72.7	11.2	10.9	15.8	16.4
Pakistan	48.1	42.8	18.0	19.7	33.9	36.9
Sri Lanka	43.2	27.8	20.4	26.1	36.4	46.1
South Korea	58.0	44.2	15.9	23.2	26.1	32.7

Source ILO (2016)

Two countries, that is, Maldives and Sri Lanka in the South Asian region, are having employed workforce which is lowest but the rate of decline is also very high (Table 3). On the whole, the services sector has employed a higher proportion of the workforce compared with the industrial sector of the South Asian countries. This is counter-intuitive when we compare it with the structural transformation experience of the now advanced countries as well as newly industrializing countries of East Asia. The contributing factor in the case of developed countries and newly industrializing countries was the faster growth of industrial sector, whereas the South Asian countries are mostly witnessing a higher growth rate of the services sector.

The various indicators of competitive industrial performance (CIP) index developed by UNIDO (2015) are shown in Table 4. A comparative analysis of South Asian countries and newly industrializing countries of East Asia shows that there exists a wide gap between them. When we compare the manufacturing value added (MVA) per person for the year 2013 at 2005 prices in US dollars, South Korea has MVA $7180.7, whereas Nepal has only MVA $26.3 per person. Among the South Asian countries, Sri Lanka has the highest per person MVA $357.2, which is very low. The East Asian countries are fast catching-up with the developed countries in terms of manufacturing value added and had improved industrial competitiveness index. Their ranks are very high such as South Korea, China and Malaysia. However, India has the highest rank, that is, 43 among the 131 countries for which the UNIDO has provided a relative ranking. Pakistan, Bangladesh and Sri Lanka are ranked as 75, 77 and 81, respectively. But Nepal is ranked 126 among the 131 sampled countries. This clearly brings out the fact that South Asian countries have to improve substantially in generating various capabilities in their respective industrial sectors. The share of manufacturing sector in the GDP is also very low in the South Asian countries compared with the East Asian countries.

Table 4 Indicators of industrial competitiveness across South Asian countries

Country	MVA per capita 2005 $ 2013	Industrial competitiveness index 2013	Share of MVA in GDP (%) 2013	Medium and high-tech exports as % of total exports 2013
India	161.7	43	14	28.7
Nepal	26.3	128	6	20.3
Pakistan	139.1	75	17	10.4
Sri Lanka	357.2	81	19	8.2
Bangladesh	118.28	77	19	2.0
China	1142.6	5	33	58.3
South Korea	7180.7	3	29	72
Malaysia	1717.0	24	25	58.4

Source UNIDO (2015)

As far as the innovation-led high-tech and medium-tech manufactured exports are concerned, the South Asian countries had recorded very low proportions compared with the East Asian countries. Among South Asian countries, India was having the share as high as 28.7%. This share was very low for rest of the South Asian countries. The indicators of competitive industrial performance index show relatively dismal performance of the South Asian countries and sustainability of this sector is under a question mark. Its low industrial base, technological backwardness and small-scale production are the factors responsible for the low ranking of CIP index. Furthermore, these trends are supported by the stagnation witnessed by the manufacturing sector across South Asian countries (Table 5). The share of value added in the GDP of the South Asian countries declined from 14.3% from 1980–1984 to 13.5% in 2010–2013. The analysis of Table 5 shows that the 5-year average has either remained constant or has declined over the period from 1980–1984 to 2010–2013. Contrary to this, the share of employment in the manufacturing sector has marginally gone up between the period 1980–1984 and 1985–1989. Thereafter, there is a steady rise in the employment shares and the share of manufacturing employment in total employment increased to 12.2% during the period 2010–2013. The foregoing analysis of the South Asian countries clearly brings out the fact that the industrial base, innovation and competitiveness are relatively very weak. The low per capita income and poverty is the main root cause of weak industrial sector of the South Asian countries.

Table 5 Share of manufacturing value added and employment of South Asian countries

Year	MVA as % of GDP in South Asia	Share of manufacturing employment in total employment
1980–84	14.3	9.6
1985–89	14.3	10.1
1990–94	14.2	10.3
1995–99	14.5	11.4
2000–04	13.9	12.1
2005–09	14.8	11.9
2010–13	13.5	12.2

Source UNIDO (2015)

4   Skill Mismatch in South Asian Countries

South Asian countries are trapped in relatively low per capita income and small industrial sectors. The average productivity of the industrial sector is also very low. The industrial sector has not been remained dynamic enough to provide the leadership role in the transformation process of the South Asian countries. This kind of deceptive structural transformation process has generated mismatch between higher shares of income generation of the services sector in the economy but the higher share of workforce continues to stay in the agriculture sector of the economy. This kind of mismatch in the production structure has generated mismatch in a higher level of dependence of workforce and population on agriculture sector and low level of urbanization and industrial sector workforce. The consequences of this were twofold, that is, on the one hand, the skill formation of the workforce engaged in the agriculture sector is very low, which was also reflected in the low ranking of the social indicators (Dreze and Sen 2013) and mismatch of existing skills with the existing and expected employment opportunities in the future on the other hand (UNDP 2017). The analysis of Table 6 shows that on an average the mean years of schooling are very low across South Asian countries. It ranges between 10.9 years in Sri Lanka and 3.1 years in Bhutan. However, India and Maldives have 6.3 and 6.2, respectively, the mean years of schooling in the year 2015. When we compare it with the expected years of schooling, then none of the South Asian countries could be able to achieve it. The adult literacy rates as reflected from the secondary school education show that it ranges between as low as 9.6% of the population of Bhutan and as high as 80.5% of the population in Sri Lanka. Although the proportion of the population having completed secondary school education is increasing over a period of time, yet 48.7% of the eligible children in the relevant age group could acquire education in India. Bangladesh, Pakistan, Maldives and Nepal had these proportions as 43.4, 35.4, 32.6 and 32%, respectively. Among the South Asian countries, two countries, that is, Afghanistan and Bhutan, recorded very low adult literacy proportions of the population. In general, the human development index and accordingly the ranking

Table 6 Social indicators across South Asian countries

Countries	HDI	Life expectancy in years	Expected mean years of schooling	Mean years of schooling	% Population with at least secondary education
Afghanistan	0.479 (169)	60.7	10.1	3.6	22.2
Bangladesh	0.579 (140)	72	10.2	5.2	43.1
Bhutan	0.607 (132)	69.9	12.5	3.1	9.6
India	0.624 (131)	68.3	11.7	6.3	48.7
Maldives	0.701 (105)	77	12.7	6.2	32.6
Nepal	0.568 (144)	70.0	12.2	4.1	32.0
Pakistan	0.550 (148)	66.4	8.1	5.1	35.4
Sri Lanka	0.766 (72)	75	14	10.9	80.5

Source UNDP (2016)

of the South Asian countries are also very low. As indicated in Table 6, the HDI rank varied from 72 for Sri Lanka to 169 for Afghanistan. Except Sri Lanka, all other South Asian countries were ranked above hundred. This gives a fairly good idea regarding the low level of social development and general skill base of the South Asian countries. There are wide differences in rural–urban skill development across South Asian countries (UNDP 2016). The education base of the rural workforce is extremely low (Brar 2016). The population living in the countryside of South Asian countries neither have skills to join the manufacturing sector nor have enough skills to shift towards precision agriculture and agribusiness activities. Therefore, it can be inferred that the transformative skills across South Asian countries are in short supply.

The other most important mismatch that has been noticed in several studies (Ribound and Tan 2009; EIU 2013; Jagannathan and Geronimo 2013) regarding technical and vocational education and training (TVET). It has been noticed on the basis of empirical evidence that the existing technical education is inadequate both in terms of quantity and quality. The workforce trained by educational institutions also lacks skills that are required for available jobs in the manufacturing sector. There is a lack of manpower planning and what is being produced by the educational institutions is not suitable for manufacturing employment opportunities being generated. It is also significant to note that the informal sector dominates over the formal sector in most of the South Asian countries and jobs available in the informal sector are neither remunerative nor having good working conditions and thus could not attract the workforce for such kind of jobs. But an important fact that needs to be noted here is that in-service training is the lowest among the world that is being imparted by the manufacturing firms across South Asian countries (Ribound and Tan 2009). The mushrooming of private commercial technical educational institutions in South Asian countries has to some extent increased the supply of technical manpower but manufacturing firms provide opportunities to only those who are having ready to use skills. Thus, manufacturing firms have declared the majority of the technical manpower unfit for employment. This kind of mismatch between availability of skilled manpower and availability of jobs simply shows the lack of manpower planning in South Asian countries.

As the production system is moving towards increasing knowledge-intensive goods and services, the national innovation system is either facing stagnation or at the most declining trends (Nakandala and Malik 2015). South Asian countries research and development (R&D) expenditure on science and technology have been remained very low and could not match with the rise of GDP. The relative share of R&D in GDP across South Asian countries has recorded wide variations but none of the South Asian countries crossed threshold level R&D, that is, one per cent R&D expenditure. It is significant to note here that the scientific and technical manpower per million population varies across South Asian countries. But, as compared with East Asian and industrially advanced countries, it has also remained very low (UNESCO 2015). The other pillars of national innovation system and knowledge economy are the educational expenditure as a proportion of GDP. The educational expenditure ranged between 5.89% in Maldives and 1.72% in Sri Lanka for the year 2012. The expenditure in higher education was as low as 0.21% in Pakistan and as high as 1.21% in India in the year 2012. A modest expenditure on the knowledge economy and research system shows that the South Asian countries are lagging behind in the race of basic requirements of the current phase of domestic and global economy. Lack of innovations, diffusion of modern technology and inadequacy of interaction of the economic actors of production had generated a hiatus in several dimensions and intensities. This has resulted in wide gaps in income distribution and employment across and within sectors of the South Asian countries (Nayyar 2017). Consequently, the process of development is not only turned out to be exclusionary in nature but also low-productivity low-wage economic activities have limited the scope of sustained economic development to pass through the low/middle-income trap (Lee 2013). Thus, the inadequacy of scientific and technical skill base of the South Asian countries has generated a mismatch between the goals and actual reality of South Asian countries in the face of opportunities to catch-up.

5   Innovation Systems, Industrialisation and Competitiveness in South Asian Countries

There has been emergence of skill mismatch required for economic transformation of the South Asian countries. The current model of economic development is driven by the market forces, where dominance of the private corporate sector is ensured by the state (Bhadhuri 2009). The education organizational structure is geared towards meeting the needs of the market economy based on individual choices. However, we have noted in the previous section that even the existing institutional arrangements could not fulfil the changing requirements of skill base desired by the private corporate sector. This mismatch has been generated between the market-led model of education and productive economic activities because of the fact that neither the state nor the private corporate sectors have made adequate investment in the desired direction. This is a typical case of a market failure both in terms of industrialization of South Asian countries and creating the adequate number and quality of skill base. Therefore, there is a dire need to develop alternative thinking for ensuring to meet the challenges and aspirations of population of South Asian countries through appropriate industrialization and skill base suitable for the stage of economic development.

South Asian countries are expected to take a detour from the current pattern of economic transformation. To overcome the distortion in the production structure, it is imperative to integrate the production, processing and marketing of the primary sector of the South Asian countries. The drive for industrialization should begin with the integration of agriculture production with the manufacturing. Since the agriculture is largely small-scale production and has huge surplus/disguisedly employed workforce, therefore, it is useful to employ this workforce in gainful manufacturing activities. It is important to note that the employment generation in gainful economic activities has a capacity to generate higher level of domestic demand for manufacturing goods to fulfil basic needs. Another source of demand is the fast expansion of the middle class across South Asian countries during the last two decades (Krishnan and Hatekar 2017; Jagannathan and Geronimo 2013). This kind of change requires entirely new skill base and organizational structure. In the era of predominance of the private corporate sector, the competition for the small-scale production is relatively very tough. Therefore, it is desirable to change the organization of the production from individual to cooperative. Taiwanese experience of industrialization, while integrating production, manufacturing and marketing activities through farmers' association/cooperatives and also directing input markets as well, is quite instructive in this respect. The local labour was employed mainly in manufacturing activities and farm activities turned out to be a part-time activity. The surpluses generated were used to develop local infrastructure and expansion of economic activities. The surplus production was sold out in the international markets while participating in the global value chains and quietly created their own value chain system and also graduated from manufacturing primary production to white goods. This was possible due to the state support in terms of generating innovation system that facilitated the small producers in developing the niche markets based on short-cycle technologies. The innovation system generated an environment of new opportunities and simultaneously created capabilities among the workforce so that these opportunities can be encashed upon. South Asian country governments should also adequately invest in developing a national innovation system so that somewhat similar kind of environment can be generated to build niche market through opening up the window of opportunity through leapfrogging in technologies.

The base of such kind of alternative opportunities needs a systematic public policy framework to impart relevant skills to the workforce. It is pertinent to note here that the workforce engaged in the primary sector of the South Asian countries lacks education. On the basis of examining the historical experience of Japan's public policymaking that not only succeeded in Japan but also remained the pillar of successful industrialization experience of the East Asian countries such as South Korea and Taiwan, Sen (2006) has argued that changing the face of education in Japan turned it from a backward to industrialized nation. The author further noted the public policy perception while citing from Kido Takayoshi in the late nineteenth century that 'our people are no different from the Americans or Europeans of today; it is all a matter of education or lack of education'. To educate the workforce, the Japanese government had spent 43% of the budget on education between 1906 and 1911. South Asian country governments should learn some lessons from public policy employed by the government of Japan and other East Asian countries for making the economic transformation to succeed.

The task of economic transformation for the South Asian countries is relatively more complex and difficult due to a different phase of globalization but still there exists window of opportunity to leapfrog and thus it requires manpower planning to synchronize with the production structure. Education to the population for generating human capital is one of the fundamental pillars of the national innovation system. South Asian countries should embark on the formation of technological capabilities and learning abilities of the human workforce. The systemic approach to address deficiencies in the innovation system is required to be adopted to address the inadequacy of skill formation of the workforce and competitiveness of the industrial sector. While redrawing priorities for investment in skill formation, the South Asian countries should emphasize on individual success to collective success. The education system should impart basic education along with entrepreneurial skills to start social/collective enterprises. The environment of institutional arrangements should be created so that collective efforts should succeed and surpluses generated should be allowed to employ both for improving the infrastructure and for living conditions as well as the expansion of the enterprises. This should be supported by the systems of innovation that not only fulfils the needs of necessary innovations for creating new products, brand names, marketing and organization skills but also develops synergy between institutional arrangements and economic actors to generate movements towards collective efforts to succeed. These skills are called transformative skills and are suitable to the cultural values of the South Asian countries. These skills can allow South Asian countries to draw advantages even in the era of 4IR. Thus, there are possible pathways that can be created if the South Asian country governments pledge to play a supportive role in build human capabilities and provide matching opportunities for the use of newly developed human capabilities. There is no other way for South Asian countries but to industrialize for economic transformation from a low/middle income to developed economies.

6 Conclusions

This chapter has examined the skill formation, competitiveness and industrial development in systems of innovation framework. The evolutionary approached has been adopted for understanding the inadequacy of the skill formation, competitiveness and industrial development in the South Asian countries. South Asian countries are undergoing structural transformation in the era of globalization. The structure is tilted towards service orientation at an early stage of economic development. However, the most important distortion of the structural transition is the overstay of workforce in the primary sector of these economies. This is the consequence of lack of matching industrialization that could have used the surplus workforce that continues to derive their livelihood from the low-paid low-productive economic activities. Consequently, the major section of the population still living in abject poverty. Lack of remunerative employment opportunities has created an unequal distribution of income. The economic theory of growth and development has argued that there is a possibility of sustained economic growth through skill development and engaging the workforce in developing new ideas and innovations through adequate investment. In this chapter, three levels of skill mismatches of the workforce of South Asian countries are identified. First, the workforce engaged in the primary sector of these economies lacks basic education or have no skills that are required to transform traditional agriculture to precision agriculture and connecting it with the agribusiness. Second, the existing technical and general education imparted by the educational institutions do not produce workforce required to be employed in the modern industrial sector of the South Asian countries. Third, the technical and scientific workforce is not only inadequate but also not producing new innovations that can provide widow of opportunity to leapfrog to the path of low-productivity low-wage to high-productivity high-wage economic activities. An alternative strategy of industrialization and skill formation is suggested to overcome these skill gaps/mismatches. The new skills formation that takes care of cultural values of the South Asian countries, that is, social enterprises for collective efforts to succeed are suggested. The public policy of South Asian countries is required to support investing in human capabilities and generate an institutional arrangement that should allow the sustainability of collective enterprises. Revamping of the national innovation system that integrates economic actors and bridges the gap of innovation requirements for transition from a traditional to industrially advanced economy is also suggested.

References

Bhadhuri A (2009) The face you were afraid to see: essays on the Indian economy. Penguin, New Delhi

Brar JS (2016) Critical evaluation of education development in Punjab. In: Singh L, Singh N (eds) Economic transformation of a developing economy: the experience of Punjab, India. Springer, New Delhi, pp 291–312

Dreze J, Sen A (2013) An uncertain glory: India and its contradictions. Allen Lane, London

EIU (2013) Skills development in South Asia: trends in Afghanistan, Bangladesh, India, Nepal, Pakistan and Sri Lanka. The Economist Intelligence Unit, London

ILO (2016) Workforce structure of the global economy. International Labour Organisation, Geneva

Jagannathan S, Geronimo D (2013) Skills for competitiveness, jobs and employability in developing Asia-Pacific. In: ADB Briefs No. 18. Asian Development Bank, Manila

Krishnan S, Hatekar N (2017) Rise of new middle class in India and its changing structure. Econ Polit Wkly 52(22):40–48

Kuznets S (1966) Modern economic growth: rate, structure and spread. Yale University Press reprinted by Oxford and IBH Public Co., New Delhi, New Haven

Lee K (2013) Schumpeterian analysis of economic catch-up: knowledge, path creation and middle income trap. Cambridge University Press, Cambridge

Lucas RE Jr (1988) On the mechanics of economic development. J Monet Econ 22(1):3–42

Nakandala D, Malik A (2015) "South Asia". In: UNESCO Science Report Towards 2030, UNESCO, Paris

Nayyar D (2017) Employment, growth and development: essays on a changing world economy. Routledge, New Delhi

Ribound M, Tan H (2009) Improving skills for competitiveness. In: Ghani E, Ahmed S (eds) Accelerating growth and job creation in South Asia. Oxford University Press, New Delhi, pp 204–245

Romer PM (1986) Increasing returns and long run economic growth. J Polit Econ 94(5):1002–1037

Schwab K (2017) The fourth industrial revolution. Portfolio Penguin, London

Sen A (2006) Identity and violence: the illusion of destiny. Allen Lane, London

UNDP (2016) Human development report 2016: human development for everyone. United Nations Development Programme, New York

UNDP (2017) India skill report 2017, United Nations Development Programme, New Delhi, http://www.in.undp.org/content/india/en/home/library/poverty/india-skills-report-2017.html accessed on October 10, 2018

UNESCO (2015) UNESCO Science Report Towards 2030. United Nations Educational Scientific and Cultural Organization, Paris

UNIDO (2015) The role of technology and innovation in inclusive and sustainable industrial development. In: Industrial Development Report 2016. United Nations Industrial Development Organization, Vienna

WEF (2016) The future of jobs report: employment, skills and workforce strategy for the fourth industrial revolution. World Economic Forum, Geneva

WEF (2017) Realizing human potential in the fourth industrial revolution: an agenda for leaders to shape future of education, gender and work. World Economic Forum, Geneva

World Bank (2016) World Development Indicators. The World Bank, Washington DC

Conclusion: Manufacturing and Employment in South Asia

Sachin Chaturvedi and Sabyasachi Saha

1 Introduction

This volume has gathered a great deal of evidence on industrial development, structural transformation and employment generation in the South Asian region. In this concluding chapter, we recapitulate the cumulative evidence and insights drawn from the chapters. For various practical reasons, South Asia shares a common development context and demography. Economies in South Asia had initiated economic liberalisation more than two decades back. This resulted in increase in capital intensity in the manufacturing sector together with falling employment intensity, even as some improvement in labour productivity is observed during this phase. However, rise in capital intensity in the industry has not necessarily contributed to technological deepening measured in terms of value addition perhaps, due to serious innovation shortfall. Although India has overwhelming presence in the region, it has almost similar challenges and opportunities in the traditional industries that are pursued in the region. India definitely has much wider industrial base and is better placed in terms of technology-intensive manufacturing.

The importance accorded to industrial development in South Asia reflects both frustration and aspiration. However, frustration with regard to industrial development in South Asia even though widespread can be at times misplaced. Higher economic growth in the region has not necessarily been riding on commensurate industrial growth—however, performance of the industrial sector needs nuanced understanding. UNIDO has stressed that the economy receives dynamism brought about by industrialisation which acts as engine of long-run growth and catch-up. It is also effective for prolonging episodes of economic growth by reducing volatility.

Industrial development as it appears from the experience of South Asia has not strictly conformed to standard predictions of structural transformation but can poten-

S. Chaturvedi (✉) · S. Saha
Research and Information System for Developing Countries (RIS), New Delhi, India
e-mail: dg@ris.org.in

© Springer Nature Singapore Pte Ltd. 2019
S. Chaturvedi and S. Saha (eds.), *Manufacturing and Jobs in South Asia*, South Asia Economic and Policy Studies,
https://doi.org/10.1007/978-981-10-8381-5_10

tially respond positively to foundations of technological capacities and accumulation of physical and human capital in the near future. Rapid economic growth for large populations with low per capita income is not sustainable if the economies ignore production that caters to domestic needs. Import dependence in manufactured items in South Asian countries has sharply grown even as these economies are more integrated with world markets. This necessitates promotion of industrial activity in these economies. However, low per capita income imposes constraints in terms of market size in the initial phase. Export-driven models would crucially promote industrialisation in such scenarios. Examples of export-driven growth models with matching domestic demand push have been a successful industrialisation strategy for the large and newly industrialised developing countries. Keeping in view dependence on agriculture in South Asia, transition from the agriculture and integration of agriculture in industrial strategy is very important for these countries.

The desire for an appropriate structural transformation that deepens industrialization needs well-informed strategy. Industrial development in South Asia has been held back due to a variety of reasons. Expansion of industrial base alone may not be helpful. Structural constraints not only interfere in the process of industrial growth but actually contribute to persistence of inefficiencies, reduced competitiveness and come in the way of economies of scale. Overall, industrial resurgence is linked with 3S—Size (of the firm linked with capital investment), Scale (in production linked with market size) and Skill (of the labour force). The ultimate policy objective is to promote and robustly facilitate the three preconditions. Industrial policy (that includes trade policy), macroeconomic policy (that generates investible surpluses) and public policy (for quality of employment and skills) all play distinct role in this regard.

The predominant character of South Asian industrial performance is that of persistent dualism. Productivity and efficiency differentials between firms (of different sizes) are the source of duality within the manufacturing sector. Dualism has been a prominent characteristic of Indian manufacturing industry dominated by a very large number of small and medium firms. Conventional approaches to measurement of productivity (for example TFPG) carry relevance only in case of organised manufacturing industry for which adequate time-series data is available. It is observed that distinct movement of the production frontier captured by TFPG, over the longer time horizon, has contributed modestly to the process of technological catch-up of the Indian industry indicating no apparent differences between large and small firms with regard to productivity. But, beyond productivity, efficiency and technological competence of firms are functions of a variety of factors including access to finance, physical and digital infrastructure, connectivity, human resources, knowledge, etc. These are also profoundly shaped, directly, by easier access to world markets through efficient trade facilitation and indirectly through regulatory reforms (easy entry and exit rules, clearances, tax benefits, etc.) popularly dubbed as 'ease of doing business'. Larger firms have stronger command over multiple resources, mentioned earlier, leading to dualism. This is an important policy lesson and South Asia is in urgent need of minimising dualism for significant improvement in value addition and competitiveness and in widening the scope of better quality jobs.

There is a persistent concern that unavailability of skills has made structural transformation (towards industrialisation) fragile. This is essentially a skill conundrum that these countries are faced with despite enjoying demographic dividend. Skills are an essential precondition for kick-starting a fresh process of industrialisation in South Asian countries that have been lagging so far. As we are aware, industrialisation has experienced distinct shifts from mechanisation to automation and from mass production to production networks. Moreover, industrialisation has traditionally followed technologies originating in high-income countries having advanced innovation ecosystems. Technical progress and catch-up in newly industrialising countries are dependent on domestic technological/absorptive capabilities that are linked with knowledge and skills eventually shaped through the national innovation system. Capability development is fundamentally based on education of the workforce and the allocation of human capital and investment in research and development (R&D). To bridge the gap of technological knowledge and advance in the process of catch-up, the developing countries are required to develop absorptive capacities. It is significant to note that the determinants of absorptive capacities are continuous investment in human capital. There is robust evidence that industrial development in the developing economies is experiencing significant transition and becoming increasingly more technology intensive. Thus, it would be important for a developing country to reap benefits of this manufacturing transition while simultaneously investing in generating skilled technicians, scientists and engineers.

2   Country Case Studies

2.1   Bangladesh

In Bangladesh, the structure and composition of the manufacturing sector have experienced shifts since the introduction of economic liberalisation policies in 1980 (with trade liberalisation initiated in the late 1980s). With preferential market access in developed countries since the late 1970s the RMG industry has achieved export-oriented growth and also made significant contribution to employment creation in the following decades. Over the last decades, non-traditional manufacturing industries have made considerable progress. These non-traditional establishments include chemical products, electrical equipment, leather products, paper products, basic metals, rubber and plastic products. However, it is also observed that a number of industries have experienced reduction in the number of establishments such as in textiles and pharmaceuticals.

Majority of enterprises across sectors are domestic market oriented. Domestic market-oriented industries include coke and refined petroleum, machinery and equipment, motor vehicles and trainers, installation of machinery and recycling, etc. Export-oriented industries include RMG (95% of total production), transport equipment (82%), leather and leather goods (74%) and textiles products (57%). A few other industries also have limited export shares, for example, paper and paper products, computer, electronic and optical products and electrical equipment, etc. Lack of competitiveness, limited capacity, poor network with buyers, low quality of products and lack of competent human resources constrain domestic market-oriented enterprises from exporting.

Majority of export-oriented industries that have experienced rise in share and increase in employment are RMG, leather, pharmaceuticals and rubber. Similarly, in the segment of domestic market-oriented industries such industries include paper products, chemical products, basic metals and furniture. Some of the sectors have diminishing contribution to employment generation. For example, a number of domestic market-oriented industries such as tobacco, wood and cork, recorded media, fabricated metal, electrical equipment and a few export-oriented industries such as food and beverages have lost their share in manufacturing employment. Without improving the level of competitiveness, these sectors would not grow fast and thereby would not contribute much to employment generation. Overall, in Bangladesh, employment in the manufacturing sector is highly concentrated in a few sectors. Also, compared to other South Asian countries, the performance of Bangladesh's manufacturing sector in terms of generating employment has not been satisfactory. In fact, share of employment in the manufacturing sector is behind those of major South Asian economies (India and Sri Lanka). It is highlighted that Bangladesh lacks diversified manufacturing base which limits opportunities for employment.

2.2 Nepal

Industrialisation in Nepal has traditionally suffered from low levels of investment. Although FDI commitment has been relatively high, the actual inflow has always been extremely low. This is notwithstanding economic reforms undertaken in the last two decades. In the total inflow, the share of Indian investment has been above 40% followed by China and other countries.

Nepal is facing problem of declining share of manufacturing in output, export and employment. Despite economic integration with SAARC countries, Nepal, which is a landlocked country, has not been able to derive the expected benefits from this arrangement. Moreover, opportunities for global value and supply chain have not been adequately internalised in the policymaking process so that the manufacturing sector is able to attract domestic and foreign investment. A flourishing manufacturing sector in Nepal would have added to sustaining the current phase of economic growth. It is imperative that a new approach on industrial policy is adopted which addresses market, government and coordination failures more effectively which in addition to enhancing growth could contribute to creating jobs.

A need is being felt for review of regional cooperation strategies encompassing investment and trade for ensuring benefits for Nepal from the regional integration. It is suggested that promotion of intra-regional value chains should be integral to regional cooperation arrangements to generate adequate benefits for countries like

Nepal. With the promulgation of new constitution in Nepal and political transition, some consensus is emerging among political parties on the imperatives of rapid economic transformation and job creation.

In case of Nepal, expansion and restructuring of industries grounded on comparative advantages will be necessary. At the same time, such a strategic shift requires investments in social and physical infrastructure including investment in new technologies, know-how and innovation. This is expected to create productive synergies within and between sectors of the economy and contribute to enhancing exports through diversification, quality improvement and changes in the structure of production and trade, among others.

2.3 Pakistan

Due to significant forward and backward linkages, manufacturing sector is considered a major and indispensable source of economic growth and job creation in Pakistan. The manufacturing sector in Pakistan contributed 13.5% to GDP and 13.8% to employment in the fiscal year 2016–17. However, lack of adequate physical infrastructure has dampened prospects of industrialisation in Pakistan. Infrastructure bottleneck is particularly serious in the case of power generation capacities. The economy moved from agriculture to services sector without consolidating the industrial sector. This is one of the probable reasons behind massive labour force remaining unemployed. The manufacturing sector is expected to provide jobs for a range of skills and can absorb more labour as compared to the service sector. This is particularly true for unskilled and semi-skilled jobs. The bypassing of manufacturing in Pakistan has left lesser room of job creation and has weakened the growth foundations of economy.

The textile industry in Pakistan is presented in detail as part of the country case study in view of its overwhelming importance in the industrial landscape of Pakistan. The textile industry in Pakistan contributes over 60% to total exports and accounts for 46% of the total manufacturing output. Production, trade and employment in this sector have been analysed with important policy lessons. The future of manufacturing (and textile) sector depends on how efficiently Pakistan moves towards export promotion-led growth and development. A well-organised plan for product diversification can contribute substantially to the future growth of the industrial sector. This requires a massive paradigm shift in policymaking towards technology enhancement, global value chains and skills, and increase in labour productivity. However, these are all longer term solution, and therefore, short-term answers might look far more attractive. The comparative advantage does exist for textiles, but it is often squandered in terms of inadequate energy supply, low quality of products and lack of price competitiveness. Essentially, industry-driven growth in Pakistan is linked to exports, which in turn is linked to a revamped policy focused on sophistication and integration into global value chains. With rising unpredictability with traditional trading partners, Pakistan should be exploring new markets for its industrial products.

Employment statistics related to the textile sector in Pakistan is seldom available mainly because of decline in textile sector capacity over time, which has badly injured employment prospects and has effectively restricted the entry of the new workforce. Non-availability of textile sector employment data is also due to the absence of comprehensive surveys. Historical trend of total employment in textile sector shows a downward trend since 2006–2007.

2.4 Sri Lanka

Sri Lanka has the most impressive record of social sector development in South Asia and has high scores on development indicators. Sri Lanka now aspires to gradually and resolutely develop an export-oriented manufacturing sector with emphasis on developing a sophisticated, high-value export portfolio. This is expected to trigger viable growth momentum by expanding export potential and increasing supply capacity. Simultaneously, such policy focus will entail a larger shift to capital-intensive production processes that increase labour productivity. However, Sri Lanka is at disadvantage with regard to its demography (the only exception in South Asia) with an ageing population that may have serious implication for an industrialisation strategy. The island's geographic proximity to large emerging economies (including India) and strategic maritime routes linking vital economic corridors makes it an ideal hub for producers wishing to target multiple high-value markets. However, a brief perusal of past history suggests that Sri Lanka has encountered mixed success in implementing reforms with regard to international trade. The advancements made in clustered waves of liberalisation have been offset by periods of economic uncertainty instigated by nationalist reforms.

A surge of foreign investment into labour-intensive segments provided added impetus to Sri Lankan manufacturing. The Textile and Apparel sector emerged as the most significant manufacturing sector, accounting for around 60% of aggregate manufacturing output and over 45% of export earnings in 2016. As some of the other South Asian peers, Sri Lanka has proved to be an ideal destination for apparel-led investments after liberalisation as the sector held comparative advantage in unskilled and semi-skilled labour. In the last 40 years, manufacturing sector composition has increased by a mere 2.2% (textile and garments, the largest export-oriented sector, has stagnated between at the 20–25% over the last decade). In comparison, the services sector has expanded by 14.1% within a similar time period. On the bright side, processed rubber products—pneumatic tyres and industrial gloves, in particular—witnessed a surge in export revenue in the latter half of the previous decade. Subsequent drops in exports can be explained by a steep decline in the price of natural rubber which resulted in a contraction in the value of agricultural exports.

3 Manufacturing Sector and Jobs: The Indian Context

The Indian context has been captured elaborately in two dedicated chapters. These chapters complement each other given the fact that the first chapter explores influence of trade on manufacturing and associated employment generation in India from a product export perspective (product-level analysis) and the other from industry export intensity perspective (disaggregated industry-level analysis), with both having a significant focus on the impact on employment.

3.1 Manufacturing Exports and Employment

There are many unresolved issues relating to the current debate on trade and employment which need to be examined in the context of India. Despite persistence of global recession, some countries are posting robust performance in manufacturing export as compared to India. As the global demand for imports is shrinking, high export performing countries are adopting inward oriented strategies for promoting their domestic absorption and also continuing with the export sector to employment in the domestic economy. However, the extent of employment generation depends upon commodity structure demanded by importers. Therefore, selection of countries/RTAs for trade partnership needs to be undertaken in such a manner that it may optimise national objects of employment generation alongside technology intensive trade for higher export earnings.

The Chapter concludes that employment intensity of exports is significant for India in certain regions in the world. India's strong export linkage with Asia is important since it serves India's export and employment interest. India's employment generation through export is expected to be in select regions such as Asia, North and West Africa, Canada and the Oceania. India's future trade engagement in the form of BFTA/FTA/CEPA/CECA with these countries can give leverage to India in generating large employment at home.

It is evident from the global trade that substantial trade takes place through the regional route since trade flows are mostly guided by the preferential trade practices. For promoting trade, India needs to engage in the process of regionalism as an emerging economy, aspiring to reach the level of $ 5 billion economy by 2025. Export activities in trade destinations are subdued due to prolongation of the global recession, but return of buoyancy to the world economy may spur export activities in those countries. If India is to enter into the exclusive club of top five economies by 2025, export has to take the driving seat to steer growth. In this context, India is likely to sign number of RTAs to strengthen its external sector engagement. The results show that 28 RTAs from the total of 84 RTAs, that have been studied, can generate high employment in India. About 37 of them would ensure moderate level and 19 of them can have low level of employment in the domestic economy.

In terms of employment generation in India, the RTAs across the globe are clearly identified in terms of their employment generation capacity. From this perspective, RTAs from Africa can generate high level of employment, followed by Asia with medium level, Europe with mix of medium and high level, LAC with low and Oceania with medium level of employment in India. In terms of levels of employment intensity of exports, specific RTAs in particular regions can be identified for BFTA/CEPA/CECA/FTA negotiations.

With rising wage rate and declining size of employment happening during the last two decades, the share of high technology trade in the total trade is rising. These phenomena are partially pointing towards gradual substitution of more of blue collar jobs by less number of white collar jobs in India. However, SMEs and cottage industry sectors have more employment-output ratio than corporate sectors. For generating more employment in the economy, SMEs need to be promoted and with support for integration with GVCs.

3.2 Industry Performance and Employment

The second study highlights that the Indian manufacturing sector has been experiencing rising output but diminishing value added in total output with the trend becoming more pronounced since mid-1990s. The share of value of production in overall value added decreased from 23% in 1996 to 18% in 2004 with a marginal increase up to 20% in 2008 and declined thereafter. The declining manufacturing value added indicates an increase in resource intensity of the manufacturing sector in India. However, it is important to note that the growth of exports is found to be higher than the growth of value-added and employment indicating increasing trade performance. However, the share of manufacturing in total merchandise exports increased from 79% in 1990 to 87% in 2002 and declined marginally thereafter.

The share of workers (unskilled) in total employment has largely remained the same over years with minor variations. At the same time, the share of female in total employment has increased from 9.97% in 1995 to 15.15% in 2002. The share has gradually declined to 12.48% in 2012 with a minor improvement afterwards. However, the share of contract workers has seen an almost threefold increase in the share from 13.34% in 1995 to 26.42% in 2004 and further to 35.39% in 2014.

It is evident that in 1990 a little over 25% of the number of industries were employment–export champions and 36% of the industries were export champions but employment laggards. These two groups of industries that displayed higher employment intensity accounted for nearly 61% of the total number of industries in India's manufacturing sector in 1991. As we move to 2000, their share further increased by 69% and declined marginally thereafter to reach 67% in 2014. The recent decline in their share notwithstanding it appears that high employment intensity appears to be the hallmark of an overwhelming majority of manufacturing industries in India. Further, there has been a steady increase in the share of export champions–employment laggards, which is evident from more than fourfold increase in the share of industries in this category from 3.6% in 1990 to over 16% in 2014. This indicates the increasing capital intensity in India's manufacturing sector.

In terms of export performance, in 1990, the employment and export champions accounted for over 55% of the total manufacturing exports, which declined over the years to reach the present level of 20%. When it comes to employment, their share has shown fluctuations from year to year and yet their contribution is over 19% in 2014. Thus, we have a situation wherein, 22% of the manufacturing industries that we have designated as export–employment champions, today account for 19% of the employment and 21% of the exports. In case of employment champions–export laggards, while their export share has increased to reach as high as 21% in 2007, there has been a decline thereafter to reach the present level of 18%. When it comes to their employment contribution, it continues to remain as high as 59%. Therefore, it is evident that these two categories of industries put together account for nearly 78% of total employment, while they account for only 38% of the total exports. From the employment generation perspective, any attempt to enhance their international competitiveness is bound to give rich dividends in terms of employment.

One important finding is that export–employment champions provide higher jobs to unskilled workers as compared to skilled workers and employs higher proportion of female labour and low-contract workers. Second, export champions–export laggards generating industries also seem to be providing a better quality of employment as evident from their skill intensity, contract intensity and female employment intensity as compared to their capital-intensive counterparts. Hence, promotion of export orientation in these employment generating industries would further increase both quantity and quality of employment.

From a long-term development perspective, a large economy like India has to adopt a strategy of reaping both static and dynamic comparative advantages. It is rather salutary note that export champions–employment laggards that accounted for over 50% of total manufacturing exports in 2014–2015 are either medium- or high-tech industries. The presence of a few medium- and high-tech industries in the other two categories—employment–export champions and employment champions–export laggards is observed. However, the available evidence tends to suggest that most of these industries that are presumably reaping dynamic comparative advantage because of their high technological base are showing poor performance with respect to the quality of employment that they generate. Though these industries have the potential for building dynamic comparative advantage based on their deep science, technology and knowledge base, the current strategy appears to involve building competitiveness based on low labour cost advantage. Hence, we make the case for appropriate policy interventions towards dynamic comparative advantage based on product, process and other innovations. It also appears that there is the need for appropriate institutional interventions to ensure that innovation-induced value addition and depth of manufacturing contributes towards the generation of high-quality employment such that international competitiveness and growth leads to shared prosperity.

4 Industry, Employment and Competitiveness: Concluding Observations

Apart from industrialisation and the manufacturing sector, this volume (in Chap. 8) has looked into the question of employment in great detail against patterns of structural transformation in the context of South Asia and globally. This chapter brings out the rationale rather unambiguously why manufacturing needs to be relentlessly pursued as a policy objective in South Asia and how quality of employment may be improved in the process. This chapter also draws attention to the imbalances that services-led economic growth can bring for large developing countries.

South Asian economies are labour-surplus dual economies. The GDP growth is independent of employment growth in such economies; labour is in excess supply so that no 'labour constraint' on growth exists. On the other hand, most people do not have access to any kind of institutionalised social security and must work to survive. This means that most of those who are in the labour force are also employed. But many engage in work sharing (in self-employment and in casual wage employment) and many others engage in very low-productivity work. Very few remain unemployed and these few are educated (hence looking for good jobs in the formal sector) and generally belong to relatively well-off households (so that they can afford to remain unemployed). The employment problem manifests itself in poverty (which results from underemployment and low-productivity employment) and not in unemployment (which does not imply poverty). Employment growth reflects labour force growth and tells us little about growth in the demand for labour associated with economic growth. In case of South Asia, except for Sri Lanka, the formal sector employs a very small proportion of the workforce; a large majority (between 80 and 90%) of the workers work in the informal sector, either as self-employed or as casual wage employees. Even in Sri Lanka, where the formal sector employs 37% of all workers, the majority is still in the informal sector.

Therefore, underemployment, not unemployment, shows up to be the major problem. However, the estimates of underemployment are not robust. In Nepal, for example, underemployment has almost certainly been seriously underestimated. In Sri Lanka, too, underemployment appears to be underestimated. Change in employment conditions, therefore, cannot be discerned from employment growth or change in unemployment. Employment growth in the formal sector and change in underemployment in the informal sector can tell us much about the change in employment conditions, but time-series data on these indicators are in general unavailable.

The pattern of growth in East Asia was far more effective in improving employment conditions than the pattern of growth in South Asia. This can be seen most clearly from a comparison of India's experience during 2000–2015 with Korea's during 1963–1990 (the period during which Korea's economy underwent transformation from a low-income economy to a high-income economy). The growth rates of GDP in the two countries were not radically different: 7.2% in India and 7.5% in Korea. The rate of growth of agriculture was virtually the same: 3% in India and 2.9% in Korea. The rate of growth of non-agriculture was exactly the same: 8.2% in both countries. The big difference was in the composition of non-agricultural growth. This was driven by the growth of manufacturing (14.8% per annum) in Korea and by the growth of services (8.9% per annum) in India. Manufacturing recorded a growth of 7.5% in India and services recorded a growth of 6.6% in Korea.

We can draw two conclusions. First, the employment effect of growth depends on both the pace and the pattern of growth. In South Asian countries, growth did not significantly improve employment conditions due to the fact that economic growth remained suboptimum and at the same time did not allow desirable structural transformation. Only India had rapid economic growth but the particular pattern of this growth blunted its effectiveness in improving the employment conditions. Growth was slower in Nepal, Pakistan and Sri Lanka and the pattern of growth was similar to India; the improvement in employment conditions was naturally less significant in these countries than in India. Bangladesh did have manufacturing-led growth with better effects on employment but the growth was not rapid enough.

South Asian countries, the workforce is either disguisedly employed or employed in low productive economic activities that do not match with the skill requirements for competitiveness of their industrial sector and thus results in mass poverty. To overcome the industrial stagnation and skill formation gaps, the South Asian countries need to revamp their national innovation system for harnessing the ongoing industrial revolution and move onto the path of self-sustained economic development. On average, the mean years of schooling are very low across South Asian countries. The education among rural workforce is extremely low. The rural population in South Asian countries neither has skills to join manufacturing sector nor has enough skills to shift towards precision agriculture and agribusiness activities. Therefore, it can be inferred that the transformative skills across South Asian countries are in short supply. The task of economic transformation in the South Asian countries is relatively more complex and difficult, but there exists window of opportunity to leapfrog aided by manpower planning in sync with the production structure. Revamping of national innovation system that integrates economic actors and bridges the gap of innovation requirements for transition from a traditional to industrially advanced economy is strongly suggested.

CPI Antony Rowe
Eastbourne, UK
August 21, 2020